low-calorie
cooking

low-calorie
cooking

igloo

Published by Igloo Books Limited
Henson Way
Kettering
Northants
NN16 8PX
info@igloo-books.com

This edition printed in 2005

ISBN 1-84193-309-0

Printed in China

Author: Victoria Chow
With thanks to Yew Yuan Chow and James Mitchell

Project management by Metro Media Limited

Contents

Introduction

Whether you are on a diet to lose weight or just trying to eat more healthily, calorie counting is often an effective way to get results. In scientific terms, 1000 calories = 1 kilocalorie = the energy it takes to raise the temperature of 1kg of water by 1°C. However, in nutritional terms, the words 'calorie' and 'kilocalorie' are used interchangeably. Some food packaging will also give kilojoule (kJ) values. For your reference, 1 kilocalorie = 4.2 kilojoules, however this book uses calories throughout so as to fit in with calorie-counting diets and health plans.

Too many people still believe that weight loss programmes or healthy eating diets means bland food. This recipe book will prove these diet myths completely false. Every sumptious dish has a calorie count per serving and there is a wide choice of dishes. While we cannot guarantee you miraculous results, we aim to make counting your calories taste a lot better.

In the starters chapter you will find everything from Devilled eggs to Steamed crab cakes and Prawn & sesame seed triangles. The soup chapter provides warming treats such as Vegetable minestrone and Chinese cabbage soup. So whether you want a starter, a tasty lunch or just something to warm you up on a cold winter's day, this chapter is sure to please.

Salads are perhaps the most traditional diet fare, but we have something to add to the standard lettuce and tomato combination. With Lobster & avocado salad, Hot potato & bean salad and Pear & grape salad to choose from, there are some mouth-watering combinations to be found here.

Main courses include Moussaka and Spicy masala chicken. There is also a vegetarian main course chapter incorporating influences from around the world, including Spring vegetable stir-fry or Tofu & green bean curry.

In the desserts chapter there are recipes that include Blueberry sundae, Pears with strawberry sauce and Chocolate & orange angel cake, all with calorie counts to ensure you don't stray too far from your chosen diet plan.

Starters

Watching your weight and counting the calories does not necessarily mean skipping starters! With mouth-watering recipes such as Chicken tikka, Steamed crab cakes and Smoked salmon pancakes with pesto in this chapter, you will be able to find a tasty appetiser without worrying about the calorie content. Alternatively each starter can also make a great light lunch or snack.

Salmon-filled mushroom caps

SERVES 6
150 calories per serving

INGREDIENTS:

200g/7oz canned salmon
25g/1oz fine dry breadcrumbs
2 tablespoons chopped onion
2 tablespoons chopped parsley
Salt and freshly ground black pepper

18 large fresh mushrooms (caps about
4cm/1½in diameter, stalks removed
and wiped with damp kitchen paper)
2 tablespoons red pepper (diced)

- Preheat the oven to 180°C/350°F/Gas mark 4.
- In a small mixing bowl, combine the salmon, breadcrumbs, onion and parsley. Season with a pinch of salt and pepper.
- Place the mushroom caps in a baking tray, crown side down. Mould the salmon mixture into the caps. Place a little red pepper on top of each cap.
- Bake for 15 to 20 minutes or until tender.

Prunes stuffed with mussels

SERVES 4
190 calories per serving

INGREDIENTS:

3 tablespoons port
1 tablespoon clear honey
2 garlic cloves (crushed)
Salt and pepper

24 large stoned prunes
24 fresh mussels
12 rashers smoked streaky bacon

- Mix the port, honey and garlic together, then season to taste with salt and pepper. Put the prunes in a small bowl and pour the port mixture on top. Cover and leave to marinate for at least 4 hours.
- Clean the mussels by scrubbing or scraping the shells and pulling out any beards

that are attached to them. Put the mussels in a large saucepan, but do not add extra water – the water that clings to their shells should be sufficient. Cook, covered, over a high heat for 3 to 4 minutes, or until the mussels have opened. Discard any mussels that remain closed.

- Strain the mussels, reserving the cooking liquid. Leave to cool, then remove the mussels from their shells.
- Using the back of a knife, stretch the bacon rashers, then cut in half widthways.
- Lift the prunes from their marinade, reserving any that remains.
- Stuff each prune with a mussel, then wrap with a piece of bacon. Secure with a cocktail stick. Repeat with the remaining prunes.
- Simmer the mussel cooking liquid and remaining marinade together in a saucepan until reduced and syrupy. Brush the stuffed prunes with this mixture.
- Place under a medium grill and cook for 3 to 4 minutes on each side, turning regularly and brushing with the marinade mixture, until the bacon is crisp and golden. Serve while still hot.

Tuna-stuffed tomatoes

SERVES 4
200 calories per serving

INGREDIENTS:
- Preheat the oven to 200°C/400°F/Gas mark 6.

4 plum tomatoes
2 tablespoons tomato purée
2 egg yolks
2 teaspoons lemon juice
Grated zest of 1 lemon

4 tablespoons olive oil
125g/4½oz canned tuna (drained)
2 tablespoons capers (rinsed)
Salt and pepper

- Halve the tomatoes and scoop out the seeds. Divide the tomato purée among the tomato halves and spread around the inside.
- Place on a baking tray and roast in the oven for 12 to 15 minutes. Leave to cool.
- To make the mayonnaise, blend the egg yolks and lemon juice in a blender or food processor with the lemon zest until smooth. Once mixed and with the blender still on, add the olive oil. Stop blending as soon as it has thickened.
- Add the tuna and capers to the mayonnaise and season.
- Spoon the tuna mixture into the tomato shells and return to the oven for a few minutes. Serve warm.

Spinach meatballs

SERVES 4

140 calories per serving

INGREDIENTS:

125g/4½oz pork
1 egg
1cm/½in piece root ginger
(peeled and chopped)
1 small onion (finely chopped)
½ teaspoon salt and black pepper
1 tablespoon boiling water
25g/1oz canned bamboo shoots
(drained, rinsed and chopped)
2 slices smoked ham (chopped)
2 teaspoons cornflour

450g/1lb fresh spinach
2 teaspoons sesame seeds

For the sauce:
150ml/5fl oz vegetable stock
½ teaspoon cornflour
1 teaspoon cold water
1 teaspoon soy sauce
½ teaspoon sesame oil
1 tablespoon chopped fresh chives

- Mince the pork very finely in a blender or food processor. Lightly beat the egg in a bowl and stir into the pork.
- Put the ginger and onion in a separate bowl, add the boiling water and leave to stand for 5 minutes. Drain and add to the pork mixture with the bamboo shoots, ham and cornflour. Mix thoroughly, add salt and pepper, and roll into 12 balls.
- Wash the spinach and remove the stalks. Blanch in boiling water for 10 seconds, drain well then slice into very thin strips and mix with the sesame seeds. Roll the meatballs in the mixture to coat. Then place the meatballs on a heatproof plate in the base of a steamer. Cover and steam for 8–10 minutes, until tender.
- To make the sauce, put the stock in a saucepan and bring to the boil. Mix together the cornflour and water to a smooth paste and stir it into the stock. Stir in the soy sauce, sesame oil and chives. Transfer the cooked meatballs to a warm plate and serve with the sauce.

Fruit cocktail

SERVES 6
95 calories per serving

INGREDIENTS:

½ *honeydew melon*
225g/8oz canned pineapple chunks
in juice

225g/8oz seedless white grapes
(halved)
125ml/4fl oz white grape juice

- Remove the seeds from the melon half and use a melon baller to scoop out even-sized balls.
- Combine all the fruits in a glass bowl and pour the pineapple and grape juices over the top.
- Cover and chill until required.

Salmon yakitori

SERVES 4
250 calories per serving

INGREDIENTS:

350g/12oz salmon fillet
8 baby leeks

For the sauce:
75ml/3fl oz soy sauce

75ml/3fl oz fish stock
25g/1oz caster sugar
75ml/3fl oz dry white wine
50ml/2fl oz sweet sherry
1 garlic clove (crushed)

- Skin the salmon and cut the flesh into 5cm/2in chunks. Trim the leeks and cut them into 5cm/2in lengths.
- Thread the salmon and leeks alternately on to 8 wooden skewers. Leave in the refrigerator until needed.
- To make the sauce, place all the ingredients in a small saucepan and heat gently over a low heat, stirring, until the sugar dissolves. Bring to the boil, then reduce the heat and simmer for 2 minutes. Strain the sauce and leave to cool. Pour about one-third of the sauce into a small dish.
- Brush plenty of the remaining sauce over the kebabs and transfer to a barbecue or a medium-high grill. Baste frequently with the sauce and cook for 10 minutes.
- Serve hot with the reserved sauce for dipping.

Baked garlic mushrooms

SERVES 4
100 calories per serving

INGREDIENTS:

25g/1oz low-fat spread
8 large, flat mushrooms
2 garlic cloves (finely chopped)

Salt and pepper
150ml/¼pt dry white wine
150ml/¼pt low-fat single cream

- Preheat the oven to 190°C/375°F/Gas mark 5. Use the low-fat spread to grease a large, shallow ovenproof dish.
- Peel the mushrooms, remove and discard the stalks. Place the mushrooms in the prepared dish, gill sides up. Sprinkle with the garlic and a little salt and pepper.
- Mix the wine with the cream and pour over the mushrooms.
- Cover the dish with aluminium foil and bake in the oven for about 20 minutes or until the mushrooms are tender. Transfer to serving plates and spoon the garlicky juices over. Serve immediately.

Spinach & potato galette

SERVES 6
260 calories per serving

INGREDIENTS:

900g/2lb large potatoes
450g/1lb fresh spinach
2 eggs
400g/14oz low-fat soft cheese

1 tablespoon wholegrain mustard
50g/2oz chopped chives
Salt and pepper

- Preheat the oven to 180°C/350°F/Gas mark 4. Line a deep 23cm/9in cake tin with non-stick baking parchment.
- Place the potatoes in a large saucepan and cover with cold water. Bring to the boil and cook for about 10 minutes. Drain well and allow to cool slightly before slicing thinly.
- Wash the spinach and place in a large pan with only the water that is clinging to the leaves. Cover and cook, stirring once, until the spinach has wilted. Drain well in a sieve and squeeze out the excess moisture. Chop finely.
- Beat the eggs with the soft cheese and mustard then stir in the chopped spinach and chives.

- Place a layer of sliced potatoes in the lined tin, arranging them in concentric circles. Top with a spoonful of the soft cheese mixture and spread out. Continue layering, seasoning with salt and pepper as you go, until all the potatoes and the soft cheese mixture are used up.
- Cover the tin with aluminium foil and place in a roasting tin. Fill the roasting tin with enough boiling water to come halfway up the sides, then cook in the oven for 40 to 45 minutes. Serve hot or cold.

Melon & strawberries

SERVES 4
60 calories per serving

INGREDIENTS:

¼ honeydew melon
½ cantaloupe melon
150ml/¼pt rosé wine

3 teaspoons rose water
175g/6oz small strawberries (washed and hulled)

- Scoop out the seeds from both melons with a spoon, then carefully remove the peel. Cut the melon flesh into thin strips and place in a bowl. Pour the wine and rose water over. Mix together gently, cover and leave to chill in the refrigerator for at least 2 hours.
- Halve the strawberries and carefully mix into the melon. Allow the melon and strawberries to stand at room temperature for about 15 minutes. Arrange on individual serving plates and serve.

Melon with Parma ham

SERVES 6
90 calories per serving

INGREDIENTS:

1 honeydew melon (cut into 6 wedges)
6 slices wafer-thin Parma ham

6 cherry tomatoes

- Remove the peel from the melon and cut each wedge into 2 thin wedges. Halve the ham slices widthways. Wrap a piece of ham round the centre of each piece of melon and arrange on serving plates. Garnish with a cherry tomato.

Cheese & spinach puffs

SERVES 6
100 calories per serving

INGREDIENTS:

150g/5oz cooked spinach (chopped)
175g/6oz cottage cheese
1 teaspoon grated nutmeg
Salt and pepper

2 egg whites
25g/1oz Parmesan cheese (grated)

- Preheat the oven to 220°C/425°F/Gas mark 7. Oil 6 individual ramekins.
- Mix together the spinach and cottage cheese in a small bowl, then add the nutmeg and seasoning to taste.
- Whisk the egg whites in a separate bowl until stiff enough to hold soft peaks.
- Fold them evenly into the spinach mixture using a large metal spoon, then spoon the mixture into the prepared ramekins. Smooth the tops.
- Sprinkle with the Parmesan and place on a baking tray. Bake for 15 to 20 minutes, or until well risen. Serve immediately.

Baked mozzarella with tomatoes

SERVES 5
145 calories per serving

INGREDIENTS:

6 beefsteak tomatoes (sliced)
100g/4oz Mozzarella cheese (grated)
6 black olives (stoned and sliced)
12 basil leaves

1 tablespoon extra-virgin olive oil
1 tablespoon lemon juice
2 slices white bread (diced)

- Preheat the oven to 200°C/400°F/Gas mark 6.
- Lay the tomato slices overlapping in 6 individual shallow ovenproof dishes.
- Sprinkle the cheese, olives and basil leaves over. Add a few drops of olive oil to each, then a small splash of lemon juice.
- Place the bread on a baking tray. Place the bread and individual dishes in the oven and bake for 8 to 10 minutes. Sprinkle the croûtons over the cheese to serve.

Baked stuffed tomatoes

SERVES 8
125 calories per serving

INGREDIENTS:

8 tomatoes (seeded)
1 garlic clove (chopped)
1 tablespoon chopped fresh parsley
1 tablespoon chopped fresh basil
3 tablespoons dry white wine

2 tablespoons olive oil
50g/2oz fresh breadcrumbs
Butter for greasing
100g/4oz low-fat Mozzarella cheese (shredded)

- Preheat the oven to 220°C/425°F/Gas mark 7. Grease a large baking dish.
- Remove the pulp from the tomatoes, leaving a 5mm/½in shell.
- With a fork, mix the tomato pulp with the garlic, parsley and basil in a medium-sized mixing bowl. Combine the wine and olive oil and blend into the mixture.
- Add the breadcrumbs and mix well. Spoon the mixture into each tomato shell.
- Arrange the tomatoes in the baking dish. Bake in the oven for about 10 minutes.
- Top each tomato with Mozzarella cheese. Return to the oven and cook for a further 10 minutes.

Szechuan beaten chicken

SERVES 4
85 calories per serving

INGREDIENTS:

1 litre/1¾pt water
2 chicken quarters
1 cucumber (cut into matchsticks)

For the sauce:
2 tablespoons soy sauce
1 teaspoon granulated sugar

1 tablespoon finely chopped spring onions
1 teaspoon red chilli oil
¼ teaspoon black pepper
1 teaspoon sesame seeds
2 tablespoons smooth peanut butter (creamed with a little sesame oil)

- Bring the water to a rolling boil in a wok or a large saucepan. Add the chicken pieces, reduce the heat, cover and cook for 30 to 35 minutes.
- Remove the chicken from the wok or pan and immerse in a bowl of cold water for at least 1 hour to cool it, ready for shredding.
- Remove the chicken pieces, drain and dry on absorbent kitchen paper. Take the

→

←

meat off the bones. On a flat surface, pound the chicken with a rolling pin, then tear the meat into shreds with 2 forks. Mix the chicken with the cucumber and arrange in a serving dish.

- To serve, mix together all the sauce ingredients until thoroughly combined and pour over the chicken and cucumber in the serving dish.

Baked fennel

SERVES 4
115 calories per serving

INGREDIENTS:

2 fennel bulbs
2 celery sticks (cut into 7.5cm/3in sticks)
6 sun-dried tomatoes (halved)

200g/7oz passata
2 teaspoons dried oregano
50g/2oz Parmesan cheese (grated)

- Preheat the oven to 190°C/375°F/Gas mark 5.
- Using a sharp knife, trim the fennel, discarding any tough outer leaves, and cut the bulb into quarters.
- Bring a large saucepan of water to the boil, add the fennel and celery and cook for 8 to 10 minutes or until just tender. Remove with a slotted spoon and leave to drain.
- Place the fennel, celery and sun-dried tomatoes in a large ovenproof dish.
- Mix the passata and oregano together and pour the mixture over the fennel in the dish. Sprinkle with the Parmesan and bake for 20 minutes.

Greek-style tomato platter

SERVES 6
100 calories per serving

INGREDIENTS:

8 tomatoes (sliced)
100g/4oz Feta cheese (crumbled)
8 black olives (stoned and sliced)

1 tablespoon chopped fresh oregano
1 tablespoon white wine vinegar
1 tablespoon olive oil

- Arrange the tomato slices on 6 small serving plates. Scatter the cheese, olives and oregano on top. Whisk together the vinegar and oil and drizzle over.

Cheese & onion herb sticks

SERVES 10
215 calories per serving

INGREDIENTS:

300ml/½pt warm water
1 teaspoon dried yeast
Pinch of granulated sugar
1 tablespoon sunflower oil
1 red onion (finely chopped)

450g/1lb white flour
1 teaspoon salt
1 teaspoon dry mustard
3 tablespoons chopped fresh sage
75g/3oz low-fat Cheddar cheese

- Put the water in a jug and sprinkle the yeast on top. Add the sugar, mix well and leave for 10 minutes.
- Heat the oil in a small frying pan and fry the onion until it is well coloured.
- Stir the flour, salt and mustard into a mixing bowl, then add the sage. Set aside 2 tablespoons of the cheese. Stir the rest into the flour mixture and make a well in the centre. Add the yeast mixture with the fried onions and oil, then gradually incorporate the flour and mix to a soft dough, adding extra water if necessary.
- Turn the dough on to a floured surface and knead for 5 minutes until smooth and elastic. Return to the clean bowl, cover with a damp tea towel and leave in a warm place to rise for about 2 hours until doubled in bulk. Lightly grease 2 baking trays.
- Turn the dough on to a floured surface, knead briefly, then divide the mixture in half and roll each piece into a 30cm/12in long stick. Place each stick on a baking tray and make diagonal cuts along the top.
- Sprinkle the sticks with the reserved cheese. Cover and leave for 30 minutes until well risen. Preheat the oven to 220°C/425°F/Gas mark 7.
- Bake the sticks for 25 minutes or until they sound hollow when tapped underneath.

Cheese-stuffed mushrooms

SERVES 4
150 calories per serving

INGREDIENTS:

16 large mushrooms
1 large onion (sliced)
15g/½oz margarine

100g/4oz low-fat cottage cheese
1½ teaspoons prepared mustard
½ teaspoon Worcestershire sauce

→

←
- Preheat the oven to 190°C/375°F/Gas mark 5.
- Remove the stems from the mushrooms and chop the stems. Set the mushroom caps aside. Fry the mushroom stems and onion in the margarine until the vegetables are tender. Remove from the heat. Combine the cottage cheese, mustard and Worcestershire sauce. Add the cooked mushroom mixture and mix.
- Fill the mushroom caps with the mixture. Place on a baking tray and bake for 8 to 10 minutes. Drain on kitchen paper.

Chicken tikka

SERVES 6
135 calories per serving

INGREDIENTS:

450g/1lb chicken without skin or bone (cubed)
1 teaspoon grated fresh root ginger
1 garlic clove (crushed)
1 teaspoon chilli powder
¼ teaspoon ground turmeric

1 teaspoon salt
150ml/¼pt low-fat natural yogurt
50ml/2fl oz lemon juice
1 tablespoon chopped fresh coriander
1 tablespoon sunflower oil

- In a medium-sized bowl, mix together the chicken pieces, ginger, garlic, chilli powder, turmeric, salt, yogurt, lemon juice and coriander, and leave to marinate for at least 2 hours.
- Place on a grill tray in a flameproof dish lined with aluminium foil and baste with the oil.
- Preheat the grill to medium. Grill the chicken for about 15 to 20 minutes until cooked, turning and basting 3 times.

Artichoke & prawn cocktail

SERVES 6
150 calories per serving

INGREDIENTS:

900g/2lb canned artichoke hearts (drained and quartered)
225g/8oz peeled, cooked prawns
3 tablespoons olive oil

2 tablespoons lemon juice
Salt and pepper
150ml/¼pt sour cream

- Put the artichokes in a bowl and add the peeled prawns. Drizzle the oil and lemon juice over and season with a little salt and lots of pepper. Toss gently and chill until ready to serve.
- Just before serving, spoon into 6 wine goblets. Top each with a spoonful of sour cream and serve.

Tiger prawn rolls

SERVES 4

175 calories per serving

INGREDIENTS:

For the dip:
1 small red chilli (deseeded and finely chopped)
1 teaspoon clear honey
4 tablespoons soy sauce

For the rolls:
2 tablespoons chopped fresh coriander
1 garlic clove (finely chopped)
1½ teaspoon Thai red curry paste
16 wonton wrappers
1 egg white (beaten lightly)
16 raw tiger prawns (peeled, with tails intact)
600ml/1pt sunflower oil for deep-frying

- To make the dip, mix the chilli with the honey and soy sauce and stir well.
- Reserve until required.
- To make the prawn rolls, mix the coriander, garlic and red curry paste.
- Brush each wonton wrapper with egg white and place a small amount of the coriander mixture in the centre. Place a prawn on top. Fold the wonton wrapper over, enclosing the prawn and leaving the tail exposed. Repeat with the other prawns.
- Fill a deep-fat fryer or deep saucepan about one-third full with sunflower oil and heat until a cube of bread turns brown in 30 seconds. Add the prawn rolls in small batches and fry for 1 to 2 minutes each until golden brown and crisp. Drain on kitchen paper and transfer to a large serving plate. Garnish with fresh chillies and serve with the dip.

Sweetcorn pancakes

SERVES 4
165 calories per serving

INGREDIENTS:

100g/4oz self-raising flour
1 egg white
150ml/¼pt skimmed milk

200g/7oz canned sweetcorn (drained)
Oil for brushing
Salt and pepper

- Place the flour, egg white and milk in a blender or food processor with half the sweetcorn and process until smooth.
- Season well and add the remaining sweetcorn.
- Heat a frying pan and brush with oil. Drop in tablespoons of batter and cook until set. Turn over the pancakes and cook the other side until golden. Serve hot.

Avocado cream

SERVES 4
150 calories per serving

INGREDIENTS:

1 tablespoon powdered gelatine
50ml/2fl oz cold water
150ml/¼pt vegetable stock
1 large avocado
2 teaspoons lemon juice

4 tablespoons low-calorie mayonnaise
1 teaspoon Worcestershire sauce
1 teaspoon Tabasco sauce
2 tablespoons snipped fresh chives

- Mix the gelatine with the cold water in a small bowl and leave to soften for a few minutes. Stand the bowl in a pan of gently simmering water and stir until the gelatine completely dissolves. Stir in the stock and leave to cool.
- Halve the avocado, remove the stone and scoop the flesh into a bowl. Mash well with the lemon juice. Beat in the mayonnaise and flavour with the Worcestershire and Tabasco sauces. Stir in the chives. Stir the cool stock into the avocado mixture.
- Divide between 4 small dishes and chill until set.

Minted melon & grapefruit

SERVES 4
100 calories per serving

INGREDIENTS:

1 small galia melon
2 pink grapefruit
1 yellow grapefruit
1 teaspoon Dijon mustard

1 teaspoon sherry vinegar
1 teaspoon clear honey
1 tablespoon chopped fresh mint
Sprigs of fresh mint, to garnish

- Halve the melon and remove the seeds with a teaspoon. With a melon baller, carefully scoop the flesh into balls.
- With a small sharp knife, peel the grapefruit and remove all the white pith.
- Remove the segments by cutting between the membranes, holding the fruit over a small bowl to catch any juices.
- Whisk the mustard, vinegar, honey, mint and grapefruit juices together in a mixing bowl. Add the melon balls together with the grapefruit and mix well.
- Chill for 30 minutes.
- Ladle into 4 glass dishes and serve garnished with sprigs of fresh mint.

Prawn & sesame seed toast

SERVES 4
240 calories per serving

INGREDIENTS:

225g/8oz cooked peeled prawns
1 spring onion
¼ teaspoon salt
1 teaspoon soy sauce
1 tablespoon cornflour

1 egg white (beaten)
3 thin slices white bread (crusts removed)
4 tablespoons sesame seeds
600ml/1pt vegetable oil for deep-frying

- Put the prawns and spring onion into a blender or food processor and process until finely chopped. Transfer to a bowl and stir in the salt, soy sauce, cornflour and egg white.
- Spread the mixture on to one side of each slice of bread. Spread the sesame seeds on top of the mixture, pressing down well. Cut each slice into 4 equal triangles.
- Heat the vegetable oil for deep-frying in a wok over a medium-high heat.
- Carefully place the triangles in the oil, coated side down, and cook for 2 to 3

→

←

minutes until golden brown. Remove with a slotted spoon and drain on kitchen paper. Serve immediately.

Tomato & cheese tarts

SERVES 4
60 calories per serving

INGREDIENTS:

2 sheets filo pastry
1 egg white
100g/4oz low-fat soft cheese

Salt and pepper
Handful fresh basil leaves
3 small tomatoes (sliced)

- Preheat the oven to 200°C/400°F/Gas mark 6.
- Brush the sheets of filo pastry lightly with egg white and cut into 16 squares measuring 10cm/4in.
- Layer the squares in twos, in 8 patty tins. Spoon the cheese into the pastry cases.
- Season and top with basil leaves.
- Arrange the tomatoes on the tarts, add seasoning and bake for 10 to 12 minutes, until golden. Serve warm.

Sweet & sour baby onions

SERVES 4
135 calories per serving

INGREDIENTS:

350g/12oz baby onions
2 tablespoons olive oil
2 fresh bay leaves (torn into strips)
Thinly pared zest of 1 lemon

1 tablespoon demerara sugar
1 tablespoon clear honey
4 tablespoons red wine vinegar

- Soak the onions in a bowl of boiling water for 15 minutes. Using a sharp knife, peel and halve the onions.
- Heat the oil in a large frying pan. Add the onions and bay leaves to the pan and cook for 5 to 6 minutes over a medium-high heat until browned all over.
- Cut the lemon zest into thin matchsticks. Add to the frying pan with the sugar and honey. Cook for 2 to 3 minutes, stirring occasionally, until the onions are lightly caramelized.

- Add the vinegar to the frying pan. Cook for about 5 minutes, stirring, until the onions are tender. Transfer the onions to a dish and serve immediately.

Stuffed celery

SERVES 6
100 calories per serving

INGREDIENTS:

225g/8oz low-fat cottage cheese
2 teaspoons lemon juice
½ teaspoon soy sauce
1 teaspoon prepared mustard
50g/2oz red pepper (chopped)

50g/2oz chives (chopped)
1 garlic clove (crushed)
6 celery sticks (washed, with leaves removed)

- Place all the ingredients except the celery into a blender or food processor and blend until smooth. Stuff the celery sticks with the cheese mixture. Refrigerate for at least 30 minutes before serving.

Steamed crab cakes

SERVES 4
160 calories per serving

INGREDIENTS:

2 garlic cloves (crushed)
1 teaspoon finely chopped lemon grass
½ teaspoon ground black pepper
2 tablespoons chopped fresh coriander
3 tablespoons creamed coconut
1 tablespoon lime juice

200g/7oz cooked crabmeat (flaked)
1 tablespoon Thai fish sauce
2 egg whites
1 egg yolk (lightly beaten)
600ml/1pt sunflower oil for deep-frying

- Line 8 x 125ml/4fl oz ramekins with aluminium foil.
- Mix the garlic, lemon grass, pepper and coriander together in a bowl.
- Mash the coconut with the lime juice until smooth. Stir it into the other ingredients with the crabmeat and fish sauce.
- Whisk the egg whites in a clean bowl until stiff, then lightly and evenly fold them into the crab mixture. Spoon the mixture into the prepared ramekins and press down lightly. Brush the tops with egg yolk.

→

←
- Place in a steamer half-filled with boiling water, then cover with a close-fitting lid and steam for 15 minutes, or until firm to the touch. Pour off any excess liquid and remove from the ramekins.
- Fill a deep saucepan about one-third full with sunflower oil and heat until a cube of bread browns in 30 seconds. Add the crab cakes in batches and deep-fry for about 1 minute, turning once, until golden brown. Drain on kitchen paper.

Lemony stuffed courgettes

SERVES 4
130 calories per serving

INGREDIENTS:

4 courgettes (about 175g/6oz each)
1 teaspoon sunflower oil
1 garlic clove (crushed)
1 teaspoon ground lemon grass
Grated zest and juice of ½ lemon

100g/4oz long-grain rice
175g/6oz cherry tomatoes (halved)
25g/1oz toasted cashew nuts
Salt and pepper

- Preheat the oven to 200°C/400°F/Gas mark 6. Grease a medium-sized baking tin.
- Halve the courgettes lengthways and use a teaspoon to scoop out the centres, reserving the flesh. Blanch the shells in boiling water for 1 minutes, then drain.
- Chop the courgette flesh finely and place in a saucepan with the oil and garlic.
- Stir over a moderate heat until softened, but not browned.
- Stir in the lemon grass, lemon zest and juice, rice, tomatoes and nuts. Season well and spoon into the courgette shells. Place the shells in the baking tin and cover with aluminium foil.
- Bake for 25 to 30 minutes or until the courgettes are tender. Serve hot.

Parma ham & pepper pizzas

SERVES 4
100 calories per serving

INGREDIENTS:

½ loaf ciabatta bread
1 red pepper (roasted and peeled)
1 yellow pepper (roasted and peeled)

4 slices Parma ham (cut into thick strips)
50g/2oz reduced-fat Mozzarella cheese

- Cut the bread into 4 thick slices and toast until golden.
- Cut the peppers into thick strips and arrange on the bread with the Parma ham.
- Preheat the grill.
- Thinly slice the Mozzarella and arrange on top. Grill for 2 to 3 minutes, until the cheese is bubbling. Serve hot.

Crab & cucumber savouries

SERVES 6
150 calories per serving

INGREDIENTS:

1 large cucumber (diced)
50g/2oz low-fat spread
225g/8oz button mushrooms (sliced)
2 teaspoons plain flour
150ml/¼pt fish stock (made with
½ stock cube)

1 tablespoon dry sherry
75ml/3fl oz low-fat single cream
175g/6oz canned white crabmeat
Salt and pepper

- Boil the cucumber in lightly salted water for 3 minutes then drain well. In the same pan, melt the low-fat spread and cook the mushrooms, stirring, for 2 minutes.
- Add the cucumber, cover and cook over a gentle heat for 2 minutes.
- Stir in the flour, remove from the heat and add the stock, sherry and cream.
- Return to the heat, bring to the boil and cook for 2 minutes, stirring.
- Add the crabmeat and season to taste.
- Heat through, then spoon into 6 serving dishes.

Baked stuffed beetroot

SERVES 6
150 calories per serving

INGREDIENTS:

6 large cooked beetroot
25g/1oz low-fat spread
100g/4oz button mushrooms (chopped)
25g/1oz plain flour
200ml/7fl oz skimmed milk
1 teaspoon lemon juice

75g/3oz Emmental cheese (grated)
Salt and pepper
2 tablespoons chopped fresh parsley
75ml/3fl oz water
2 teaspoons caraway seeds

→

←
- Preheat the oven to 200°C/400°F/Gas mark 6.
- Peel the beetroot if necessary and trim the roots. Cut a slice off the top of each.
- Using a metal spoon, scoop out the flesh, leaving a 1cm/½in thick wall of beetroot. Stand the beetroot shells in a deep baking dish.
- Melt the low-fat spread in a saucepan, add the mushrooms and cook gently, stirring, for 2 minutes. Blend in the flour. Remove from the heat and gradually stir in the milk.
- Return to the heat and bring to the boil, stirring, until thickened. Simmer for 2 minutes. Stir in the lemon juice and half the cheese and season to taste. Stir in the parsley. Spoon the mixture into the beetroot shells and sprinkle with the remaining cheese.
- Pour the water around the beetroots and bake in the oven for about 30 minutes, until the cheese is bubbling. Transfer to serving plates and sprinkle with caraway seeds before serving.

Griddled smoked salmon

SERVES 4
120 calories per serving

INGREDIENTS:

350g/12oz sliced smoked salmon   *2 teaspoons sherry vinegar*
1 teaspoon Dijon mustard   *4 tablespoons olive oil*
1 garlic clove (crushed)   *Salt and pepper*
2 teaspoons chopped fresh dill   *100g/4oz mixed salad leaves*

- Fold the slices of smoked salmon, making 2 folds, accordion-style, so they form little parcels.
- To make the vinaigrette, whisk the mustard, garlic, dill, vinegar, oil and seasoning together in a small bowl.
- Heat a ridged griddle pan over a medium heat until smoking. Add the salmon parcels and cook on one side only for 2 to 3 minutes until heated through.
- Meanwhile, dress the salad leaves with some of the vinaigrette and divide between 4 serving plates. Top with the smoked salmon, cooked side up. Drizzle with the remaining vinaigrette.

Devilled eggs

SERVES 4
80 calories per serving

INGREDIENTS:

100g/4oz low-fat cottage cheese
50g/2oz low-fat mayonnaise
50g/2oz onion (finely diced)
50g/2oz celery (finely diced)
¼ teaspoon celery seed
¼ teaspoon salt

1 teaspoon Dijon mustard
8 eggs (hard-boiled, halved with
yolks removed)
2 tablespoons chopped fresh parsley

- In a medium-sized bowl, beat the cottage cheese and mayonnaise until fluffy. Add all the remaining ingredients, except for the eggs and parsley, and beat well.
- Stuff the eggs with the mixture and refrigerate. Before serving, scatter with the parsley.

Pineapple boats

SERVES 6
100 calories per serving

INGREDIENTS:

1 pineapple
225g/8oz low-fat cottage cheese
1 red pepper (chopped)

1 green chilli (seeded and chopped)
Salt and pepper

- Cut the pineapple into 6 wedges, cut most of the flesh from the skin and roughly chop, discarding any tough central core. Place the flesh in a bowl with the cottage cheese, pepper and chilli. Mix well and season to taste.
- Place the pineapple skins on individual serving plates. Spoon the cheese mixture on to the skins and chill for at least 1 hour before serving.

Soups

When it is cold outside, there is nothing more comforting than a bowl of soup. Whether you want a warm starter, a lunchtime treat or just something to fend off the winter chill – choose from a selection that includes classics such as Vegetable minestrone and Chicken & pasta soup, as well as a few more unusual dishes, such as Medieval apple soup, Chinese egg flower soup and Curried carrot & apple soup.

Consommé

SERVES 6

115 calories per serving

INGREDIENTS:

1.25 litres/2¼pt beef stock
225g/8oz extra lean minced beef
2 tomatoes (chopped)
2 large carrots (chopped)
1 large onion (chopped)
2 celery sticks (chopped)

1 turnip (chopped)
1 bouquet garni
2 egg whites
Shells of 2 eggs (crushed)
Salt and pepper
1 tablespoon sherry

- Put the stock and minced beef in a saucepan. Add the tomatoes, carrots, onion, celery, turnip, bouquet garni, egg whites, egg shells and plenty of seasoning.
- Bring almost to boiling point, whisking all the time with a flat whisk.
- Cover and simmer for 1 hour, taking care not to allow the layer of froth on top of the soup to break. Pour the soup through a scalded fine cloth, keeping the froth back. Repeat if necessary until the liquid is clear. Add the sherry and reheat.

Chicken & pasta soup

SERVES 6

130 calories per serving

INGREDIENTS:

900ml/1½pt chicken stock
1 bay leaf
4 spring onions (sliced)
225g/8oz button mushrooms (sliced)
100g/4oz cooked chicken breast
(skinned and thinly sliced)

Salt and pepper
50g/2oz soup pasta
150ml/¼pt dry white wine
1 tablespoon chopped fresh parsley

- Put the stock and bay leaf into a pan and bring to the boil. Add the spring onions and mushrooms.
- Add the chicken to the soup and season to taste. Heat through for 2 to 3 minutes.
- Add the pasta, cover and simmer for 7 to 8 minutes. Just before serving, add the wine and parsley, heat through for 2 to 3 minutes, then season to taste.

Potato & pork soup

SERVES 4
170 calories per serving

INGREDIENTS:

1 litre/1³/₄pt chicken stock
2 large potatoes (diced)
2 tablespoons rice wine vinegar
25g/1oz cornflour
4 tablespoons water
100g/4oz pork fillet (sliced)
1 tablespoon soy sauce

1 teaspoon sesame oil
1 carrot (cut into matchsticks)
1 teaspoon chopped fresh root ginger
3 spring onions (sliced thinly)
1 red pepper (sliced)
225g/8oz canned bamboo shoots
(drained)

- Add the chicken stock, potatoes and 1 tablespoon vinegar to a saucepan and bring to the boil. Reduce the heat until the stock is just simmering.
- Mix the cornflour with the water to make a paste, then stir into the hot stock.
- Bring the stock back to the boil, stirring until thickened, then reduce the heat until it is just simmering again.
- Place the pork in a dish and season with the remaining vinegar, the soy sauce and sesame oil.
- Add the pork, carrot and ginger to the stock and cook for 10 minutes. Stir in the spring onions, pepper and bamboo shoots. Cook for a further 5 minutes. Pour into warmed serving bowls and serve immediately.

Watercress soup mimosa

SERVES 6
100 calories per serving

INGREDIENTS:

15g/¹/₂oz low-fat spread
1 onion (chopped)
350g/12oz watercress (roughly chopped)
1 tablespoon plain flour
1 litre/1³/₄pt chicken stock

Salt and pepper
¹/₄ teaspoon grated nutmeg
50ml/2fl oz low-fat single cream
2 eggs (hard-boiled and finely chopped)

- Heat the low-fat spread in a large saucepan and fry the onion for 2 minutes.
- Add the watercress to the onion mixture and cook, stirring, for a further 2

→

← minutes. Stir in the flour.
- Remove from the heat and gradually blend in the stock. Return to the heat and bring to the boil, stirring. Season with salt, pepper and nutmeg. Reduce the heat and simmer for 20 minutes.
- Purée the mixture in a blender or food processor and return to the heat. Stir in the cream and reheat. Ladle into soup bowls and sprinkle the chopped egg on top.

Lentil soup

SERVES 8
130 calories per serving

INGREDIENTS:

3 litres/5/4pt cold water
700g/1½lb red lentils
225g/8oz stewing beef
1 leek (finely chopped)
3 large carrots (finely chopped)

100g/4oz celery (chopped)
225g/8oz onion (finely chopped)
25g/1oz plain flour
50ml/2fl oz white wine

- Place the water in a large casserole dish and bring to the boil. Add the lentils, beef, leek, carrots and celery. Return the mixture to the boil, reduce the heat, cover and simmer for 40 minutes.
- Remove the beef and brown in a frying pan over a low heat. When it is very hot, add the onions. Cook for 15 minutes, stirring frequently. Sprinkle the flour over and stir until the flour browns.
- Pour 225ml/8fl oz of the lentil mixture over the meat and onions and stir well.
- Add the wine and cook for a further 1 minute. Add the contents of the frying pan to the lentils and simmer for a further 30 minutes, then serve immediately.

White onion soup

SERVES 6
150 calories per serving

INGREDIENTS:

4 large onions (thinly sliced)
50g/2oz low-fat spread
Salt and pepper
450ml/³/4pt vegetable stock

450ml/³/4pt skimmed milk
2 egg yolks
½ teaspoon lemon juice
2 thick slices wholemeal bread (cubed)

- Preheat the oven to 200°C/400°F/Gas mark 6.
- Heat the low-fat spread in a saucepan, add the onions and cook gently, covered, for 10 minutes, stirring from time to time, until soft. Add a little seasoning and the stock. Bring to the boil, reduce the heat and simmer gently for 30 minutes.
- Stir in the milk and heat through.
- Whisk the egg yolks with the lemon juice. Add 2 ladlefuls of the hot soup and whisk well. Return to the pan and heat through gently until slightly thickened but do not allow to boil.
- Spread out the bread cubes on a baking tray and bake in the oven for 10 minutes until a deep golden brown. Ladle the soup into individual bowls and sprinkle with the croûtons just before serving.

Chinese cabbage soup

SERVES 4
70 calories per serving

INGREDIENTS:

450g/1lb pak choi
600ml/1pt vegetable stock
1 tablespoon rice wine vinegar
1 tablespoon soy sauce
1 tablespoon caster sugar

1 tablespoon dry sherry
1 red chilli (seeded and thinly sliced)
1 tablespoon cornflour
2 tablespoons water

- Wash the pak choi thoroughly under cold running water, rinse and drain. Pat dry with kitchen paper. Trim the stems from the pak choi and shred the leaves.
- Heat the stock in a large saucepan. Add the pak choi and cook for 10 to 15 minutes.
- Mix together the vinegar, soy sauce, sugar and sherry in a small bowl. Add this mixture to the stock, together with the chilli. Bring to the boil, lower the heat and cook for 2 to 3 minutes.
- Blend the cornflour with the water to form a paste and gradually stir into the soup. Cook, stirring constantly, until it thickens. Cook for a further 4 to 5 minutes, then ladle the soup into individual serving bowls and serve immediately.

Red onion & beetroot soup

SERVES 6
80 calories per serving

INGREDIENTS:

2 teaspoons olive oil
350g/12oz red onions (sliced)
2 garlic cloves (crushed)
275g/10oz cooked beetroot (cut into sticks)

1.2 litres/2pt vegetable stock
50g/2oz cooked soup pasta
2 tablespoons raspberry vinegar
Salt and pepper

- Heat the oil in a casserole dish and add the onion and garlic. Cook gently for about 20 minutes or until soft and tender.
- Add the beetroot, stock, pasta and vinegar and heat through. Season to taste and serve hot.

Smooth cheese soup

SERVES 4
150 calories per serving

INGREDIENTS:

1 large potato (diced)
1 large carrot (diced)
1 small onion (diced)
1 celery stick (diced)
600ml/1pt vegetable stock

½ teaspoon dried mixed herbs
100g/4oz low-fat Cheddar cheese (grated)
150ml/¼pt skimmed milk

- Put the vegetables in a saucepan with the stock and herbs. Bring to the boil, reduce the heat, part-cover and simmer gently for 15 minutes until the vegetables are soft.
- Purée in a blender or food processor and return to the pan. Add the cheese and milk and heat until the cheese melts. Ladle into bowls and serve hot.

Creamy scallop soup

SERVES 4

100 calories per serving

INGREDIENTS:

50g/2oz butter
1 onion (finely chopped)
450g/1lb potatoes (diced)
Salt and pepper
600ml/1pt fish stock

350g/12oz scallops
300ml/½pt milk
2 egg yolks
75ml/3fl oz double cream

- Melt the butter in a large saucepan over a very low heat. Add the onion and cook for 10 minutes until softened, but not coloured. Add the potatoes and salt and pepper to taste, cover and cook for a further 10 minutes.
- Pour in the stock, bring to the boil and simmer for a further 10 to 15 minutes, until the potatoes are tender.
- Meanwhile, prepare the scallops. Roughly chop the white meat and put into a second saucepan with the milk. Bring to a gentle simmer and cook for 6 to 8 minutes until the scallops are just tender.
- When the potatoes are cooked, transfer them and their cooking liquid to a blender or food processor and process to a purée. Return the mixture to a clean saucepan with the scallops and the milk and heat through.
- Remove the pan from the heat. Whisk the egg yolks and cream together and add to the soup. Return to a very gentle heat and, stirring constantly, reheat the soup until thickened slightly. Do not boil or the soup will curdle. Adjust the seasoning to taste and serve.

Mushroom & corn soup

SERVES 4

150 calories per serving

INGREDIENTS:

25g/1oz low-fat spread
25g/1oz plain flour
100g/4oz button mushrooms (sliced)
1 onion (finely chopped)
300ml/½pt vegetable stock

300ml/½pt skimmed milk
350g/12oz canned sweetcorn (drained)
Salt and pepper
4 teaspoons low-fat single cream

→

←
- Heat the low-fat spread in a saucepan, add the mushrooms and onion, and cook, stirring constantly, for 3 minutes. Add the flour and cook, stirring, for 1 minute.
- Remove from the heat and gradually blend in the stock, then the milk and sweetcorn. Return to the heat, bring to the boil, reduce the heat and simmer gently for 10 minutes, stirring occasionally. Season to taste. Ladle into warm bowls and garnish each with a swirl of cream.

Tomato & carrot soup

SERVES 4
100 calories per serving

INGREDIENTS:

400g/14oz canned chopped tomatoes
2 large carrots (grated)
1 small onion (finely chopped)
300ml/¹/₂pt vegetable stock (made with
1 stock cube)

1 teaspoon dried oregano
Pinch of grated nutmeg
Pinch of salt
1 bay leaf
1 tablespoon chopped fresh parsley

- Put all the ingredients except the parsley in a saucepan and bring to the boil, stirring. Reduce the heat, part-cover and simmer for 30 minutes.
- Discard the bay leaf, ladle into bowls and serve garnished with the parsley.

Curried carrot & apple soup

SERVES 4
120 calories per serving

INGREDIENTS:

2 teaspoons sunflower oil
1 tablespoon mild korma curry powder
500g/1lb 2oz carrots (chopped)
1 large onion (chopped)

1 cooking apple (chopped)
900ml/1¹/₂pt chicken stock
Salt and pepper

- Heat the oil in a saucepan and gently fry the curry powder for 2 to 3 minutes.
- Add the carrots, onion and apple, stir well, then cover the pan and cook over a

very low heat for about 15 minutes, shaking the pan occasionally, until softened.
- Spoon the vegetable mixture into a blender or food processor, then add half the stock and blend until smooth.
- Return the mixture to the pan and pour in the remaining stock. Bring the soup to the boil and adjust the seasoning before serving.

Medieval apple soup

SERVES 6
100 calories per serving

INGREDIENTS:

2 large cooking apples (cored and chopped)
1 litre/1³/₄pt lamb stock
2.5cm/1in cinnamon stick

½ teaspoon grated fresh root ginger
Salt and pepper
50g/2oz long-grain rice (cooked)

- Place the apple in a pan with the stock, cinnamon and ginger. Bring to the boil, reduce the heat, part-cover and simmer gently for 20 minutes until the apples are pulpy. Remove the cinnamon stick. Purée the soup in a blender or food processor and return to the pan.
- Season to taste and add the rice. Heat through then serve.

Vegetable minestrone

SERVES 8
90 calories per serving

INGREDIENTS:

Large pinch of saffron strands
1 tablespoon boiling water
1 onion (chopped)
1 leek (sliced)
1 celery stick (sliced)
2 carrots (diced)
3 garlic cloves (crushed)
600ml/1pt chicken stock

800g/1³/₄lb canned chopped tomatoes
50g/2oz frozen peas
50g/2oz soup pasta
1 teaspoon caster sugar
Salt and pepper
1 tablespoon chopped fresh parsley
1 tablespoon chopped fresh basil

- Soak the saffron strands in the boiling water and leave to stand for 10 minutes.

→

←
- Put the onion, leek, celery, carrot and garlic into a large pan. Add the stock, bring to the boil, cover and simmer for about 10 minutes.
- Add the tomatoes, the saffron with its liquid and the peas. Bring to the boil and add the soup pasta. Simmer for 10 minutes until tender.
- Season with the sugar and salt and pepper to taste. Stir in the parsley and basil just before serving.

Green soup

SERVES 4

125 calories per serving

INGREDIENTS:

1 tablespoon olive oil
1 onion (chopped)
1 garlic clove (chopped)
200g/7oz potato (cut into 2.5cm/1in cubes)
700ml/1¼pt vegetable stock

1 small cucumber (cut into chunks)
75g/3oz watercress
100g/4oz green beans (trimmed and halved)
Salt and pepper

- Heat the oil in a large saucepan and fry the onion and garlic for 3 to 4 minutes or until softened. Add the potato and cook for a further 2 to 3 minutes.
- Stir in the stock, bring to the boil and leave to simmer for 5 minutes.
- Add the cucumber to the saucepan and cook for a further 3 minutes or until the potatoes are tender.
- Add the watercress and allow to wilt. Then place the mixture in a blender or food processor and purée until smooth.
- Bring a small saucepan of water to the boil and cook the beans for 3 to 4 minutes or until tender. Add the beans to the soup, season and warm through.

Oriental noodle soup

SERVES 6

150 calories per serving

INGREDIENTS:

1.8 litres/3pt beef stock
1 teaspoon finely chopped lemon grass
2 teaspoons soy sauce

175g/6oz vermicelli (broken into small pieces)

- Bring the stock to the boil with the lemon grass and soy sauce. Add the vermicelli and simmer for 6 minutes, or until the noodles are tender.

Winter vegetable soup

SERVES 6
100 calories per serving

INGREDIENTS:

25g/1oz low-fat spread
2 onions (finely chopped)
2 large carrots (finely diced)
1 small swede (finely diced)
1 potato (finely diced)
1 leek (thinly sliced)

600ml/1pt vegetable stock
1 bay leaf
Salt and pepper
100g/4oz frozen peas
300ml/½pt skimmed milk
1 tablespoon cornflour

- Heat the low-fat spread in a saucepan and fry the onions for 2 minutes until soft but not brown. Add the carrots, swede, potato and leek and toss for 1 minute.
- Add the stock, bay leaf and a little seasoning.
- Bring to the boil, reduce the heat, part cover and simmer gently for 15 minutes.
- Add the peas and cook for a further 3 minutes.
- Blend a little of the milk with the cornflour to make a smooth paste. Stir in the remaining milk. Add to the pan and bring to the boil, stirring, until thickened slightly. Simmer for 2 minutes. Discard the bay leaf and serve immediately,

Greek lemon soup

SERVES 4
150 calories per serving

INGREDIENTS:

1 tablespoon cornflour
1 litre/1¾pt chicken stock
50g/2oz long-grain rice

4 tablespoons fresh lemon juice
3 eggs

- Stir the cornflour into 225ml/8fl oz chicken stock until it has dissolved. Pour into a saucepan and add the remaining stock. Heat over a medium heat, add the rice and cook until tender. Remove from the heat.
- Beat the lemon juice and eggs together. Whisk half the stock, a little at a time,

→

← into the egg mixture. Pour the egg mixture into pan with remaining stock, mixing well. Return to a low heat and cook, stirring constantly, until the soup is just thickened. Serve immediately.

Lamb & rice soup

SERVES 4
120 calories per serving

INGREDIENTS:

150g/5oz lean lamb
Salt
50g/2oz long-grain rice
900ml/1½pt lamb stock
1 leek (sliced)

1 garlic clove (thinly sliced)
2 teaspoons soy sauce
1 teaspoon rice wine vinegar
1 medium open-cap mushroom (thinly sliced)

- Using a sharp knife, trim any fat from the lamb and cut the meat into thin strips. Set aside until required.
- Bring a large pan of lightly salted water to the boil and add the rice. Bring back to the boil, stir once, reduce the heat and cook for 10 to 15 minutes, until tender.
- Drain the rice, rinse under cold running water, drain again and set aside until required.
- Put the stock in a large saucepan and bring to the boil. Add the lamb strips, leek, garlic, soy sauce and vinegar, reduce the heat, cover and leave to simmer for 10 minutes, or until the lamb is tender and cooked through.
- Add the mushroom and the rice to the pan and cook for a further 2 to 3 minutes, or until the mushroom is completely cooked through. Serve immediately.

Rich kidney soup

SERVES 4
150 calories per serving

INGREDIENTS:

25g/1oz low-fat spread
225g/8oz lambs' kidneys (finely chopped)
1 small onion (finely chopped)
25g/1oz plain flour

750ml/1¼pt lamb stock
1 small bay leaf
Salt and pepper
2 tablespoons port

- Heat the low-fat spread in a saucepan and add the kidneys and onion. Fry for 1 minute, stirring over a gentle heat so the kidneys do not toughen. Add the flour and cook for 1 minute.
- Remove from the heat and blend in the stock. Add the bay leaf and seasoning to taste.
- Return to the heat and bring to the boil, stirring, until thickened. Reduce the heat, part-cover and simmer gently for 30 minutes. Remove the bay leaf.
- Purée in a blender or food processor and return to the saucepan. Stir in the port, heat through and serve.

Prawn wonton soup

SERVES 4
100 calories per serving

INGREDIENTS:

For the wontons:
175g/6oz cooked prawns (peeled)
1 garlic clove (crushed)
1 spring onion (finely chopped)
1 tablespoon soy sauce
1 tablespoon Thai fish sauce
1 tablespoon chopped fresh coriander
1 small egg (separated)
12 wonton wrappers

For the soup:
1 litre/1³/₄pt beef stock
1 tablespoon Thai fish sauce
1 tablespoon soy sauce
1 tablespoon Chinese rice wine
2 small red chillies (seeded and sliced)
2 spring onions (sliced)

- Finely chop the prawns. Put them into a bowl and stir in the garlic, spring onion, soy sauce, fish sauce, coriander and egg yolk.
- Lay the wonton wrappers on a work surface in a single layer and place about 1 tablespoon of the filling mixture in the centre of each. Brush the edges with egg white and fold each one into a triangle, pressing lightly to seal. Bring the 2 bottom corners of the triangle around to meet in the centre, securing with a little egg white to hold in place.
- To make the soup, place the stock, fish sauce, soy sauce and rice wine in a large saucepan and bring to the boil over a medium heat. Add the chillies and spring onions. Drop the wontons into the pan and simmer for 4 to 5 minutes, until thoroughly heated. Serve immediately.

Red pepper soup

SERVES 6
90 calories per serving

INGREDIENTS:

1 tablespoon olive oil
4 red peppers (seeded and chopped)
1 large onion (chopped)
1 garlic clove (crushed)
1 small red chilli (seeded and sliced)

50ml/2fl oz tomato purée
900ml/1½pt chicken stock
Finely grated zest and juice of 1 lime
Salt and pepper

- Heat the oil in a saucepan and add the peppers and onion. Cook gently, with the saucepan covered, for about 5 minutes, shaking the pan occasionally. Stir in the garlic, then add the chilli with the tomato purée. Stir in half the stock, then bring to the boil. Cover the pan and simmer for 10 minutes.
- Cool slightly, then purée in a blender or food processor. Return to the pan, then add the remaining stock, the lime zest and juice, and seasoning to taste. Bring the soup to the boil, then serve immediately.

Cream of artichoke soup

SERVES 6
25 calories per serving

INGREDIENTS:

750g/1lb 11oz Jerusalem artichokes
(peeled and sliced)
1 lemon (sliced thickly)
50g/2oz butter
2 onions (chopped)
1 garlic clove (crushed)
1.5 litres/2¼pt vegetable stock

Salt and pepper
2 bay leaves
¼ teaspoon ground nutmeg
1 tablespoon lemon juice
150ml/¼pt single cream
Salt and pepper

- Put the artichokes into a bowl of water with the lemon slices.
- Melt the butter in a large saucepan. Add the onions and garlic and fry gently for 3 to 4 minutes until soft.
- Drain the artichokes, discarding the lemon, and add to the pan. Mix well and cook gently for 2 to 3 minutes without allowing to colour.
- Add the stock, seasoning, bay leaves, nutmeg and lemon juice. Bring slowly to

the boil, then cover and simmer gently for about 30 minutes.
- Discard the bay leaves. Cool the soup slightly then process in a blender or food processor until smooth.
- Pour into a clean pan and bring to the boil. Stir in the cream and cook gently, without boiling, for 2 minutes. Serve immediately.

Cream of lettuce soup

SERVES 6
80 calories per serving

INGREDIENTS:

600ml/1pt chicken stock
1 small lettuce (shredded)
25g/1oz low-fat spread
1 small onion (chopped)
1/2 teaspoon ground nutmeg

Salt and pepper
300ml/1/2pt skimmed milk
1 egg yolk
2 tablespoons low-fat single cream

- Bring the stock to the boil, add the lettuce and boil for 5 minutes. Take out about 2 tablespoons of the lettuce shreds with a slotted spoon and reserve.
- In a separate pan, heat the low-fat spread and then add the onion. Cook for 3 minutes until soft. Add the lettuce and stock and season to taste with the nutmeg, salt and pepper. Simmer for 5 minutes until the onion is very soft.
- Purée in a blender or food processor and return to the saucepan. Stir in the milk.
- Whisk the egg yolk and cream together. Whisk in a little of the hot soup. Pour the mixture back into the remaining soup and heat through. Add the reserved lettuce and ladle into serving bowls.

Hot & sour prawn soup

SERVES 6
50 calories per serving

INGREDIENTS:

450g/1lb raw king prawns
1 litre/1³/4pt chicken stock
3 lemon grass stalks
10 kaffir lime leaves (torn in half)
225g/8oz canned straw mushrooms

3 tablespoons Thai fish sauce
50ml/2fl oz lime juice
2 tablespoons chopped spring onions
1 tablespoon chopped fresh coriander
4 red chillies (seeded and chopped)

→

←
- Shell and devein the prawns and set aside. Rinse the prawn shells, place them in a large saucepan with the stock and bring to the boil.
- Bruise the lemon grass stalks with the blunt edge of a chopping knife and add them to the stock together with half the lime leaves. Simmer gently for 5 to 6 minutes, until the stalks change colour and the stock is fragrant.
- Strain the stock, return to the saucepan and reheat. Drain the mushrooms and add them and the prawns, then cook until the prawns turn pink. Stir in the fish sauce, lime juice, spring onions, coriander, chillies and the rest of the lime leaves.

Cucumber soup

SERVES 4
90 calories per serving

INGREDIENTS:

1 cucumber
Salt
2 teaspoons dried dill

2 tablespoons cider vinegar
300ml/¹/₂pt low-fat plain yogurt
300ml/¹/₂pt skimmed milk

- Cut 4 thin slices off the cucumber and reserve for the garnish. Grate the remainder into a large bowl and sprinkle with salt. Leave to stand for 10 minutes. Squeeze out all the moisture and drain off.
- Stir in the dill, vinegar and yogurt. Chill for 30 minutes.
- Just before serving, stir in the milk, pour into individual serving bowls and garnish with the reserved cucumber slices.

Cream of pea soup

SERVES 10
240 calories per serving

INGREDIENTS:

675g/1¹/₂lb quick-cooking dried split peas
3 litres/5pt chicken stock
50g/2oz margarine
3 small carrots (peeled and grated)

2 small onions (peeled and grated)
1 large leek (chopped)
1¹/₂ teaspoons granulated sugar
375g/13oz canned evaporated skimmed milk

- Rinse the split peas, drain, and place in a large casserole dish. Add the stock and bring to the boil, reduce the heat and simmer for 10 minutes. Skim the froth from the top of the soup.
- Melt 40g/1½oz margarine in a frying pan and fry the carrots and onion until golden. Add the leek and cook for 10 minutes over a low heat. Stir the vegetable mixture and sugar together into the stock. Simmer for about 2 hours, until the split peas are tender.
- Rub the soup through a fine sieve, or purée in a blender or food processor.
- Return to the casserole dish and stir in the evaporated milk. Heat without boiling, stirring occasionally. Just before serving, add the remaining margarine.

Pea & ham soup

SERVES 4
150 calories per serving

INGREDIENTS:

225g/8oz frozen peas
1.2 litres/2pt ham stock
50g/2oz cooked ham (chopped)

50ml/2fl oz skimmed milk
Salt and pepper
Pinch of grated nutmeg

- Simmer the peas in the stock in a saucepan for 3 minutes. Purée in a blender or food processor and return to the pan.
- Add the chopped ham and milk and heat through. Season to taste with the salt, pepper and nutmeg and serve hot.

Sweetcorn chowder

SERVES 4
145 calories per serving

INGREDIENTS:

25g/1oz low-fat spread
25g/1oz plain flour
1 bunch spring onions (finely chopped)
1 large potato (diced)
300ml/½pt vegetable stock

300ml/½pt skimmed milk
200g/7oz canned sweetcorn (drained)
Salt and pepper
50g/2oz low-fat Cheddar cheese
(grated)

→

←
- Heat the low-fat spread in a saucepan and add the spring onions and potato.
- Gently fry for 5 minutes. Add the flour and cook for 1 minute, stirring.
- Remove from the heat and gradually blend in the stock, then add the milk and sweetcorn.
- Return to the heat, bring to the boil, stirring, then reduce the heat and simmer very gently for 15 minutes. Season to taste. Stir in the cheese and ladle into individual bowls to serve.

Tomato & coriander soup

SERVES 4
120 calories per serving

INGREDIENTS:

700g/1½lb small fresh tomatoes
2 tablespoons vegetable oil
1 bay leaf
4 spring onions (cut into 2.5cm/1in pieces)
1 teaspoon salt

1 teaspoon garlic pulp
1 teaspoon crushed black peppercorns
2 tablespoons chopped fresh coriander
750ml/1¼pt water
1 tablespoon cornflour
50ml/2fl oz single cream

- To skin the tomatoes, plunge them into very hot water for 30 seconds, then transfer to a bowl of cold water. The skin should now peel off quickly and easily.
- Chop the peeled tomatoes into large chunks.
- Heat the oil in a large saucepan, add the bay leaf and spring onions, then stir in the tomatoes. Cook, stirring, for a few minutes more until the tomatoes are softened.
- Add the salt, garlic, peppercorns, coriander and water, bring to the boil, then simmer for 15 minutes.
- Dissolve the cornflour in a little water. Remove the soup from the heat and press through a sieve or purée in a blender or food processor.
- Return the soup to the pan, add the cornflour mixture and stir over a gentle heat until boiling and thickened.
- Ladle the soup into shallow soup plates, then swirl in a tablespoon of cream into each bowl before serving.

Chinese egg flower soup

SERVES 4
100 calories per serving

INGREDIENTS:

900ml/1½pt chicken stock
1 tablespoon soy sauce
2 tablespoons dry sherry
A pinch of ground ginger

25g/1oz frozen peas
½ red pepper (seeded and diced)
1 egg (beaten)

- Put all the ingredients except the egg in a saucepan and bring to the boil.
- Simmer for 5 minutes until the peas are tender. Remove from the heat and pour the egg in a thin stream through the prongs of a fork so it 'flowers'.
- Let the soup stand for 20 seconds to allow the egg to set, then serve.

Melon & basil soup

SERVES 6
70 calories per serving

INGREDIENTS:

2 cantaloupe melons
75g/3oz caster sugar
175ml/6fl oz water

Finely grated zest and juice of 1 lime
3 tablespoons shredded fresh basil

- Cut the melons in half across the middle. Scrape out the seeds and discard. Using a melon baller, scoop out 18 balls and set aside for the garnish. Scoop out the remaining flesh and place in a blender or food processor.
- Place the sugar, water and lime zest in a small pan over a low heat. Stir until the sugar has dissolved, bring to the boil and simmer for 2 to 3 minutes. Remove from the heat and leave to cool slightly. Pour half the mixture into a blender or food processor with the melon flesh. Purée until smooth, adding the remaining syrup and lime juice to taste.
- Pour the mixture into a bowl, stir in the basil and chill. Serve garnished with melon balls.

Spicy oatmeal soup

SERVES 8
160 calories per serving

INGREDIENTS:

15g/½oz margarine
1 tablespoon groundnut oil
2 large leeks (thinly sliced)
4 carrots (sliced)
2 medium potatoes (diced)
2 celery sticks (sliced)
1.2 litres/2pt chicken stock

1 tablespoon dried chives
1 tablespoon dried shallots
½ tablespoon dried tarragon
½ tablespoon dried basil
1 teaspoon salt
100g/4oz oatmeal
225ml/8fl oz white wine

- Heat the margarine and groundnut oil in a large saucepan and add the leeks.
- Cook for 2 to 3 minutes over a medium-high heat. Add the carrots, potatoes, celery and chicken stock. Bring to the boil.
- Add the chives, shallots, tarragon, basil and salt. Boil gently for 20 minutes. Add the oatmeal and cook for a further 5 minutes. Add the wine, cook for 15 minutes more and serve.

Artichoke soup

SERVES 4
160 calories per serving

INGREDIENTS:

1 tablespoon olive oil
1 onion (chopped)
1 garlic clove (crushed)
850g/1¾lb canned artichoke hearts
(drained)
600ml/1pt hot vegetable stock

150ml/¼pt single cream
2 tablespoons chopped fresh thyme
leaves
2 sun-dried tomatoes (cut into strips),
to garnish

- Heat the olive oil in a large saucepan and fry the onion and garlic until just softened. Using a sharp knife, roughly chop the artichoke hearts. Add the artichoke pieces to the pan. Pour in the hot vegetable stock, stirring.
- Bring the mixture to the boil, then reduce the heat and leave to simmer, covered, for about 3 minutes.
- Place the mixture in a blender or food processor and purée until smooth. Return

the soup to the saucepan. Stir the cream and thyme into the soup.
- Transfer the soup to a large bowl, cover and leave to chill in the refrigerator for about 3 to 4 hours. Transfer the chilled soup to individual soup bowls and garnish with strips of sun-dried tomato.

Crab & ginger soup

SERVES 4
40 calories per serving

INGREDIENTS:

1 carrot (chopped)
1 leek (chopped)
1 bay leaf
900ml/1½pt fish stock
2 medium-sized cooked crabs

2.5cm/1in piece fresh root ginger
(peeled and grated)
1 teaspoon soy sauce
½ teaspoon ground star anise
Salt and pepper

- Place the carrot and leek in a large saucepan with the bay leaf and the fish stock. Bring to the boil, reduce the heat, cover and leave to simmer for 10 minutes, or until the vegetables are nearly tender.
- Remove all of the meat from the crabs. Break off and reserve the claws, break the joints and remove the meat using a fork.
- Add the crabmeat to the pan together with the ginger, soy sauce and star anise and bring to the boil. Leave to simmer for about 10 minutes, or until the vegetables are tender and the crab is heated through.
- Season the soup then ladle into individual serving bowls and garnish with the crab claws. Serve immediately.

Pumpkin soup

SERVES 4
100 calories per serving

INGREDIENTS:

25g/1oz low-fat spread
700g/1½lb pumpkin (diced)
600ml/1pt vegetable stock
600ml/1pt skimmed milk

Salt and pepper
1 teaspoon granulated sugar
1 tablespoon chopped fresh parsley, to garnish

→

←
- Melt the low-fat spread in a saucepan. Add the pumpkin and cook gently, stirring, for 2 minutes. Add the stock, bring to the boil, reduce the heat and simmer for 15 to 20 minutes until the pumpkin is tender.
- Purée in a blender or food processor until smooth, then return to the saucepan.
- Stir in the milk, seasoning and sugar. Heat, but do not boil. Ladle into individual bowls and garnish with parsley.

Cabbage soup

SERVES 6
85 calories per serving

INGREDIENTS:

1 medium cabbage head (shredded)
2 large onions (thinly sliced)
2 carrots (thinly sliced)
1 large potato (diced)
700ml/1pt 3½fl oz skimmed milk

2 tablespoons low-fat yogurt
1 bay leaf
½ teaspoon dill weed
½ teaspoon rosemary

- Place the cabbage, onions, carrots and potato in a heavy-based saucepan with a little water. Cover and cook slowly until tender.
- Add the milk, yogurt, bay leaf, dill weed and rosemary. Continue to cook for a further 15 minutes.

Cullen skink

SERVES 4
110 calories per serving

INGREDIENTS:

225g/8oz smoked haddock fillet
25g/1oz butter
1 onion (finely chopped)
600ml/1pt milk
350g/12oz potatoes (diced)

350g/12oz cod (boned, skinned and cubed)
150ml/¼pt double cream
2 tablespoons chopped fresh parsley
Salt and pepper

- Put the haddock fillet into a large frying pan and cover with boiling water.
- Leave for 10 minutes. Drain, reserving 300ml/½pt of the water. Flake the fish, taking care to remove all the bones.

- Heat the butter in a large saucepan over a low heat. Add the onion and cook gently for 10 minutes until softened. Add the milk and bring to a gentle simmer before adding the potatoes. Cook for 10 minutes.
- Add the reserved haddock flakes and cod. Simmer for a further 10 minutes until the cod is tender.
- Remove about one-third of the fish and potatoes, place in a blender or food processor and process until smooth. Return to the soup with the cream, parsley and salt and pepper to taste. Add a little of the reserved water if the soup seems too thick.

Clam chowder

SERVES 4
140 calories per serving

INGREDIENTS:

900g/2lb live clams
4 rashers rindless streaky bacon
(chopped)
25g/1oz butter

1 onion (chopped)
1 large potato (peeled and diced)
300ml/¹/₂pt milk
150ml/¹/₄pt double cream

- Scrub the clams and put into a large saucepan with a splash of water. Cook over a high heat for 3 to 4 minutes until all the clams have opened, discarding any that remain closed. Strain the clams, reserving the cooking liquid. Remove the clams from their shells and roughly chop if large.
- Dry-fry the bacon in a clean saucepan over a medium-low heat until browned and crisp. Drain on kitchen paper. Add the butter to the same pan and when it has melted, add the onion. Cook for 4 to 5 minutes until softened. Add the potato, reserved cooking liquid and milk. Bring to the boil and simmer for 10 minutes until the potato is tender. Transfer to a blender or food processor and process until smooth.
- Add the clams, bacon and cream. Simmer for 2 to 3 minutes until heated through.

Salads

Salads are a great way to eat fewer calories while still enjoying a tasty meal. Whether as a main course, a lunch or a snack, they are refreshing in the hot summer months, and can serve as an ideal accompaniment to a hot course when you have guests. From Bean sprout & pepper salad to Asparagus salad with mustard dressing, these diet dishes are anything but dull!

Mussel & red pepper salad

SERVES 4
180 calories per serving

INGREDIENTS:

2 large peppers
350g/12oz cooked shelled mussels
1 head of radicchio
25g/1oz rocket leaves

For the dressing:
1 tablespoon olive oil
1 tablespoon lemon juice
1 teaspoon finely grated lemon zest
2 teaspoons clear honey
1 teaspoon French mustard
1 tablespoon snipped fresh chives
Salt and pepper

- Halve and deseed the peppers and place them skin side up on a grill pan. Cook under a hot grill for 8 to 10 minutes until the skin is charred and blistered and the flesh is soft. Leave to cool for 10 minutes, then peel off the skin.
- Slice the pepper flesh into thin strips and place in a bowl. Gently mix in the mussels and reserve.
- To make the dressing, mix all of the ingredients together in a small bowl. Mix into the pepper and mussel mixture until well coated.
- Remove the central core of the radicchio and shred the leaves. Place in a serving bowl with the rocket leaves and toss together.
- Pile the mussel mixture into the centre of the leaves and serve.

Waldorf salad

SERVES 6
175 calories per serving

INGREDIENTS:

2 green apples (chopped)
2 celery sticks (chopped)
100g/4oz walnuts (coarsely chopped)
100g/4oz raisins

100g/4oz low-fat sour cream
1 tablespoon clear honey
12 lettuce leaves

- Mix the apples, celery, walnuts and raisins with the sour cream. Add the honey and stir to blend. Line 6 individual serving bowls with 2 lettuce leaves each and spoon the apple mixture evenly between them and serve.

Greek cucumber salad

SERVES 4
50 calories per serving

INGREDIENTS:

1 cucumber
1 teaspoon salt
3 tablespoons finely chopped fresh mint

1 garlic clove (crushed)
1 teaspoon caster sugar
200ml/7fl oz low-fat Greek yogurt

- Peel the cucumber and cut in half lengthways. Remove the seeds with a teaspoon and discard. Slice the cucumber thinly and combine with the salt. Leave for at least 15 minutes.
- Combine the mint, garlic, sugar and yogurt in a bowl.
- Rinse the cucumber in a sieve under cold running water to flush away the salt.
- Drain well and combine with the yogurt mixture. Chill for 15 minutes and serve.

Curly endive salad

SERVES 4
50 calories per serving

INGREDIENTS:

½ curly endive
½ small onion (very thinly sliced)
Grated zest and juice of ½ lemon
1 teaspoon clear honey

Salt and pepper
2 teaspoons walnut oil
2 teaspoons water

- Tear the curly endive into neat pieces and place in a large salad bowl. Scatter the onion over.
- Whisk together the lemon zest, juice, honey, salt and pepper, oil and water.
- Drizzle over the endive and serve.

Baked seafood salad

SERVES 6
260 calories per serving

INGREDIENTS:

1 small green pepper (chopped)
1 small onion (chopped)
225g/8oz celery (chopped)
450g/1lb crabmeat (cooked)
450g/1lb small scallops (cooked)

225g/8oz low-fat sour cream
1 teaspoon salt
1 teaspoon Worcestershire sauce
225g/8oz breadcrumbs
25g/1oz margarine

- Preheat the oven to 180°C/350°F/Gas mark 4.
- Mix all the ingredients except the breadcrumbs and margarine in a casserole dish. Sprinkle the breadcrumbs over the top and dot with margarine. Bake for 30 minutes and serve warm.

Chinese prawn salad

SERVES 6
100 calories per serving

INGREDIENTS:

175g/6oz beansprouts
1 small red pepper (chopped)
100g/4oz cooked, peeled prawns
2 teaspoons soy sauce
2 teaspoons white wine vinegar

½ teaspoon granulated sugar
2 tablespoons sesame oil
Salt and pepper
6 large lettuce leaves
1 spring onion (chopped)

- Put the beansprouts in a bowl with the pepper and prawns.
- Mix together the remaining ingredients except the lettuce and spring onion and pour over the prawn mixture. Toss well.
- Place a lettuce leaf on each of 6 individual serving bowls. Spoon prawn mixture on to each lettuce leaf and scatter the spring onion over before serving.

Prawn noodle salad

SERVES 4
170 calories per serving

INGREDIENTS:

100g/4oz cellophane noodles (soaked in hot water until soft)
16 cooked prawns (peeled)
1 small red pepper (seeded and cut into strips)
½ cucumber (cut into matchsticks)
1 tomato (chopped)
2 shallots (finely sliced)
Salt and pepper

For the dressing:
1 tablespoon rice vinegar
2 tablespoons Thai fish sauce
2 tablespoons lime juice
Pinch of salt
½ teaspoon grated fresh root ginger
1 lemon grass stalk (finely chopped)
1 red chilli (seeded and finely sliced)
2 tablespoons roughly chopped fresh mint
1 tablespoon snipped fresh chives

- Combine all the dressing ingredients in a small bowl or jug and whisk well.
- Drain the noodles, then plunge them in a saucepan of boiling water for 1 minute. Drain, rinse under cold running water and drain again.
- In a large bowl, combine the noodles with the prawns, pepper, cucumber, tomato and shallots. Lightly season with salt and pepper, then toss with the dressing.
- Spoon the noodles on to individual plates. Serve at once.

Brown rice & chicken salad

SERVES 8
270 calories per serving

INGREDIENTS:

450g/1lb brown rice
450ml/³/₄pt water
450g/1lb cooked chicken (diced)
12 spring onions (sliced)
2 celery sticks (chopped)
2 medium green peppers (chopped)
100g/4oz black olives (halved)

50g/2oz pimiento (minced)
100g/4oz cherry tomatoes (halved)
100g/4oz parsley (chopped)
100g/4oz radishes (sliced)
50ml/2fl oz olive oil
50ml/2fl oz white wine vinegar

→

← • In a covered saucepan, cook the rice in the water over a medium heat for about 25 minutes, or until the liquid is absorbed and the rice is fluffy. Remove from heat and leave to cool. Add all the remaining ingredients and toss well.

Warm tuna salad

SERVES 4
180 calories per serving

INGREDIENTS:

50g/2oz Chinese leaves (shredded)
3 tablespoons Chinese rice wine
2 tablespoons Thai fish sauce
1 tablespoon finely shredded fresh root ginger
1 garlic clove (finely chopped)
½ red chilli (deseeded, finely chopped)

2 teaspoons demerara sugar
2 tablespoons lime juice
400g/14oz fresh tuna steak
1 tablespoon sunflower oil
100g/4oz cherry tomatoes

• Place a small pile of shredded Chinese leaves on a large serving plate.
• Place the rice wine, fish sauce, ginger, garlic, chilli, brown sugar and 1 tablespoon lime juice in a screw-top jar and shake well to mix.
• Cut the tuna into strips, then sprinkle with the remaining lime juice.
• Brush a wide frying pan with the sunflower oil and heat until very hot. Arrange the tuna strips in the pan and cook until just firm and light golden, turning them over once. Remove and reserve.
• Add the tomatoes to the pan and cook over a high heat until lightly browned.
• Spoon the tuna and tomatoes over the Chinese leaves and spoon over the dressing over the top. Serve warm.

Nutty rice salad

SERVES 4
250 calories per serving

INGREDIENTS:

175g/6oz long-grain rice
175ml/6fl oz water
50g/2oz frozen peas
50g/2oz raisins

50g/2oz toasted flaked almonds
2 tablespoons sunflower oil
1 tablespoon white wine vinegar
Salt and pepper

- In a covered saucepan, cook the rice in the water over a medium-high heat for about 20 minutes. Add the peas and cook for a further 5 minutes. Drain, rinse with cold water, and drain again. Empty into a salad bowl.
- Add the raisins, almonds, oil, vinegar and seasoning. Toss well and serve.

Antipasti salad

SERVES 8
170 calories per serving

INGREDIENTS:

425g/15oz canned chickpeas (drained)
175g/6oz canned artichoke hearts
100g/4oz red pepper
50g/2oz black olives (pitted and sliced)
1 red leaf lettuce (shredded)
100g/4oz low-fat salami (sliced)
100g/4oz low-fat Mozzarella cheese
50g/2oz Parmesan cheese (grated)

For the garlic dressing:
2 tablespoons olive oil
1 tablespoon tarragon vinegar
¼ teaspoon prepared mustard
¼ teaspoon Worcestershire sauce
1 garlic clove (crushed)

- Place the chickpeas, artichoke hearts, pepper, olives and lettuce in a salad bowl.
- Make the dressing by placing all the ingredients in a screw-top jar and shaking well. Pour over the salad and toss well.
- Arrange the salami on the top and sprinkle the cheeses over.

Rocket salad

SERVES 4
50 calories per serving

INGREDIENTS:

1 slice white bread (cubed)
1 garlic clove (quartered)
15g/½oz low-fat spread
100g/4oz rocket leaves
1 coriander sprig (torn into leaves)

1 flat leaf parsley sprig (torn into leaves)
1 red onions (sliced)
1 tablespoon tarragon vinegar
Salt and pepper

- Put the bread, garlic and low-fat spread in a small frying pan and toss over a gentle heat until golden.

$\rightarrow$

- Discard the garlic and drain the croûtons on kitchen paper.
- Put the rocket and herbs in a small salad bowl. Scatter the onion and croûtons over. Sprinkle with vinegar and season well.

Beetroot & orange salad

SERVES 4
50 calories per serving

INGREDIENTS:

1 Little Gem lettuce (separate leaves)
2 oranges
2 large cooked beetroot (diced)

1 tablespoon orange juice
1 teaspoon balsamic vinegar
Salt and pepper

- Arrange the lettuce leaves evenly on 4 small plates.
- Holding the oranges over a bowl, remove all pith and zest from them and cut into segments. Squeeze any juice from the membranes into the bowl, then discard them.
- Pile the beetroot in the centre of the lettuce leaves with the orange segments surrounding them. Add the orange juice to the bowl with the vinegar. Season to taste. Spoon over the beetroot and serve.

Sweet & sour seafood salad

SERVES 4
100 calories per serving

INGREDIENTS:

18 live mussels
6 large scallops
200g/7oz baby squid (cleaned)
2 shallots (finely chopped)
6 raw tiger prawns (peeled and deveined)
1/4 cucumber (sliced)
1 carrot (peeled and sliced)
1/4 head Chinese leaves (shredded)

For the dressing:
4 tablespoons lime juice
2 garlic cloves (finely chopped)
2 tablespoons Thai fish sauce
1 teaspoon sesame oil
1 tablespoon brown sugar
2 tablespoons chopped fresh mint
1/4 teaspoon pepper
Pinch of salt

- Clean the mussels by scrubbing or scraping the shells and pulling out any 'beards' that are attached to them. Discard any with broken shells or any that refuse to close when tapped. Put the mussels into a large saucepan with just the water that clings to their shells and cook, covered, over a high heat for about 3 to 4 minutes, shaking the pan occasionally, until the mussels are opened. Discard any that remain closed. Strain the mussels, reserving the liquid in the pan.
- Separate the corals from the scallops and cut the whites in half horizontally. Cut the tentacles from the squid and slice the body cavities into rings.
- Add the shallots to the liquid in the pan and cook over a high heat until the liquid is reduced to about 3 tablespoons. Add the scallops, squid and prawns and stir for 2 to 3 minutes until cooked. Remove from the pan and spoon the mixture into a large bowl.
- Toss the cucumber and carrot with the Chinese leaves in a separate bowl.
- To make the dressing, place all the ingredients in a screw-top jar and shake well until evenly combined.
- Toss the vegetables and seafood together. Spoon the dressing over the vegetables and seafood and serve immediately.

Seafood salad with herbs

SERVES 6
80 calories per serving

INGREDIENTS:

225ml/8fl oz fish stock
350g/12oz squid (cleaned and cut into rings)
12 king prawns (shelled)
12 scallops
50g/2oz bean thread/cellophane noodles (soaked in warm water for 30 minutes)
½ cucumber (cut into matchsticks)
1 lemon grass stalk (finely chopped)

2 kaffir lime leaves (finely shredded)
2 shallots (finely sliced)
Juice of 1 lime
2 tablespoons Thai fish sauce
25g/1oz spring onions (sliced)
2 tablespoons chopped coriander leaves
12 mint leaves (roughly torn)
4 red chillies (seeded and sliced)

- Pour the stock into a medium-sized saucepan, set over a high heat and bring to the boil.
- Cook each type of seafood separately in the stock. Do not overcook – it will only take a few minutes for each seafood. Remove and set aside.
- Drain the noodles and cut them into short lengths, about 5cm/2in long. Combine the noodles with the cooked seafood.
- Add all the remaining ingredients, mix together well and serve.

→

Asparagus salad

SERVES 8
80 calories per serving

INGREDIENTS:

425g/15oz canned artichoke hearts
425g/15oz canned white asparagus
(drained and chopped)
425g/15oz canned green asparagus
(drained and chopped)
225g/8oz mushrooms (sliced)
8 Romaine lettuce leaves
100g/4oz celery (chopped)
50g/2oz red pepper (diced)
100g/4oz black olives (seeded)

For the dressing:
125ml/4fl oz olive oil
1 garlic clove (crushed)
50ml/2fl oz lemon juice
2 tablespoons chopped fresh parsley
1 teaspoon capers
1 tablespoon Dijon mustard
Salt and pepper

- Prepare the dressing by placing all the ingredients in a screw-top jar, shaking well and refrigerating for at least 30 minutes.
- Place the artichoke hearts, asparagus and mushrooms in a bowl and pour the dressing over them. Cover and refrigerate for about 2 hours. Remove the vegetables with a slotted spoon and reserve the dressing.
- Place the lettuce leaves in a large salad bowl and arrange the vegetables on the top. Garnish with the celery, red pepper and olives. Serve with the reserved dressing.

Beetroot, chicory &
orange salad

SERVES 4
50 calories per serving

INGREDIENTS:

2 medium cooked beetroot (diced)
2 heads chicory (sliced)
1 large orange

4 tablespoons natural low-fat yogurt
2 teaspoons wholegrain mustard
Salt and pepper

- Mix together the beetroot and chicory in a large serving bowl.
- Finely grate the zest from the orange. With a sharp knife, remove all the peel and white pith. Cut out the segments, catching the juice in a bowl. Add the segments to the salad.
- Add the orange zest, yogurt, mustard and seasonings to the orange juice. Mix thoroughly, then spoon over the salad.

Hot potato & bean salad

SERVES 4
150 calories per serving

INGREDIENTS:

450g/1lb potatoes (scrubbed and diced)　*2 teaspoons chopped fresh mint*
100g/4oz French beans　*Salt and pepper*
75ml/3fl oz low-fat crème fraîche

- Cook the potatoes in boiling, lightly salted water for 5 minutes. Top and tail the beans and cut into short lengths.
- Add to the potatoes and cook for a further 5 to 10 minutes, until the potatoes are tender. Drain and return to the pan. Add the crème fraîche, mint and seasoning. Toss and serve warm.

Lobster & avocado salad

SERVES 4
320 calories per serving

INGREDIENTS:

2 cooked lobsters (about 400g/14oz each)
1 large avocado
1 tablespoon lemon juice
225g/8oz green beans
4 spring onions (thinly sliced)
2 tablespoons chopped fresh chervil
1 tablespoon snipped fresh chives

For the dressing:
1 garlic clove (crushed)
1 teaspoon Dijon mustard
Pinch of granulated sugar
1 tablespoon balsamic vinegar
Salt and pepper
75ml/3fl oz olive oil

→

←

- To prepare the lobsters, cut them in half lengthways. Remove the intestinal vein that runs down the tail, the stomach sac and any grey 'beards' from the body cavity at the head end of the lobster. Crack the claws and remove the meat – in one piece if possible. Remove the meat from the tail of each lobster. Roughly chop all the meat and reserve.
- Split the avocado lengthways and remove the stone. Cut each half in half again and peel away the skin. Cut the avocado into chunks and toss with the lemon juice. Add to the lobster meat.
- Bring a large saucepan of lightly salted water to the boil over a medium heat.
- Add the beans and cook for 3 minutes, then drain and immediately refresh under cold water. Drain again and leave to go completely cold. Cut the beans in half, then add to the avocado and lobster.
- Meanwhile, make the dressing by whisking the garlic, mustard, sugar, vinegar and seasoning together in a bowl. Gradually add the olive oil, whisking, until thickened.
- Add the spring onions, chervil and chives to the lobster and avocado mixture and toss gently together. Drizzle the dressing over and serve immediately.

Fresh salad with raspberry vinaigrette

SERVES 10
185 calories per serving

INGREDIENTS:

1 bunch watercress (torn)
2 heads Bibb lettuce (torn into bite-size pieces)
450g/1lb mushrooms (sliced)
425g/15oz canned artichoke hearts
1 bunch white radishes (sliced)
225g/8oz fresh raspberries

For the vinaigrette:
125ml/4fl oz raspberry vinegar
½ teaspoon salt
225g/8oz olive oil
½ teaspoon Dijon mustard
½ teaspoon freshly ground pepper

- Place the watercress, lettuce, mushrooms, artichoke hearts and radishes in a large bowl.
- Shake the vinaigrette ingredients together in a screw-top jar and drizzle over the salad, then toss well. Serve with raspberries on top.

Beetroot & chive salad

SERVES 4

50 calories per serving

INGREDIENTS:

4 cooked beetroot (chopped)
2 tablespoons low-fat crème fraîche

Salt and pepper
1 tablespoon snipped fresh chives

- Put the beetroot in a bowl. Add the crème fraîche, seasoning and chives, toss and serve.

Crab salad

SERVES 4

230 calories per serving

INGREDIENTS:

225g/8oz mayonnaise
125ml/4fl oz evaporated skimmed milk
50ml/2fl oz chilli sauce
50g/2oz green pepper (chopped)
50g/2oz onions (chopped)
2 tablespoons pitted green olives
(chopped)

1 Iceberg lettuce
475g/1lb 1oz crabmeat (cooked)
50g/2oz chives (minced)
Juice of ½ lemon

- For the dressing, mix the mayonnaise, evaporated milk and chilli sauce together in a screw top jar and shake well.
- Place the rest of the ingredients in a large serving bowl, garnish with chives and lemon juice and serve with the dressing.

Turnip salad

SERVES 4

50 calories per serving

INGREDIENTS:

350g/12oz turnips
2 spring onions (white part only, chopped)
1 tablespoon caster sugar

Pinch of salt
2 tablespoons horseradish cream
2 teaspoons caraway seeds

- Peel, slice and shred the turnips. Add the spring onions, sugar and salt, then rub together with your hands to soften the turnip.
- Fold in the horseradish cream and caraway seeds and serve.

Smoked haddock salad

SERVES 4

230 calories per serving

INGREDIENTS:

350g/12oz smoked haddock fillet
4 tablespoons olive oil
1 tablespoon lemon juice
2 tablespoons sour cream
1 tablespoon hot water
2 tablespoons snipped fresh chives

Salt and pepper
1 plum tomato (diced)
8 quail's eggs
4 thick slices granary bread
100g/4oz mixed salad leaves

- Fill a large frying pan with water and bring to the boil over a medium heat. Add the haddock, cover and remove from the heat. Leave for 10 minutes until the fish is tender. Lift from the water, drain and leave until cool enough to handle.
- Flake the flesh, removing any small bones. Reserve, discarding the poaching water.
- For the dressing, whisk the olive oil, lemon juice, sour cream, hot water, chives and seasoning together. Stir in the tomato.
- Bring a small saucepan of water to the boil over a medium heat. Carefully lower the quail's eggs into the water. Cook the eggs for 3 to 4 minutes from when the water returns to the boil. Drain immediately and refresh under cold running water. Carefully peel the eggs and cut in half lengthways.
- Toast the bread and cut each piece diagonally. Arrange 2 halves on each of 4

serving plates. Top with the salad leaves, then the flaked fish, then the quail's eggs. Spoon the dressing over and serve.

Mustard carrot salad

SERVES 4
50 calories per serving

INGREDIENTS:

450g/1lb carrots (coarsely grated)
Salt and pepper
25g/1oz low-fat spread

1 tablespoon mustard seeds
1 tablespoon lemon juice

- Put the carrots in a salad bowl and season with salt and pepper to taste.
- Melt the low-fat spread in a frying pan and add the mustard seeds. When they start to pop, add the lemon juice, stir and pour over the salad. Toss well and serve straight away, while still warm.

Banana & pecan salad

SERVES 6
150 calories per serving

INGREDIENTS:

50g/2oz finely chopped lean back bacon
50g/2oz pecan nuts (chopped)
200g/7oz banana (sliced)

300g/11oz celery (sliced)
½ lime (thinly sliced)
250g/9oz natural low-fat yoghurt
6 lettuce leaves

- Grill the bacon until crisp, then cut into small pieces.
- Combine the bacon, pecan nuts, banana, celery, lime and yoghurt. Place 1 lettuce leaf in each of 6 individual bowls and divide the mixture between each bowl.

Basque tomatoes

SERVES 8
140 calories per serving

INGREDIENTS:

8 firm ripe tomatoes
100g/4oz fresh parsley (chopped)
1 garlic clove (crushed)
1 teaspoon salt
1 teaspoon granulated sugar

¼ teaspoon pepper
100g/4oz black olives
50ml/2fl oz olive oil
2 tablespoons tarragon vinegar
1 teaspoon Dijon mustard

- Slice the tomatoes, spread them in a shallow dish and sprinkle with parsley.
- Combine the remaining ingredients in a mixing bowl, mix well and pour over the tomatoes. Cover and refrigerate for at least 2 hours.

Spinach & bacon salad

SERVES 4
150 calories per serving

INGREDIENTS:

1 slice white bread (crusts removed)
15g/½oz low-fat spread
3 rashers streaky bacon (rinded and diced)
175g/6oz spinach leaves (torn into pieces)

1 small onion (thinly sliced and separated into rings)
1 tablespoon olive oil
2 teaspoons red wine vinegar
1 teaspoon Worcestershire sauce
Freshly ground black pepper

- Spread the bread with the low-fat spread on both sides and cut into small dice.
- Fry in a frying pan until golden. Drain on kitchen paper.
- Dry-fry the bacon until crisp and drain on kitchen paper.
- Put the spinach in a salad bowl with the onion. Whisk together the oil, vinegar, Worcestershire sauce and some pepper. Drizzle dressing over the salad and top with the breadcrumbs.

Bamboo shoot salad

SERVES 4
80 calories per serving

INGREDIENTS:

400g/14oz canned whole bamboo shoots
25g/1oz long-grain rice
2 tablespoons chopped shallots
1 tablespoon chopped garlic
3 tablespoons chopped spring onion

2 tablespoons Thai fish sauce
2 tablespoons lime juice
1 teaspoon granulated sugar
½ teaspoon dried flaked chillies
20 small fresh mint leaves
1 tablespoon toasted sesame seeds

- Rinse and drain the bamboo shoots, then slice and set aside.
- Dry roast the rice in a frying pan until it is golden brown. Remove and grind to fine crumbs with a pestle and mortar.
- Tip the rice into a bowl. Add the shallots, garlic, spring onions, fish sauce, lime juice, sugar, chillies and half the mint leaves.
- Mix thoroughly, then pour over the bamboo shoots and toss together. Serve sprinkled with sesame seeds and the remaining mint leaves.

Beansprout & pepper salad

SERVES 4
50 calories per serving

INGREDIENTS:

175g/6oz beansprouts
1 red pepper (cut into thin rings)
1 green pepper (cut into thin rings)
1 onion (thinly sliced and separated into rings)

For the dressing:
2 tablespoons soy sauce
1 tablespoon sherry
2 tablespoons water
Salt and pepper

- To make the dressing, place all the ingredients in a screw-top jar and shake well.
- Mix together the beansprouts, peppers and onion in a large salad bowl. Add the dressing, toss and serve.

Cranberry cream salad

SERVES 6
200 calories per serving

INGREDIENTS:

75g/3oz cherry gelatine
225ml/8fl oz hot water
450g/1lb cranberry sauce

100g/4oz celery (diced)
50g/2oz raisins
225g/8oz low-fat sour cream

- Dissolve the gelatine in the hot water and chill until slightly thickened. Fold the cranberry sauce into the gelatine and add the celery and raisins.
- Fold in the sour cream and pour the mixture into a mould. Chill until firm.

Sweet & sour tofu salad

SERVES 6
150 calories per serving

INGREDIENTS:

250g/9oz block firm tofu

For the marinade:
2 tablespoons sunflower oil
150ml/¼pt soy sauce
2 tablespoons red wine vinegar
Pinch of granulated sugar
¼ teaspoon English mustard

1 tablespoon grated fresh root ginger
2 garlic cloves (crushed)
25ml/1fl oz tomato juice

To serve:
175g/6oz beansprouts
1 red pepper (sliced)
2 spring onions (chopped)

- Cut the tofu into small cubes and place in a shallow dish.
- Mix together the marinade ingredients and pour over the tofu. Cover and chill for 24 hours, turning occasionally.
- When ready to serve, mix the beansprouts with the red pepper and shape into nests on 6 individual serving plates. Pile the marinated tofu in the centre, drizzle any remaining marinade over and sprinkle with the spring onion.

Fruity pasta & prawn salad

SERVES 6
175 calories per serving

INGREDIENTS:

175g/6oz pasta shells
225g/8oz frozen prawns (thawed and drained)
1 large cantaloupe melon

2 tablespoons olive oil
1 tablespoon tarragon vinegar
2 tablespoons snipped fresh chives
200g/7oz Chinese leaves (shredded)

- Cook the pasta in boiling salted water according to the instructions on the packet. Drain well and allow to cool.
- Peel the prawns and discard the shells.
- Halve the melon and remove the seeds with a teaspoon. Scoop the flesh into balls with a melon baller and mix with the prawns and pasta.
- Whisk the oil, vinegar and chives together. Pour on to the prawn mixture and turn to coat. Cover and chill for at least 30 minutes.
- Use the Chinese leaves to line a shallow bowl. Pile the prawn mixture onto the leaves and serve.

Hot bulgur salad

SERVES 4
200 calories per serving

INGREDIENTS:

100g/4oz bulgur wheat
250ml/9fl oz boiling water
1 teaspoon salt
2 tablespoons olive oil
2 tablespoons lemon juice
1 garlic clove (finely chopped)
2 tablespoons chopped fresh parsley

1 tablespoon chopped fresh mint
1 teaspoon chopped fresh coriander
3 tomatoes (chopped)
5cm/2in piece cucumber (chopped)
1 green pepper (chopped)
4 black olives (pitted and halved)

- Put the bulgur in a pan. Add the boiling water and sprinkle with the salt. Stir and leave to stand for 20 minutes until the bulgur has absorbed all the water.
- Add the oil, lemon juice, garlic, herbs, tomatoes, cucumber and green pepper.
- Toss over a gentle heat for 1 minute.
- Pile on to plates and garnish with olives before serving.

Cucumber salad

SERVES 6
110 calories per serving

INGREDIENTS:

3 large cucumbers (peeled and thinly sliced)
1 large red onion (sliced and separated into rings)
125ml/4fl oz white vinegar

3 tablespoons granulated sugar
1 teaspoon salt
¼ teaspoon pepper
¼ teaspoon ground ginger
1 tablespoon snipped fresh chives

- Layer the cucumbers in a bowl. Add the onion.
- In a screw-top jar, combine the vinegar, sugar, salt, pepper, ginger and chives.
- Shake well. Pour the dressing over the cucumbers and refrigerate for at least 1 hour.

Banana & chicory salad

SERVES 4
150 calories per serving

INGREDIENTS:

2 bananas (thickly sliced)
Grated zest and juice of 1 lemon
2 heads chicory
1 tablespoon sunflower oil
1 teaspoon granulated sugar

Salt and pepper
1 tablespoon chopped fresh coriander
1 tablespoon desiccated coconut (toasted)

- Toss the bananas in a little of the lemon juice to prevent browning.
- Cut a cone-shaped core out of the base of each chicory head, then separate into leaves. Arrange on a serving plate and pile the bananas in the centre.
- Whisk together the remaining lemon juice, zest, oil, sugar, salt and pepper and pour over. Sprinkle the leaves with coriander and the coconut.

Green lentil & cabbage salad

SERVES 6
230 calories per serving

INGREDIENTS:

225g/8oz green lentils
1.3 litres/2¼pt cold water
3 garlic cloves (1 peeled, 2 crushed)
1 bay leaf
1 onion (peeled and studded with 2 cloves)
1 tablespoon olive oil

1 red onion (finely sliced)
1 tablespoon fresh thyme leaves
350g/12oz cabbage (finely shredded)
Grated zest and juice of 1 lemon
1 tablespoon raspberry vinegar
Salt and pepper

- Rinse the lentils in cold water and place in a large pan with the water, peeled garlic clove, bay leaf and onion. Bring to the boil and cook for about 10 minutes.
- Reduce the heat, cover the pan, and simmer gently for a further 15 to 20 minutes.
- Drain and remove the onion, garlic and bay leaf.
- Heat the oil in a large pan. Add the red onion, crushed garlic and thyme, and cook for 5 minutes, until softened.
- Add the cabbage and cook for a further 3 to 5 minutes until just cooked but still crunchy.
- Stir in the cooked lentils, lemon zest and juice and raspberry vinegar. Season to taste and serve.

Orange & chicory salad

SERVES 4
100 calories per serving

INGREDIENTS:

1 head radicchio
1 head chicory
2 oranges
75g/3oz raspberries

Freshly ground black pepper
1 tablespoon raspberry vinegar
1 tablespoon pure orange juice

- Separate the radicchio into leaves and tear into small pieces. Cut a cone-shaped core out of the base of the chicory, cut the head into chunks, then separate the layers.

→

←
- Cut off all the zest and pith from the oranges. Cut the fruit into thin rounds, then slice each round into quarters. Mix together with the salad leaves and spoon on to 4 individual serving plates.
- Dot the raspberries around and add a good grinding of pepper. Whisk together the vinegar and orange juice and drizzle over just before serving.

Broccoli salad

SERVES 4
220 calories per serving

INGREDIENTS:

900g/2lb fresh broccoli
225g/8oz fresh mushrooms (sliced)
100g/4oz low-fat sour cream
100g/4oz low-fat mayonnaise
1 teaspoon granulated sugar

Pinch of freshly ground black pepper
1 teaspoon grated onion
1 garlic clove (crushed)
225g/8oz canned water chestnuts
(drained and sliced)

- Cut off and discard the tough ends of the broccoli stalks. Break the florets into small clusters and steam for about 10 minutes or until al dente.
- In a small bowl, combine the mushrooms, sour cream, mayonnaise, sugar, pepper, onion and garlic.
- In a large salad bowl, combine the cooked broccoli and water chestnuts. Add the creamed mixture and toss lightly. Cover and refrigerate for at least 4 hours before serving.

Thai beef salad

SERVES 6
105 calories per serving

INGREDIENTS:

75g/3oz lean sirloin steaks
1 red onion (finely sliced)
½ cucumber (finely sliced into matchsticks)
1 lemon grass stalk (finely chopped)

2 tablespoon chopped spring onions
Juice of 2 limes
2 tablespoons Thai fish sauce
3 red chillies (finely sliced)

- Grill the sirloin steaks until they are medium-rare, then allow to rest for 10 to 15

minutes. When cool, thinly slice the beef and put the slices in a large bowl.
- Add the sliced onion, cucumber and lemon grass.
- Add the spring onions. Toss and season with lime juice and fish sauce. Serve at room temperature, garnished with the chillies.

Tomato & spring onion salad

SERVES 4
50 calories per serving

INGREDIENTS:

8 tomatoes
3 spring onions (finely sliced)
1 tablespoon olive oil

1 tablespoon white wine vinegar
½ teaspoon granulated sugar
Salt and pepper

- Place the tomatoes in a bowl of just-boiled water for 30 seconds. Remove with a slotted spoon, then skin and cut into wedges.
- Put the tomatoes in a dish and sprinkle with the spring onions.
- Whisk together the remaining ingredients and drizzle over. Leave to stand for 30 minutes before serving.

Pear & grape salad

SERVES 4
110 calories per serving

INGREDIENTS:

2 teaspoons skimmed milk
225g/8oz low-fat cottage cheese
(whipped)
1 teaspoon granulated sugar

2 large pears (halved and peeled)
8 iceberg lettuce leaves
20 seedless white grapes (halved)

- Mix the milk with the cottage cheese and sugar and blend until of a spreading consistency.
- Place the pear halves on the lettuce leaves, cut-side down, and frost generously with the cottage cheese.
- Press the grapes, cut side down, into the cottage cheese.
- Chill for at least 20 minutes before serving.

Main courses

To prove that good food does not necessarily come with a high calorie count, here are a selection of fine dishes from around the world. Whether you are entertaining friends or feeding the family, you can choose from meat, poultry and seafood with recipes as diverse as Beef, tomato & olive kebabs, Noodles with cod and mango or Minty lime chicken.

Layered fish & potato pie

SERVES 4

120 calories per serving

INGREDIENTS:

900g/2lb potatoes (sliced)
75g/3oz butter
1 red onion (halved and sliced)
50g/2oz plain flour
150ml/¼pt milk
150ml/¼pt double cream
225g/8oz smoked haddock fillet
(cubed)

225g/8oz cod fillet (cubed)
1 red pepper (diced)
100g/4oz broccoli florets
Salt and pepper
50g/2oz Parmesan cheese (grated)

- Bring a large saucepan of lightly salted water to the boil over a medium heat.
- Add the sliced potatoes and cook for 10 minutes. Drain and reserve.
- Meanwhile, melt the butter in a saucepan over a low heat. Add the onion and fry gently for 3 to 4 minutes.
- Add the flour and cook, stirring, for 1 minute. Blend in the milk and cream and bring to the boil, stirring, until the sauce has thickened.
- Arrange half of the potato slices in the base of a shallow ovenproof dish. Preheat the oven to 180°C/350°F/Gas mark 4.
- Add the fish, red pepper and broccoli to the sauce and cook over a low heat for about 10 minutes. Season to taste with salt and pepper, then spoon the mixture over the potatoes in the dish.
- Arrange the remaining potato slices in a layer over the fish mixture and then sprinkle the Parmesan cheese over the top. Cook in the oven for 30 minutes or until the potatoes are cooked and the topping is golden.

Hot & sour cod

SERVES 4

350 calories per serving

INGREDIENTS:

4 pieces skinned cod fillet, about
175g/6oz each
50g/2oz low-fat spread
3 tablespoons lemon juice

1 teaspoon Tabasco sauce
Salt and pepper
8 spring onions (trimmed)
2 red peppers (quartered)

- Place the cod in a large shallow dish.
- Melt the low-fat spread with the lemon juice, Tabasco sauce, salt and pepper and pour over the fish. Leave to marinate for 1 hour.
- Transfer to a grill rack. Add the spring onions and peppers. Melt any remaining marinade and brush over.
- Grill for about 5 minutes on each side under a medium-high grill, until the fish is cooked through. Serve hot with rice.

Orange & ginger beef

SERVES 4

180 calories per serving

INGREDIENTS:

450g/1lb lean beef rump fillet (cut into thin strips)
Grated zest and juice of 1 orange
1 tablespoon soy sauce
1 teaspoon cornflour

2.5cm/1in piece root ginger (finely chopped)
2 teaspoons sesame oil
1 large carrot (cut into thin strips)
2 spring onions (thinly sliced)

- Place the beef strips in a bowl and sprinkle over the zest and juice of the orange. Leave to marinate for at least 30 minutes.
- Drain the liquid from the meat and set aside, then mix the meat with the soy sauce, cornflour and ginger.
- Heat the oil in a wok or large frying pan and add the beef. Stir-fry for 1 minute until lightly coloured, then add the carrot and stir-fry for a further 2 to 3 minutes.
- Stir in the spring onions and reserved liquid, then cook, stirring, until boiling and thickened. Serve hot with rice noodles or plain boiled rice.

Turkey spirals

SERVES 4

130 calories per serving

INGREDIENTS:

4 turkey breast steaks, about 100g/4oz each (thinly sliced)
4 teaspoons tomato purée
15g/¹/₂oz basil leaves

1 garlic clove (crushed)
Salt and pepper
1 tablespoon skimmed milk
2 tablespoons wholemeal flour

→

←
- Place the turkey steaks on a board and flatten them slightly with a rolling pin.
- Spread each one with tomato purée, then top with a few leaves of basil, a little garlic and seasoning.
- Roll up firmly around the filling and secure with a cocktail stick. Brush with the milk and sprinkle with the flour to coat lightly. Season with salt and pepper.
- Place the spirals on an aluminium foil-lined grill-pan. Cook under a medium-hot grill for 15 to 20 minutes, turning them occasionally, until thoroughly cooked.
- Place on a serving plate and serve hot.

Loin of pork in wine sauce

SERVES 4
210 calories per serving

INGREDIENTS:

1 tablespoon vegetable oil
1 garlic clove (crushed)
5 peppercorns (crushed)
4 pork chops
50g/2oz plain flour

1 onion (finely chopped)
50g/2oz red pepper (chopped)
50ml/2fl oz beef stock
50ml/2fl oz dry white wine
1 tablespoon red wine vinegar

- Heat the oil in a frying pan and add the garlic and peppercorns. Pat the pork dry with kitchen paper and dredge in flour. Sauté on both sides until golden brown. Remove from the pan.
- Add the onion and red pepper to the pan and sauté until softened. Add the stock, wine and vinegar and stir well.
- Return the pork to the pan and simmer slowly, uncovered, for 30 minutes, turning halfway through. Serve with boiled rice.

Garlic & herb chicken

SERVES 4
280 calories per serving

INGREDIENTS:

4 chicken breasts (skin removed)
100g/4oz full fat soft cheese (flavoured with herbs and garlic)
8 slices Parma ham

150ml/¼pt red wine
150ml/¼pt chicken stock
25g/1oz demerara sugar

- Using a sharp knife, make a horizontal slit along the length of each chicken breast to form a pocket.
- Beat the cheese with a wooden spoon to soften it. Spoon the cheese into the pocket of the chicken breasts.
- Wrap 2 slices of Parma ham around each chicken breast and secure firmly in place with a length of string.
- Pour the wine and stock into a large frying pan and bring to the boil. When just starting to boil, add the sugar and stir well to dissolve.
- Add the chicken breasts to the mixture in the frying pan. Leave to simmer for 12 to 15 minutes or until the chicken is tender and the juices run clear.
- Remove the chicken from the pan, set aside and keep warm. Reheat the sauce and boil until reduced and thickened. Remove the string from the chicken and cut into slices. Pour the sauce over the chicken and serve with a green salad.

Barbecued monkfish

SERVES 4
225 calories per serving

INGREDIENTS:

4 tablespoons olive oil
Grated zest of 1 lime
2 teaspoons Thai fish sauce
2 garlic cloves (crushed)
1 teaspoon grated fresh root ginger
2 tablespoons chopped fresh basil

Salt and pepper
700g/1½lb monkfish fillet (cut into chunks)
2 limes (each cut into 6 wedges)

Noodles or rice, to serve

- Mix the olive oil, lime zest, fish sauce, garlic, ginger and basil together. Season to taste with salt and pepper.
- Wash the monkfish under cold running water and pat dry with kitchen paper.
- Add to the marinade and mix well. Cover and leave to marinate in the refrigerator for 2 hours, stirring occasionally.
- Lift the monkfish pieces from the marinade and thread them onto skewers, alternating with the lime wedges.
- Transfer the skewers to a hot barbecue or grill and cook for 5 to 6 minutes, turning regularly, until the fish is tender.
- Serve with noodles or rice.

Chicken in spicy yogurt

SERVES 6
180 calories per serving

INGREDIENTS:

3 dried chillies
2 tablespoons coriander seeds
2 teaspoons ground turmeric
2 teaspoons garam masala
4 garlic cloves (crushed)
½ large onion (chopped)
2.5cm/1in piece fresh root ginger (grated)

2 tablespoons lime juice
1 teaspoon salt
125ml/4fl oz low-fat natural yogurt
1 tablespoon olive oil
6 chicken pieces weighing about 2kg/4½lb in total

- Grind together the chillies, coriander seeds, turmeric, garam masala, garlic, onion, ginger, lime juice and salt with a pestle and mortar.
- Gently heat a frying pan and add the spice mixture. Stir for 2 minutes and then turn into a shallow dish. Add the yogurt and oil to the spice paste and mix well to combine.
- Remove the skin from the chicken pieces and make 3 slashes in the flesh of each piece. Add the chicken to the dish containing the yogurt and spice mixture and coat the pieces completely in the marinade. Cover with clingfilm and chill for at least 4 hours. Remove the dish from the refrigerator, take off the clingfilm and leave covered at room temperature for 30 minutes before cooking.
- Wrap the chicken pieces in aluminium foil, sealing well so the juices cannot escape.
- Cook the chicken pieces over a very hot barbecue or under a very hot grill for about 15 minutes, turning once.
- Remove the foil and brown the chicken for 5 minutes. Serve hot.

Turkey spinach lasagne

SERVES 8
260 calories per serving

INGREDIENTS:

100g/4oz frozen chopped spinach
Vegetable oil for greasing
50g/2oz low-fat ricotta cheese
475g/1lb 1oz chopped cooked turkey

500ml/18fl oz spaghetti sauce
225g/8oz low-fat Mozzarella cheese (sliced)
50g/2oz Parmesan cheese (grated)

- Preheat the oven to 180°C/350°F/Gas mark 4.
- Thaw the spinach and squeeze out any liquid. Put about one-third of the spinach in the bottom of a lightly oiled casserole dish. Spread half of the ricotta over the spinach. Sprinkle on half of the turkey and spoon on half of the spaghetti sauce.
- Top with half of the Mozzarella.
- Repeat the layering process, finishing with the final third of spinach. Sprinkle the Parmesan cheese over the top. Bake in the oven for 45 to 50 minutes.

Chilli con carne

SERVES 4

350 calories per serving

INGREDIENTS:

1 onion (chopped)
1 garlic clove (crushed)
225g/8oz lean minced beef
½ teaspoon chilli powder
1 teaspoon ground cumin
½ teaspoon dried oregano
400g/14oz canned chopped tomatoes

425g/15oz canned red kidney beans (drained and rinsed)
1 tablespoon tomato purée
Salt and pepper
175g/6oz long-grain rice (cooked), to serve

- Put the onion, garlic and beef in a saucepan. Fry, stirring, until the meat is browned. Pour off any fat.
- Add the remaining ingredients except the rice and stir well. Bring to the boil, reduce the heat and simmer for 20 minutes until a rich colour and reduced.
- Serve with the rice.

Cod Creole

SERVES 4

140 calories per serving

INGREDIENTS:

450g/1lb cod fillets (skinned and cut into bite-sized pieces)
1 tablespoon lime juice
2 teaspoons olive oil
1 medium onion (finely chopped)

1 green pepper (seeded and sliced)
½ teaspoon cayenne pepper
½ teaspoon garlic salt
400g/14oz canned chopped tomatoes

→

- Sprinkle the cod with the lime juice.
- In a large, non-stick frying pan, heat the oil and fry the onion and pepper gently until softened. Add the cayenne pepper and garlic salt.
- Stir in the cod with the chopped tomatoes. Bring to the boil, then cover and simmer for about 5 minutes, or until the fish flakes easily. Serve with boiled rice or potatoes.

Duck with pineapple

SERVES 4
190 calories per serving

INGREDIENTS:

3 tablespoons vegetable oil
1 small onion (thinly shredded)
3 slices ginger root (thinly shredded)
1 spring onion (thinly shredded)
1 small carrot (thinly shredded)
175g/6oz cooked duck meat (cut into thin strips)

100g/4oz canned pineapple (cut into small slices, drained, with 2 tablespoons syrup reserved)
½ teaspoon salt
1 tablespoon red rice vinegar
1 teaspoon cornflour (mixed to a paste with 1½ teaspoons water)

- Heat the oil in a wok or large heavy-based frying pan. Add the onion and stir-fry until opaque. Add the ginger, spring onion and carrot and stir-fry for 1 minute.
- Add the duck meat and pineapple to the wok together with the salt, vinegar and pineapple syrup. Stir until the mixture is well-blended.
- Add the cornflour paste and stir for 1 to 2 minutes until the sauce has thickened.

Pork chow mein

SERVES 4
250 calories per serving

INGREDIENTS:

250g/9oz egg noodles
4 tablespoons vegetable oil
2 tablespoons soy sauce
250g/9oz pork fillet (cooked and sliced into thin shreds)
100g/4oz French beans (topped, tailed)

1 teaspoon salt
½ teaspoon sugar
1 tablespoon Chinese rice wine
2 spring onions (finely shredded)
½ teaspoon sesame oil

- Cook the noodles in boiling water according to the instructions on the packet, then drain and rinse under cold water. Drain again then toss with 1 tablespoon vegetable oil.
- Heat 1 tablespoon vegetable oil in a wok until hot. Add the noodles and stir-fry for 2 to 3 minutes with 1 tablespoon soy sauce, then remove to a serving dish and keep warm.
- Heat the remaining oil and stir-fry the pork and beans for 2 minutes. Add the salt, sugar, wine, the remaining soy sauce and half the spring onions to the wok.
- Stir the mixture in the wok, adding a little water if necessary, then pour on top of the noodles and sprinkle with sesame oil and the remaining spring onions.
- Serve hot.

Squid with wine & rosemary

SERVES 4
280 calories per serving

INGREDIENTS:

8 squid (cleaned and gutted)
6 canned anchovies (chopped)
2 garlic cloves (chopped)
2 tablespoons fresh rosemary (chopped)
2 sun-dried tomatoes (chopped)

150g/5oz breadcrumbs
1 tablespoon olive oil
1 onion (finely chopped)
200ml/7fl oz white wine
200ml/7fl oz fish stock

- Remove the tentacles from the squid bodies and chop them finely.
- Grind the anchovies, garlic, rosemary and tomatoes to a paste with a pestle and mortar. Add the breadcrumbs and the squid tentacles and mix to form a paste, adding water if necessary.
- Spoon the paste into the body sacs of the squid, then tie around the end of each sac with cotton to fasten.
- Heat the oil in a frying pan. Add the onion and cook, stirring, for 3 to 4 minutes, or until golden. Add the stuffed squid to the pan and cook for 3 to 4 minutes, or until they are brown all over.
- Add the wine and stock and bring to the boil. Reduce the heat, cover, then leave to simmer for 15 minutes.
- Remove the lid and cook for a further 5 minutes, or until the squid is tender and the juices reduced. Serve with boiled rice or noodles.

Grilled chicken with hot salsa

SERVES 4

270 calories per serving

INGREDIENTS:

4 boneless, skinless chicken breasts
(about 175g/6oz each)
Pinch of celery salt
Pinch of cayenne pepper
2 tablespoons vegetable oil

For the salsa:
275g/10oz watermelon
175g/6oz cantaloupe melon
1 small red onion (finely chopped)
2 green chillies (deseeded and chopped)
2 tablespoons lime juice
4 tablespoons chopped fresh coriander
Pinch of salt

- Preheat a moderate grill. Slash the chicken breasts deeply to speed up the cooking time.
- Season the chicken with celery salt and cayenne pepper, brush with oil and grill for about 15 minutes.
- For the salsa, remove the rind and seeds from the melons. Finely dice the flesh and put it into a bowl. Mix in the onion and chillies.
- Add the lime juice and chopped coriander and season with salt. Turn the salsa out into a small mixing bowl.
- Arrange the grilled chicken on a plate and serve with the salsa.

Spicy haddock with beans

SERVES 4

350 calories per serving

INGREDIENTS:

25g/1oz low-fat spread
750g/1½lb haddock fillet (skinned and cut into 4 pieces)
225g/8oz canned chopped tomatoes
1 tablespoon tomato purée
275g/10oz canned chopped green

beans (drained)
½ teaspoon chilli powder
½ teaspoon granulated sugar
175g/6oz long-grain rice (cooked), to serve

- Melt the low-fat spread in a large frying pan. Fry the haddock for 5 minutes on one side, then turn over.
- Add the remaining ingredients except the rice to the pan and cover with aluminium foil or a lid. Simmer for 5 minutes or until the fish is tender. Serve on a bed of boiled rice.

Chicken & vegetable terrine

SERVES 6
300 calories per serving

INGREDIENTS:

1 small green pepper (diced)
1 small red pepper (diced)
2 small carrots (diced)
1 courgette (diced)
1 butternut squash (diced)
750g/1½lb boned and skinned chicken breasts (diced)
1 garlic clove (crushed)

½ teaspoon ground nutmeg
2 tablespoons lemon juice
3 eggs
350ml/12fl oz evaporated skimmed milk
75g/3oz mixed fresh herbs (such as basil, tarragon, dill and parsley)

- Blanch the peppers, carrots, courgette and squash lightly in boiling water. Drain and reserve.
- In a blender or food processor, purée the chicken. Add the garlic, nutmeg and lemon juice. Process and add the eggs, one at a time. Process again and add the evaporated milk and chopped herbs. Mix well.
- Pour the chicken mixture into a bowl and chill for 1 hour.
- Preheat the oven to 180°C/350°F/Gas mark 4.
- Fold the vegetables into the chicken mixture, then spoon the mixture into a 9 x 20cm/3½ x 8in loaf pan.
- Bake in the oven for 1 to 1½ hours. Leave to cool, then chill overnight in the refrigerator. To serve, cut into slices.

Roast baby chickens

SERVES 4
190 calories per serving

INGREDIENTS:

4 small poussins, weighing about 350-500g/12oz-1lb 2oz each
175g/6oz wild rice (cooked)

For the marinade:
4 garlic cloves (peeled)
2 fresh coriander roots
1 tablespoon light soy sauce

Salt and pepper

For the stuffing:
4 stalks lemon grass
4 kaffir lime leaves
4 slices ginger root
75ml/3fl oz coconut milk, for brushing

- Preheat the oven to 180°C/355°F/Gas mark 4. Wash the poussins and dry on kitchen paper.
- To make the marinade, place the garlic, coriander and soy sauce in a blender or food processor and purée until smooth. Season to taste with salt and pepper.
- Rub the marinade mixture evenly into the skin of the poussins.
- Place a stalk of lemon grass, a lime leaf and a piece of ginger in the cavity of each poussin. Place the poussins in a roasting tin and brush lightly with the coconut milk. Roast for about 30 minutes in the oven.
- Remove from the oven, brush again with coconut milk, return to the oven and cook for a further 15 to 25 minutes until golden and cooked through, depending on the size of the poussins. The juices should run clear.
- Serve the poussins on a bed of wild rice with the pan juices poured over.

Indian charred chicken

SERVES 4
230 calories per serving

INGREDIENTS:

4 chicken breasts (skinned and boned)
2 tablespoons curry paste
1 tablespoon sunflower oil
1 tablespoon light muscovado sugar
1 teaspoon ground ginger
½ teaspoon ground cumin

For the cucumber raita:
¼ cucumber (cut in half lengthways)
Salt
150ml/¼pt low-fat natural yogurt
¼ teaspoon chilli powder

- Place the chicken breasts between 2 sheets of baking parchment or clingfilm.
- Pound them with the flat side of a meat mallet or a rolling pin to flatten them.
- Mix together the curry paste, oil, sugar, ginger and cumin in a small bowl.
- Spread the mixture over both sides of the chicken. Leave to marinate for at least 2 hours.
- To make the raita, peel the cucumber and scoop out the seeds with a spoon.
- Grate the flesh, sprinkle with salt and leave to stand for 10 minutes. Rinse off the salt and squeeze out any moisture by pressing the cucumber with the back of a spoon.
- Mix the cucumber with the yogurt and stir in the chilli powder. Refrigerate until required.
- Transfer the chicken to an oiled rack and barbecue over hot coals for 10 minutes, turning once. Serve with the raita.

Peppered liver

SERVES 4
350 calories per serving

INGREDIENTS:

1 tablespoon plain flour
2 tablespoons peppercorns (crushed)
225g/8oz lambs' liver (very thinly sliced)
25g/1oz low-fat spread

1 tablespoon lemon juice
1 small onion (grated)
2 tablespoons chopped fresh parsley
3 tablespoons Worcestershire sauce

- Mix the flour with the peppercorns and use to coat the liver.
- Melt the low-fat spread in a large frying pan and fry the liver on one side until golden underneath. Turn over and cook until the pink juices rise to the surface.
- Remove from the pan and transfer to warmed serving plates.
- Add the remaining ingredients to the juices in the pan and cook, stirring, for 1 minute, scraping up any residue in the pan. Spoon over the liver and serve.

Lamb & tomato koftas

SERVES 4

190 calories per serving

INGREDIENTS:

225g/8oz finely minced lean lamb
1½ onions
2 garlic cloves (crushed)
1 dried red chilli (finely chopped)
2 teaspoons garam masala
2 tablespoons chopped fresh mint
2 teaspoons lemon juice
Salt

2 tablespoons vegetable oil
4 small tomatoes (quartered)

For the dressing:
150ml/¼pt low-fat natural yogurt
5cm/2in piece cucumber (grated)
2 tablespoons fresh mint
½ teaspoon toasted cumin seeds

- Place the lamb in a bowl. Finely chop 1 onion and add to the bowl with the garlic and chilli. Stir in the garam masala, mint and lemon juice and season well with salt. Mix well.
- Divide the mixture in half, then divide each half into 10 equal portions and form each into a small ball. Roll balls in half the oil to coat. Quarter the remaining onion half and separate into layers.
- Thread 5 of the meatballs, 4 tomato quarters and some of the onion layers on to each of 4 skewers.
- Brush the vegetables with the remaining oil and cook the koftas under a hot grill for about 10 minutes, turning frequently until they are browned all over.
- Meanwhile, prepare the dressing. In a small bowl, mix together the yogurt, cucumber, mint and cumin seeds.
- Serve the koftas hot with the yogurt dressing.

Prawn omelette

SERVES 4

320 calories per serving

INGREDIENTS:

3 tablespoons sunflower oil
2 leeks (sliced)
4 tablespoons cornflour
1 teaspoon salt
350g/12oz raw tiger prawns (peeled)

175g/6oz mushrooms (sliced)
175g/6oz beansprouts
6 eggs
3 tablespoons cold water

- Heat the oil in a preheated wok or large frying pan over a medium heat. Add the leeks and stir-fry for 3 minutes.
- Mix the cornflour and salt together in a large bowl.
- Add the prawns to the cornflour and salt mixture and toss to coat all over.
- Add the prawns to the wok and stir-fry for 2 minutes, or until the prawns have changed colour and are almost cooked through.
- Add the mushrooms and beansprouts to the wok and stir-fry for a further 2 minutes.
- Beat the eggs with the water in a small bowl. Pour the egg mixture into the wok and cook, stirring, until the egg sets, carefully turning the omelette over once.
- Turn the omelette out on to a clean board, divide into 4 and serve hot.

Thai chicken & vegetable stir-fry

SERVES 4

110 calories per serving

INGREDIENTS:

2 tablespoons sunflower oil
1 stalk lemon grass (thinly sliced)
1cm/½in piece fresh root ginger (peeled and chopped)
1 large garlic clove (finely chopped)
275g/10oz lean chicken (thinly sliced)
½ red pepper (seeded and sliced)
½ green pepper (seeded and sliced)

4 spring onions (chopped)
2 medium carrots (cut into matchsticks)
100g/4oz green beans
25g/1oz peanuts (lightly crushed)
2 tablespoons oyster sauce
Pinch of granulated sugar
Salt and pepper

- Heat the oil in a frying pan over a high heat. Add the lemon grass, ginger and garlic and stir-fry for 30 seconds until brown.
- Add the chicken and stir-fry for 2 minutes. Add all the vegetables and stir-fry for 4 to 5 minutes, until the chicken is cooked and the vegetables are almost cooked.
- Finally, stir in the peanuts, oyster sauce, sugar and seasoning to taste. Stir-fry for 1 minute to blend the flavours, then serve immediately.

Tuscan chicken

SERVES 4
250 calories per serving

INGREDIENTS:

1 teaspoon olive oil
8 chicken thighs (skinned)
1 medium onion (thinly sliced)
2 red peppers (seeded and sliced)
1 garlic clove (crushed)
300ml/½pt passata

150ml/¼pt dry white wine
1 teaspoon dried oregano
400g/14oz canned cannellini beans
(drained)
3 tablespoons fresh breadcrumbs

- Heat the oil in a non-stick pan and fry the chicken until golden. Remove the chicken from the pan and keep hot. Add the onion and peppers to the pan and gently sauté until softened, but not brown. Stir in the garlic.
- Return the chicken to the pan and add the passata, wine and oregano. Season well, bring to the boil, then cover the pan tightly.
- Lower the heat and simmer gently, stirring occasionally for 30 to 35 minutes or until the chicken is tender and the juices run clear.
- Stir in the beans and simmer for a further 5 minutes until heated through.
- Sprinkle with the breadcrumbs and cook under a hot grill until golden brown.

Duck with leek & cabbage

SERVES 4
200 calories per serving

INGREDIENTS:

4 duck breasts
350g/12oz green cabbage (thinly shredded)
225g/8oz leeks (sliced)

Finely grated zest of 1 orange
125ml/4fl oz oyster sauce
1 teaspoon toasted sesame seeds

- Heat a large wok and dry-fry the duck breasts with the skin on for about 5 minutes on each side. Remove from the wok, transfer to a clean board and slice thinly with a sharp knife.
- Remove all but 1 tablespoon of the duck fat from the wok and discard.
- Add the cabbage, leeks and orange zest to the wok and stir-fry for about 5 minutes, or until the vegetables have softened.

- Return the duck to the wok and heat through for 2 to 3 minutes. Drizzle the oyster sauce over the mixture in the wok, toss well until all the ingredients are combined, and heat through.
- Scatter the stir-fry with the sesame seeds, transfer to a warm serving dish and serve hot.

Keema curry

SERVES 4
350 calories per serving

INGREDIENTS:

1 onion (finely chopped)
1 garlic clove (crushed)
450g/1lb lean minced beef
1 teaspoon grated fresh root ginger
1 tablespoon garam masala
½ teaspoon chilli powder
1 teaspoon ground cumin

1 teaspoon ground turmeric
225g/8oz canned chopped tomatoes
2 tablespoons tomato purée
150ml/¼pt low-fat plain yogurt
Salt and pepper
175g/6oz basmati rice (rinsed and boiled)

- Put the onion and garlic in a pan with the beef. Cook, stirring, until the grains are brown and separate. Pour off any fat. Add all the remaining ingredients, except the rice.
- Bring to the boil, reduce the heat, cover and cook gently for 40 minutes, stirring occasionally. Remove the lid after 20 minutes. Taste and adjust the seasoning if necessary.
- Serve on a bed of rice.

Pasta with garlic sauce

SERVES 4
310 calories per serving

INGREDIENTS:

475g/1lb low-fat cottage cheese
4 tablespoons evaporated skimmed milk
Pinch of white pepper
8 garlic cloves (crushed)

2 teaspoons soy sauce
3 tablespoons chives (minced)
450g/1lb thin spaghetti (cooked)
100g/4oz Parmesan cheese (grated)

→

- Place the cottage cheese, evaporated milk, pepper, garlic, soy sauce and chives in a blender or food processor and purée until completely smooth.
- Place the mixture in a saucepan over a medium heat and warm until bubbly round the edges. Drain the spaghetti, place in a serving dish and pour the sauce over. Sprinkle with the Parmesan and serve immediately.

Skate with black butter

SERVES 4

390 calories per serving

INGREDIENTS:

*900g/2lb skate wings (cut into 4
pieces)*
175g/6oz butter
50ml/2fl oz red wine vinegar
15g/½oz capers (drained)
1 tablespoon chopped fresh parsley

For the court-bouillon:
900ml/1½pt cold water
900ml/1½pt dry white wine
3 tablespoons white wine vinegar

2 large carrots (chopped roughly)
1 onion (chopped roughly)
2 celery sticks (chopped roughly)
2 leeks (chopped roughly)
2 garlic cloves (chopped roughly)
2 bay leaves
4 fresh parsley sprigs
4 fresh thyme sprigs
6 black peppercorns
1 teaspoon salt

- Begin by making the court-bouillon. Put all of the ingredients into a large saucepan and bring slowly to the boil over a low heat. Cover and simmer gently for 30 minutes. Strain the liquid through a fine sieve into a clean pan. Bring to the boil again and simmer rapidly, uncovered, for 15 to 20 minutes, until reduced to 600ml/1pt.
- Place the skate in a wide shallow pan and pour over the court-bouillon. Bring to the boil over a low heat and simmer very gently for 15 minutes, or a little longer depending on the thickness of the skate. Drain the fish, reserve and keep warm.
- Meanwhile, melt the butter in a frying pan over a medium heat. Cook until the butter turns dark brown. Add the vinegar, capers and parsley and simmer for 1 minute. Pour over the fish. Serve with plenty of new potatoes and French beans.

Monkfish & mussel skewers

SERVES 4
140 calories per serving

INGREDIENTS:

1 teaspoon olive oil
2 tablespoon lemon juice
1 teaspoon paprika
1 garlic clove (crushed)
Salt and pepper
450g/1lb monkfish (skinned, boned and cut into 2.5cm/1in chunks)

4 turkey rashers
8 cooked mussels
8 raw tiger prawns
1 tablespoon chopped fresh dill

- Mix together the oil, lemon juice, paprika and garlic and season to taste.
- Place the monkfish in a shallow glass dish. Pour the marinade over the fish and toss to coat evenly. Cover and leave in a cool place for 30 minutes.
- Cut the turkey rashers in half and wrap each strip around a mussel. Thread on to 4 skewers, alternating with the fish cubes and prawns. Preheat the grill to high.
- Grill the kebabs for 7 to 8 minutes, turning once and basting with the marinade.
- Sprinkle with chopped dill and salt. Serve with salad and rice.

Bacon koftas

SERVES 4
130 calories per serving

INGREDIENTS:

225g/8oz lean smoked back bacon (roughly chopped)
75g/3oz fresh wholemeal breadcrumbs
2 spring onions (chopped)
1 tablespoon chopped fresh parsley

Finely grated zest of 1 lemon
1 egg white
Pinch of black pepper
1 teaspoon paprika

- Place the bacon in a blender or food processor with the breadcrumbs, spring onions, parsley, lemon zest, egg white and pepper. Process the mixture until it is finely chopped and begins to bind together.

→

- Divide the bacon mixture into 8 even-sized pieces and shape into long ovals around 8 skewers.
- Sprinkle the koftas with paprika and cook under a hot grill or on a barbecue for about 8 to 10 minutes, turning occasionally, until browned and cooked through.
- Serve with lemon rice and salad.

Beef daube

SERVES 8
260 calories per serving

INGREDIENTS:

2 tablespoons olive oil
1 large onion (cut into wedges)
2 celery sticks (chopped)
1 green pepper (chopped)
1kg/2¼lb lean braising steak (cubed)
50g/2oz plain flour (seasoned with salt and pepper)
600ml/1pt beef stock

2 garlic cloves (crushed)
150ml/¼pt red wine
2 tablespoons red wine vinegar
2 tablespoons tomato purée
½ teaspoon Tabasco sauce
1 teaspoon chopped fresh thyme leaves
2 bay leaves
½ teaspoon Cajun spice mix

- Preheat the oven to 180°C/350°F/Gas mark 4.
- Heat the oil in a large heavy-based, flameproof casserole dish. Add the onion and cook until browned on all sides. Remove with a slotted spoon and set aside.
- Add the celery and pepper to the pan and cook until softened. Remove the vegetables with a slotted spoon and set aside.
- Coat the steak in the seasoned flour, add to the pan and sauté until browned on all sides.
- Add the stock, garlic, wine, vinegar, tomato purée, Tabasco and thyme and heat gently. Return the onions, celery and pepper to the pan. Tuck in the bay leaves and sprinkle with Cajun seasoning.
- Bring to the boil, transfer to the oven and cook for 2½ to 3 hours, or until the meat and vegetables are tender.
- Serve immediately.

French braised lamb

SERVES 6
350 calories per serving

INGREDIENTS:

½ small leg of lamb (about 900g/2lb, trimmed of all fat)
1 large onion (cut into thick wedges)
2 garlic cloves (crushed)
1 teaspoon dried mixed herbs
600ml/1pt lamb stock

4 tablespoons red wine
Salt and pepper
3 large leeks (cut into chunks)
2 turnips (cut into chunks)
450g/1lb carrots (cut into chunks)
450g/1lb small potatoes

- Preheat the oven to 180°C/350°F/Gas mark 4.
- Put the lamb in a flameproof casserole dish with the onion, garlic, herbs, stock, wine and seasoning. Bring to the boil, cover and transfer to the oven. Cook for 1½ hours.
- Add the remaining vegetables and return to the oven for a further 45 minutes or until the meat is falling off the bone and the vegetables are tender.
- Remove the meat from the bone and cut into neat pieces, discarding any remaining fat. Skim any fat from the surface of the casserole. Spoon everything into 6 warmed serving bowls and serve.

Sea bream in a salt crust

SERVES 4
190 calories per serving

INGREDIENTS:

1kg/2¼lb whole sea bream
1 shallot (sliced thinly)
1 fresh parsley sprigs
1 fresh tarragon sprig
2 garlic cloves (chopped roughly)
2.5kg/5½lb coarse sea salt
Lemon wedges, to garnish

For the sauce:
2 shallots (very finely chopped)
4 tablespoons lemon juice
300g/11oz butter (diced)
Salt and pepper

- Preheat the oven to 220°C/425°F/Gas mark 7.
- Wash the sea bream under cold running water and pat dry with kitchen paper.
- Stuff the body cavity with the shallot, parsley, tarragon and garlic.

→

←
- Sprinkle a thick layer of salt into the base of a roasting tin large enough to hold the fish with lots of space around it. Top with the fish, then pour the remaining salt over the fish to completely cover it. Sprinkle water lightly over the salt.
- Cook for about 25 minutes.
- To make the sauce, put the shallots and lemon juice into a saucepan and simmer gently over a low heat for 5 minutes. Increase the heat until the lemon juice is reduced by half. Reduce the heat and add the butter, piece by piece, whisking constantly, until all the butter is incorporated and the sauce is thick. Season to taste with salt and pepper and keep warm.
- Remove the fish from the oven and leave to stand for 5 minutes before cracking open the salt. Remove the fish, garnish with lemon wedges and serve with the sauce.

Chilli stuffed with turkey

SERVES 6
240 calories per serving

INGREDIENTS:

Vegetable oil for greasing
4 large green chillies
100g/4oz low-fat Cheddar cheese (grated)
350g/12oz cooked turkey breast (cut into 1cm/½in strips)
100g/4oz plain flour

½ teaspoon baking powder
¼ teaspoon salt
125ml/4fl oz skimmed milk
3 eggs
150g/5oz mature Cheddar cheese (grated)

- Preheat the oven to 230°C/450°F/Gas mark 8. Lightly brush a large baking dish with vegetable oil.
- Slit the chillies on one side, remove the seeds and open out flat.
- Fill each chilli with a mixture of the Cheddar cheese and turkey. Fold over the edges of the chillies and place seam-side down in the prepared baking dish.
- In a medium-sized bowl, combine the flour, baking powder and salt.
- In a small bowl whisk the milk and eggs together, then slowly add to the flour mixture, beating until smooth. Pour over the chillies. Bake in the oven for 15 minutes.
- Remove from the oven and sprinkle with the mature Cheddar cheese and serve.

Baked cod with tomatoes

SERVES 4
160 calories per serving

INGREDIENTS:

Vegetable oil for greasing
2 teaspoons olive oil
1 onion (chopped)
2 garlic cloves (finely chopped)
450g/1lb canned chopped tomatoes
(drained)
1 teaspoon tomato purée

4 tablespoons dry white wine
Salt and pepper
4 tablespoons chopped fresh flat-leaf
parsley
4 cod cutlets
2 tablespoons dried breadcrumbs

- Preheat the oven to 190°C/375°F/Gas mark 5. Lightly grease a large baking dish.
- Heat the oil in a frying pan and fry the onion for about 5 minutes. Add the garlic, tomatoes, tomato purée, wine and salt and pepper to taste.
- Bring the sauce just to the boil, then reduce the heat slightly and cook, uncovered, for 15 to 20 minutes until thick. Stir in the parsley.
- Put the cod cutlets in the prepared baking dish and spoon an equal quantity of the tomato mixture on to each. Sprinkle the breadcrumbs over the top.
- Bake for 20 to 30 minutes, basting the fish occasionally with the sauce, until the fish is tender and cooked through, and the breadcrumbs are golden and crisp.
- Serve hot with new potatoes and a green salad.

Grilled mint-glazed chops

SERVES 4
350 calories per serving

INGREDIENTS:

4 lamb chops (trimmed of any fat)
Salt and pepper

1 tablespoon mint jelly

- Place the chops on a grill rack and season well on both sides. Grill for 5 minutes on each side.
- Melt the mint jelly in a small saucepan and brush over the chops. Continue brushing and grilling for a further 3 to 4 minutes. Serve with new potatoes.

→

Jerk chicken

SERVES 4
160 calories per serving

INGREDIENTS:

4 lean chicken portions
1 bunch spring onions (trimmed)
1 Scotch Bonnet chilli (deseeded)
1 garlic clove
5cm/2in piece root ginger (peeled and roughly chopped)
1/2 teaspoon dried thyme
1/2 teaspoon paprika

1/4 teaspoon ground allspice
Pinch of ground cinnamon
Pinch of ground cloves
4 tablespoons white wine vinegar
3 tablespoons soy sauce
1/4 teaspoon freshly ground black pepper

- Rinse the chicken portions and pat dry on kitchen paper. Place in a shallow dish.
- Place all the remaining ingredients in a blender or food processor and process until smooth.
- Pour the mixture over the chicken. Turn the chicken portions so that they are well coated in the marinade.
- Transfer the chicken to the refrigerator and leave to marinate for 24 hours.
- Remove the chicken from the marinade and barbecue over medium coals, or place under a medium grill, for about 30 minutes, turning the chicken and basting occasionally with any remaining marinade, until the meat is browned and cooked through.
- Transfer the chicken to individual serving plates and serve immediately.

Beef olives in gravy

SERVES 4
385 calories per serving

INGREDIENTS:

8 ready-prepared beef olives
4 tablespoons chopped fresh parsley
4 garlic cloves (finely chopped)
4 rashers smoked streaky bacon (finely chopped)
Grated zest of 1/2 small orange

Salt and pepper
2 tablespoons olive oil
300ml/1/2pt dry red wine
1 bay leaf
1 teaspoon granulated sugar
50g/2oz pitted black olives (drained)

- Flatten out the beef olives as thinly as possible, using a meat tenderizer or mallet.
- Mix together the parsley, garlic, bacon, orange zest and salt and pepper to taste.
- Spread this mixture evenly over each beef olive. Roll up each beef olive tightly, then secure with a cocktail stick.
- Heat the oil in a frying pan and fry the beef olives on all sides for 10 minutes.
- Drain the beef olives, reserving the pan juices, and keep warm. Pour the wine into the juices, add the bay leaf, sugar and salt and pepper to taste. Bring to the boil and boil rapidly for 5 minutes to reduce slightly, stirring.
- Return the cooked beef to the pan along with the black olives and heat through for a further 2 minutes. Discard the bay leaf and cocktail sticks.
- Transfer the beef olives and gravy to a serving dish. Serve immediately.

Chicken breasts & balsamic vinegar

SERVES 4
360 calories per serving

INGREDIENTS:

4 skinless, boneless chicken breasts
2 tablespoons plain flour
1/4 teaspoon freshly ground black pepper
3 tablespoons olive oil

6 garlic cloves (peeled)
350g/12oz small mushrooms
4 tablespoons balsamic vinegar
175ml/6fl oz chicken stock

- Split each chicken breast in half lengthways.
- Season the flour with pepper and dredge the chicken in the mixture. Shake off any excess flour.
- Heat the oil in a heavy-based frying pan and cook the chicken breasts over a medium-high heat for 4 minutes, or until nicely browned on one side. Add the garlic, turn the chicken pieces and continue to cook. Add the mushrooms and cook for about 7 minutes, then add the vinegar and stock.
- Cover closely and cook over a moderately low heat for 10 minutes, turning chicken occasionally.
- Transfer the chicken to a warm platter and set aside. Let the sauce with the mushrooms cook, uncovered, over a medium-high heat for about 6 minutes.
- Remove from the heat, pour the sauce over the chicken and serve immediately.

Chilli–flavoured pork

SERVES 4
190 calories per serving

INGREDIENTS:

2 tablespoons dried wood ear mushrooms
250g/9oz pork fillet (thinly sliced)
1 teaspoon salt
1 teaspoon cornflour (mixed with 1½ teaspoons water into a smooth paste)
3 tablespoon vegetable oil
1 garlic clove (finely chopped)
½ teaspoon finely chopped ginger root

2 spring onions (finely chopped, with the white and green parts separated)
2 celery sticks (thinly sliced)
½ teaspoon granulated sugar
1 tablespoon soy sauce
1 tablespoon chilli sauce
2 teaspoons rice vinegar
1 teaspoon rice wine
A few drops of sesame oil

- Soak the wood ear mushrooms in warm water for about 20 minutes, then rinse in cold water until the water is clear. Drain well, then cut into thin shreds.
- Mix the pork in a bowl with a pinch of salt and about half the cornflour paste until well coated.
- Heat 1 tablespoon of vegetable oil in a preheated wok. Add the pork and stir-fry for about 1 minute, or until the colour changes, then remove with a slotted spoon and set aside until required.
- Add the remaining oil to the wok and heat it. Add the garlic, ginger, the white parts of the spring onions, the wood ears and celery and stir-fry for 1 minute.
- Return the pork strips together with the remaining salt, sugar, soy sauce, chilli sauce, vinegar and wine. Blend well and continue stirring for another minute.
- Finally, add the green parts of the spring onions and blend in the remaining cornflour paste and sesame oil. Stir until the sauce has thickened. Transfer the chilli-flavoured pork to a warm serving dish and serve immediately.

Crunchy-topped cod

SERVES 4
135 calories per serving

INGREDIENTS:

4 pieces skinned cod fillet (about 100g/4oz each)
2 medium tomatoes (sliced)
50g/2oz fresh wholemeal breadcrumbs
2 tablespoons chopped fresh parsley

Finely grated zest and juice of ½ lemon
1 teaspoon sunflower oil
Salt and pepper

- Preheat the oven to 200°C/400°F/Gas mark 6. Place the cod fillets in a wide ovenproof dish. Arrange the tomato slices on top.
- Mix together the breadcrumbs, fresh parsley, lemon zest and juice and oil with seasoning to taste.
- Spoon the crumb mixture evenly over the fish, then bake in the oven for 15 to 20 minutes. Serve hot.

Red mullet & coconut loaf

SERVES 6
140 calories per serving

INGREDIENTS:

225g/8oz red mullet fillets (skinned and finely chopped)
2 small tomatoes (finely chopped)
2 green peppers (finely chopped)
1 onion (finely chopped)
1 red chilli (finely chopped)
150g/5oz fresh breadcrumbs
600ml/1pt coconut milk
Salt and pepper

For the sauce:
125ml/4fl oz tomato ketchup
1 teaspoon hot pepper sauce
¼ teaspoon hot mustard

- Preheat the oven to 200°C/400°F/Gas mark 6.
- Mix the red mullet with the tomatoes, peppers, onion and chilli. Stir in the breadcrumbs, coconut milk and seasoning.
- Grease and line a 500g/1lb 2oz loaf tin and add the mullet mixture. Bake for 1 to 1½ hours, until set.

→

- To make the sauce, mix together all the sauce ingredients until smooth and creamy.
- To serve, cut the loaf into slices and serve hot or cold, drizzled with the sauce.

Red prawn curry

SERVES 4
155 calories per serving

INGREDIENTS:

2 tablespoons vegetable oil
1 garlic clove (finely chopped)
1 tablespoon red curry paste
200ml/7fl oz coconut milk
2 tablespoon Thai fish sauce
1 teaspoon granulated sugar
12 large raw prawns (peeled and deveined)
2 kaffir lime leaves (finely shredded)
1 red chilli (deseeded and finely sliced)
10 leaves fresh Thai basil, plus extra to garnish

For the curry paste:
3 dried long red chillies
½ teaspoon ground coriander
¼ teaspoon ground cumin
½ teaspoon black pepper
2 garlic cloves (chopped)
2 lemon grass stalks (chopped)
1 kaffir lime leaf (finely chopped)
1 teaspoon freshly grated root ginger
½ teaspoon salt

- To make the curry paste, put all the ingredients into a blender or food processor and process to a smooth paste, adding a little water if necessary. Transfer to a bowl and reserve.
- Heat the oil in a preheated wok or frying pan over a medium heat until almost smoking. Add the garlic and fry until golden. Add the curry paste and cook for a further minute. Add half the coconut milk, the fish sauce and the sugar. Stir well.
- The mixture should thicken slightly.
- Add the prawns and simmer for 3 to 4 minutes until they turn pink. Add the remaining coconut milk, the lime leaves and the chilli. Cook for a further 2 to 3 minutes until the prawns are just tender.
- Add the basil leaves, stir until wilted and transfer to a large serving dish.
- Garnish with basil and serve immediately.

Lamb with mushroom sauce

SERVES 4

225 calories per serving

INGREDIENTS:

2 tablespoons vegetable oil
350g/12oz lean boneless lamb fillets
(cut into thin strips)
3 garlic cloves (crushed)
1 leek (sliced)
175g/6oz mushrooms (sliced)
½ teaspoon sesame oil

For the sauce:
1 teaspoon cornflour
4 tablespoon soy sauce
3 tablespoons Chinese rice wine
3 tablespoons water
½ teaspoon chilli sauce

- To make the sauce, mix together all the sauce ingredients and set aside.
- Heat the vegetable oil in a preheated wok or frying pan. Add the lamb, garlic and leek and stir-fry for about 2 to 3 minutes.
- Add the mushrooms to the wok and stir-fry for 1 minute.
- Stir in the sauce and cook for 2 to 3 minutes or until the lamb is cooked through and tender.
- Sprinkle the sesame oil over the top and transfer to a warmed serving dish.
- Serve immediately.

Chicken pepperonata

SERVES 4

340 calories per serving

INGREDIENTS:

8 skinless chicken thighs
2 tablespoons wholemeal flour
2 tablespoons olive oil
1 small onion (thinly sliced)
1 garlic clove (crushed)
1 large red pepper (thinly sliced)

1 large green pepper (thinly sliced)
1 large yellow pepper (thinly sliced)
400g/14oz canned chopped tomatoes
1 tablespoon chopped fresh oregano,
plus extra to garnish
Salt and pepper

- Toss the chicken in the flour.
- Heat the oil in a wide frying pan and fry the chicken quickly until sealed and lightly browned, then remove from the pan.
- Add the onion to the pan and gently fry until soft. Add the garlic, peppers,

→

←

tomatoes and oregano, then bring to the boil, stirring.
- Arrange the chicken over the vegetables, season well with salt and pepper, then cover the pan tightly and simmer for 20 to 25 minutes, or until the chicken is tender and the juices run clear.
- Season to taste, garnish with oregano and serve hot.

Moussaka

SERVES 4
240 calories per serving

INGREDIENTS:

1 small aubergine (peeled and sliced)
100g/4oz minced lamb
100g/4oz minced turkey
100g/4oz onion (chopped)
100g/4oz green pepper (chopped)
1 garlic clove (minced)
125ml/4fl oz tomato sauce
75ml/3fl oz dry red wine

1 tablespoon chopped fresh parsley
2 egg whites (beaten)
4 teaspoons plain flour
Pinch of ground cinnamon
Pinch of ground nutmeg
150ml/¼pt skimmed milk
3 tablespoons grated Parmesan cheese

- Preheat the oven to 170°C/325°F/Gas mark 3.
- In a saucepan, place the aubergine in a steamer basket over boiling water. Cover and steam for about 8 minutes. Drain on kitchen paper and reserve.
- In a frying pan over a medium-high heat, cook the lamb and turkey, onion, pepper and garlic until the meat is browned. Drain, then stir in the tomato sauce, wine and parsley. Simmer uncovered for 8 minutes. Remove from the heat and gradually stir half of the hot mixture into 1 egg white, then return to the frying pan.
- To prepare the sauce, in a saucepan combine the flour, cinnamon and nutmeg, then gradually stir in the milk until smooth. Cook and stir until bubbling. Remove from the heat and gradually stir half the hot sauce into 1 egg white, then return to saucepan.
- Place half the aubergine in a large baking tin. Pour the meat mixture over the top and place the remaining aubergine over. Pour sauce over all, then sprinkle with Parmesan cheese.
- Bake for about 30 minutes, then serve immediately.

Chicken with beansprouts

SERVES 4
160 calories per serving

INGREDIENTS:

100g/4oz chicken breast fillet (skinned
and cut into thin strips)
1 teaspoon salt
1/4 egg white (lightly beaten)
1 teaspoon cornflour (mixed with 1 1/2
teaspoons water to form a paste)
300ml/1/2pt vegetable oil
1 small onion (thinly shredded)

1 small green pepper (thinly shredded)
1 small carrot (thinly shredded)
100g/4oz fresh beansprouts
1/2 teaspoon granulated sugar
1 tablespoon soy sauce
1 teaspoon rice wine
3 tablespoons water
1/4 teaspoon sesame oil

- Place the chicken in a bowl. Add a pinch of the salt, the egg white and cornflour paste and mix well.
- Heat the vegetable oil in a preheated wok or large frying pan. Add the chicken and stir-fry for about 1 minute, stirring to separate the shreds. Remove with a slotted spoon and drain on kitchen paper.
- Pour off the oil, leaving about 2 tablespoons in the wok. Add the onion, pepper and carrot and stir-fry for about 2 minutes. Add the beansprouts and stir-fry for a few seconds.
- Add the chicken with the remaining salt, sugar, soy sauce and rice wine, blend well and add the water. Sprinkle with the sesame oil and serve immediately.

Sweet & spicy duck

SERVES 4
350 calories per serving

INGREDIENTS:

125ml/4fl oz dry sherry
125ml/4fl oz strong black tea
125ml/4fl oz soy sauce
1 garlic clove (crushed)
2 tablespoons clear honey

1 teaspoon ground cloves
Salt and pepper
4 small duck breasts (skinned)
15g/1/2oz low-fat spread

- Mix together the sherry, tea, soy sauce, garlic, honey, cloves and a little salt and pepper in a shallow dish. Add the duck and leave to marinate for 1 hour.

→

←
- Remove the duck from the marinade and place on a grill rack.
- Pour the marinade into a pan and heat until reduced by half. Stir in the low-fat spread. Brush over the duck and grill for 10 to 12 minutes on each side under a medium-high grill, until golden and cooked through, brushing regularly with marinade.

Fish pasties

SERVES 4
250 calories per serving

INGREDIENTS:

450g/1lb self-raising flour, plus extra for dusting
Pinch of salt
225g/8oz butter, plus extra for greasing
3 tablespoons cold water
1 egg (beaten lightly)

For the filling:
50g/2oz butter
75g/3oz leek (diced)

75g/3oz onion (finely chopped)
75g/3oz carrot (diced)
225g/8oz potato (peeled and diced)
350g/12oz cod fillets (cut into 2.5cm/1in pieces)
4 teaspoons white wine vinegar
25g/1oz Cheddar cheese (grated)
1 teaspoon chopped fresh tarragon
Salt and pepper

- Preheat the oven to 200°C/400°F/Gas mark 6.
- To make the pastry, sift the flour and salt together into a large bowl. Add the butter and rub it in with your fingertips until the mixture resembles coarse breadcrumbs. Add enough cold water to form a dough. Knead briefly until smooth. Wrap in clingfilm and leave to chill in the refrigerator for 30 minutes.
- To make the filling, melt half the butter in a large frying pan over a low heat.
- Add the leek, onion and carrot and cook gently for 7 to 8 minutes until the vegetables are softened. Remove from the heat and leave to cool slightly.
- Put the vegetable mixture into a bowl and add the potato, cod, vinegar, remaining butter, cheese, tarragon and seasoning to taste.
- Remove the pastry from the refrigerator and roll out thinly. Using a pastry cutter, press out four 19cm/7½in discs. Divide the filling between the discs.
- Moisten the edges of the pastry and fold over. Pinch to seal. Crimp the edges and place the pastries on a lightly greased baking tray. Brush generously with the egg.
- Bake in the oven for 15 minutes. Remove from the oven and brush again with the egg glaze. Return to the oven for a further 20 minutes. Serve warm.

Beef, tomato & olive kebabs

SERVES 8
170 calories per serving

INGREDIENTS:

450g/1lb rump or sirloin steak
16 cherry tomatoes
16 large green olives (pitted)

For the baste:
4 tablespoons olive oil
1 tablespoon sherry vinegar
1 garlic clove (crushed)
Salt and pepper

For the relish:
6 plum tomatoes
1 tablespoon olive oil
½ red onion (finely chopped)
1 garlic clove (chopped)
1 tablespoon chopped fresh parsley
1 tablespoon lemon juice

- Using a sharp knife, trim any fat from the steak and cut the meat into roughly 24 evenly sized pieces.
- Thread the pieces of steak on to 8 wooden skewers, alternating the beef with the cherry tomatoes and the green olives.
- To make the baste, combine all the baste ingredients in a bowl.
- To make the relish, plunge the tomatoes in a bowl of boiling water, then drain and transfer to a bowl of cold water. Skin and chop.
- Heat the oil in a small pan and fry the onion and garlic for 3 to 4 minutes until softened. Add the tomatoes and cook for a further 2 to 3 minutes. Stir in the parsley and lemon juice and season with salt and pepper to taste. Set aside and keep warm.
- Barbecue the kebabs over hot coals for 5 to 10 minutes, basting and turning frequently. Serve with the relish.

Grilled stuffed sole

SERVES 4

210 calories per serving

INGREDIENTS:

1 tablespoon olive oil
25g/1oz butter
1 small onion (finely chopped)
1 garlic clove (chopped)
3 sun-dried tomatoes (chopped)
2 tablespoons fresh lemon thyme leaves

50g/2oz breadcrumbs
1 tablespoon lemon juice
Salt and pepper
4 small whole sole (gutted and cleaned)
Lemon wedges, to garnish

- Heat the oil and butter in a frying pan until it just begins to froth.
- Add the onion and garlic to the frying pan and cook, stirring, for 5 minutes, or until just softened.
- To make the stuffing, mix together the tomatoes, thyme, breadcrumbs and lemon juice in a bowl, then season to taste.
- Add the stuffing mixture to the pan and stir to mix.
- Using a sharp knife, pare the skin from the bone inside the gut hole of the fish to make a pocket. Spoon the stuffing into the pocket.
- Cook the fish, under a preheated grill, for 6 minutes on either side, or until golden brown. Transfer to serving plates and garnish with lemon wedges.

Turkey & macaroni cheese

SERVES 4

160 calories per serving

INGREDIENTS:

1 medium onion (chopped)
150ml/¼pt vegetable stock
25g/1oz low-fat spread
25g/1oz plain flour
300ml/½pt skimmed milk
Salt and pepper
50g/2oz low-fat Cheddar cheese

1 teaspoon dry mustard
225g/8oz macaroni
4 smoked turkey rashers (halved)
3 tomatoes (sliced)
3 fresh basil leaves
1 tablespoon grated Parmesan cheese

- Put the onion and stock into a non-stick frying pan.
- Bring to the boil, stirring occasionally, and cook for 5 to 6 minutes or until the

stock has reduced entirely and the onion is transparent.
- Put the low-fat spread, flour, milk and seasoning into a saucepan and whisk together over a medium heat until thickened and smooth. Draw aside and add the cheese, mustard and onion.
- Cook the macaroni in a large pan of boiling, salted water according to the packet instructions. Preheat the grill. Drain the macaroni thoroughly and stir into the sauce. Transfer to a shallow ovenproof dish.
- Arrange the turkey rashers and tomatoes overlapping on top of the macaroni cheese. Tuck in the basil leaves, then sprinkle with the Parmesan and grill to lightly brown the top.

Yellow bean chicken

SERVES 4
240 calories per serving

INGREDIENTS:

1 egg white (beaten)
1 tablespoon cornflour
450g/1lb skinless, boneless chicken breasts (cut into 2.5cm/1in cubes)
1 tablespoon rice wine vinegar
1 tablespoon soy sauce
1 teaspoon caster sugar

3 tablespoons vegetable oil
1 garlic clove (crushed)
1cm/½in piece fresh root ginger (grated)
1 green pepper (diced)
2 large mushrooms (sliced)
3 tablespoons yellow bean sauce

- Mix the egg white and cornflour in a bowl. Add the chicken and turn in the mixture to coat. Set aside for 20 minutes.
- Mix the rice wine vinegar, soy sauce and sugar in a bowl. Remove the chicken from the egg white mixture.
- Heat the oil in a preheated wok, add the chicken and stir-fry for 3 to 4 minutes, until golden brown. Remove the chicken from the wok with a slotted spoon, set aside and keep warm.
- Add the garlic, ginger, pepper and mushrooms to the wok and stir-fry for 1 to 2 minutes.
- Add the yellow bean sauce and cook for 1 minute. Stir in the vinegar mixture and return the chicken to the wok. Cook for 1 to 2 minutes and serve hot.

Escalopes & Italian sausage

SERVES 4
240 calories per serving

INGREDIENTS:

1 tablespoon olive oil
6 canned anchovy fillets (drained)
1 tablespoon capers (drained)
1 tablespoon chopped fresh rosemary leaves
Grated zest and juice of 1 orange

75g/3oz pepperoni (diced)
3 tomatoes (chopped)
4 turkey escalopes (about 100g/4oz each)
Salt and pepper

- Heat the oil in a large frying pan. Add the anchovies, capers, rosemary, orange zest and juice, sausage and tomatoes to the pan and cook for 5 to 6 minutes, stirring occasionally.
- Meanwhile, place the turkey between sheets of greaseproof paper. Pound with a meat mallet or the end of a rolling pin to flatten it.
- Add the turkey to the mixture in the frying pan. Season to taste with salt and pepper, cover and cook for about 3 to 5 minutes on each side. Transfer to serving plates and serve hot.

Spicy masala chicken

SERVES 6
195 calories per serving

INGREDIENTS:

12 skinless chicken thighs
75ml/3fl oz lemon juice
1 teaspoon grated fresh root ginger
1 garlic clove (crushed)
1 teaspoon crushed dried red chillies
1 teaspoon salt

1 teaspoon demerara sugar
2 tablespoons clear honey
2 tablespoons chopped fresh coriander
1 green chilli (finely chopped)
2 tablespoons sunflower oil

- Prick the chicken with a fork, rinse, pat dry and set aside in a large bowl.
- In a large mixing bowl, mix together the lemon juice, ginger, garlic, red chillies, salt, sugar and honey. Transfer the chicken to the spice mixture and coat well. Set aside for about 45 minutes.
- Preheat the grill to medium. Add the coriander and green chilli to the chicken

thighs and place them on a flameproof dish.
- Pour any remaining marinade over the chicken and baste with the oil, using a pastry brush.
- Grill the chicken thighs under the preheated grill for about 15 to 20 minutes, turning and basting occasionally, until cooked through and browned. Transfer to a serving dish and serve immediately.

Tangy pork fillet

SERVES 4
230 calories per serving

INGREDIENTS:

400g/14oz lean pork fillet
Salt and pepper
3 tablespoons orange marmalade
Grated zest and juice of 1 orange
1 tablespoon white wine vinegar
Dash of Tabasco sauce

For the sauce:
1 tablespoon olive oil
1 small onion (chopped)
1 small green pepper (thinly sliced)
1 tablespoon cornflour
150ml/¼pt orange juice

- Place a large piece of double-thickness aluminium foil in a shallow dish. Put the pork fillet in the centre of the foil and season.
- Heat the marmalade, orange zest and juice, vinegar and Tabasco sauce in a small pan, stirring until the marmalade melts and the ingredients combine. Pour the mixture over the pork and wrap the meat in the foil, making sure that the parcel is well sealed so the juices cannot run out.
- Place over hot coals and barbecue for about 25 minutes, turning the parcel occasionally.
- For the sauce, heat the oil and cook the onion for 2 to 3 minutes. Add the pepper and cook for 3 to 4 minutes.
- Remove the pork from the foil and place on to the barbecue rack. Pour the juices into the pan.
- Barbecue the pork for a further 10 to 20 minutes, turning, until cooked through and golden on the outside.
- In a small bowl, mix the cornflour with a little orange juice to form a paste. Add to the sauce and cook, stirring, until the sauce thickens. Slice the pork, spoon the sauce over, and serve with rice and a green salad.

Grapefruit bacon chops

SERVES 4

220 calories per serving

INGREDIENTS:

1 ruby grapefruit
4 lean bacon chops

3 tablespoons redcurrant jelly
Black pepper

- Cut away the pith and peel from the grapefruit using a sharp knife and carefully remove the segments, catching the juice in the bowl.
- Fry the bacon in a non-stick frying pan without fat, turning once, until golden and cooked.
- Add the reserved grapefruit juice and the redcurrant jelly to the pan and stir until melted. Add the grapefruit segments, then season with pepper and serve.

Chicken & vegetable Mornay

SERVES 4

350 calories per serving

INGREDIENTS:

25g/1oz cornflour
300ml/¹/₂pt skimmed milk
1 teaspoon low-fat spread
Salt and pepper
1 teaspoon English mustard
75g/3oz low-fat Cheddar cheese (grated)

350g/12oz mixed cooked, chopped vegetables
175g/6oz cooked, chopped chicken (skin removed)
¹/₄ teaspoon grated nutmeg

- Blend the cornflour in a saucepan with the milk. Add the low-fat spread. Bring to the boil and cook for 1 minute, stirring all the time.
- Stir in a little salt and pepper, the mustard and two-thirds of the cheese. Fold in the vegetables and the chicken and season with the nutmeg and a little more salt and pepper if required. Heat through.
- Turn into a flameproof serving dish, top with the remaining cheese and place until a medium grill until golden and bubbling.

Minty lime chicken

SERVES 6
180 calories per serving

INGREDIENTS:

*3 tablespoons finely chopped fresh
mint
4 tablespoons clear honey
4 tablespoons lime juice
Salt and pepper
12 boneless chicken thighs*

For the sauce:
*150g/5oz low-fat natural yogurt
1 tablespoon finely chopped mint
2 teaspoons finely grated lime zest*

- Combine the mint, honey and lime juice in a bowl and season with salt and pepper to taste.
- Add the chicken to the marinade, turning to coat evenly. Leave the chicken to marinate for 2 hours.
- Cook the chicken on a preheated barbecue or grill, turning frequently and basting with the marinade, until the chicken is cooked and the juices run clear.
- Meanwhile, mix together the sauce ingredients. Serve the chicken with a green salad and the sauce for dipping.

Sardinian red mullet

SERVES 4
290 calories per serving

INGREDIENTS:

*50g/2oz sultanas
150ml/5fl oz red wine
2 tablespoons olive oil
2 medium onions (sliced)
1 courgette (cut in half lengthways
and into 5cm/2in sticks)*

*2 oranges
4 red mullet (boned and filleted)
50g/2oz canned anchovy fillets
(drained)
2 tablespoons chopped fresh oregano*

- Place the sultanas in a bowl. Pour the red wine over them and leave to soak for 10 minutes.
- Heat the oil in a large frying pan. Add the onions and sauté for 2 minutes. Add the courgette to the pan and fry for a further 3 minutes, or until they are tender.
- Using a zester, pare long, thin strips from one of the oranges. Using a sharp

→

←

knife, remove all the peel and pith from both oranges, then segment them by slicing between the membrane.

- Add the orange zest to the frying pan. Add the red wine, sultanas, mullet and anchovies to the pan and leave to simmer for 10 to 15 minutes, or until the fish is cooked through.
- Stir in the oregano and orange segments, set aside and leave to cool. Place the mixture in a large bowl and leave to chill, covered, in the refrigerator for at least 2 hours. Transfer to serving plates and serve.

Lamb & anchovies with thyme

SERVES 4
300 calories per serving

INGREDIENTS:

1 teaspoon olive oil
15g/¹/₂oz butter
600g/1lb 5oz lamb shoulder or leg (cut into 2.5cm/1in chunks)
4 garlic cloves (peeled)
3 fresh thyme sprigs (stalks removed)
6 canned anchovy fillets

150ml/¹/₄pt red wine
150ml/¹/₄pt vegetable stock
1 teaspoon granulated sugar
50g/2oz black olives (stoned and halved)
2 tablespoons chopped fresh parsley, to garnish

- Heat the oil and butter in a large frying pan. Add the lamb and cook for 4 to 5 minutes, stirring, until the meat is browned all over.
- Using a pestle and mortar, grind together the garlic, thyme and anchovies to make a smooth paste.
- Add the wine and stock to the frying pan. Stir in the anchovy paste and the sugar.
- Bring the mixture to the boil, reduce the heat, cover and leave to simmer for 30 to 40 minutes, or until the lamb is tender. For the last 10 minutes of the cooking time, remove the lid in order to allow the sauce to reduce slightly.
- Stir the olives into the sauce and mix to combine.
- Transfer the lamb and its sauce to a serving bowl and garnish with parsley.

Barbecued chicken

SERVES 4
220 calories per serving

INGREDIENTS:

8 small chicken pieces

For the marinade:
2 lemon grass stalks (chopped)
2.5cm/1in piece fresh root ginger
6 garlic cloves

4 shallots
½ bunch coriander roots
1 tablespoon palm sugar
125ml/4fl oz coconut milk
2 tablespoons fish sauce
2 tablespoons soy sauce
2 limes (cut into wedges), to garnish

- To make the marinade, put all the ingredients into a blender or food processor and process until smooth.
- Put the chicken pieces in a dish and pour the marinade over. Leave in a cool place to marinate for at least 4 hours.
- Preheat the oven to 200°C/400°F/Gas mark 6. Put the chicken pieces on a rack on a baking tray. Brush with the marinade and bake in the oven for about 20 to 30 minutes or until the chicken is cooked and golden brown. Turn the pieces over halfway through and brush with more marinade.
- Garnish with lime wedges and serve with boiled rice.

French mussels

SERVES 4
200 calories per serving

INGREDIENTS:

900g/2lb live mussels
3 tablespoons olive oil
1 onion (chopped)
3 garlic cloves (chopped finely)
2 teaspoons fresh thyme leaves

150ml/¼pt red wine
850g/1¾lb canned chopped tomatoes
2 tablespoons chopped fresh parsley
Salt and pepper

- Clean the mussels by scrubbing or scraping the shells and pulling out any 'beards' that are attached to them. Discard any mussels with broken shells or any that do not close when tapped. Put the mussels into a large saucepan with just the water that clings to their shells. Cook, covered, over a high heat for 3 to 4

→

← minutes until the mussels have opened. Discard any mussels that remain closed.

- Strain, reserving the cooking liquid.
- Heat the oil in a large saucepan over a low heat. Add the onion and cook gently for 8 to 10 minutes until softened but not coloured. Add the garlic and thyme and cook for a further 1 minute. Add the wine and simmer rapidly until reduced and syrupy. Add the tomatoes and reserved cooking liquid and bring to the boil. Cover and simmer for 30 minutes. Uncover and cook for a further 15 minutes.
- Add the mussels and cook for a further 5 minutes until heated through. Stir in the parsley, season to taste with salt and pepper and serve.

Sage chicken & rice

SERVES 4
250 calories per serving

INGREDIENTS:

1 large onion (chopped)
1 garlic clove (crushed)
2 celery sticks (sliced)
2 carrots (diced)
2 sprigs fresh sage
300ml/½pt chicken stock
350g/12oz boneless, skinless chicken

breasts (cut into 2.5cm/1in cubes)
225g/8oz wild rice
400g/14oz canned chopped tomatoes
Dash of Tabasco sauce
2 medium courgettes (thinly sliced)
100g/4oz lean ham (diced)
Salt and pepper

- Place the onion, garlic, celery, carrots and sage in a large saucepan and pour in the stock. Bring to the boil, cover the pan and simmer for 5 minutes.
- Stir the chicken into the pan with the vegetables. Cover the pan and continue to cook for a further 5 minutes. Stir in the rice and tomatoes.
- Add the Tabasco sauce and season well. Bring to the boil, cover and simmer for 25 minutes.
- Stir in the courgettes and ham and continue to cook, uncovered, for a further 10 minutes, stirring occasionally, until the rice is just tender. Remove and discard the sage and serve hot.

Pork stroganoff

SERVES 4

230 calories per serving

INGREDIENTS:

350g/12oz lean pork fillet
1 tablespoon vegetable oil
1 medium onion (chopped)
2 garlic cloves (crushed)
25g/1oz plain flour
2 tablespoons tomato purée

400ml/14fl oz chicken stock
100g/4oz button mushrooms (sliced)
1 large green pepper (diced)
Salt and pepper
½ teaspoon ground nutmeg
4 tablespoons low-fat natural yogurt

- Trim away any excess fat and silver skin from the pork, then cut the meat into slices 1cm/½in thick.
- Heat the oil in a large saucepan and gently fry the pork, onion and garlic for 4 to 5 minutes until lightly browned.
- Stir in the flour and tomato purée, pour in the stock and stir to mix thoroughly.
- Add the mushrooms, pepper, seasoning and nutmeg. Bring to the boil, cover and simmer for 20 minutes until the pork is tender and cooked through.
- Remove the saucepan from the heat and stir in the yogurt. Serve the pork and sauce on a bed of rice.

Salmon burgers

SERVES 4

240 calories per serving

INGREDIENTS:

350g/12oz canned boneless, skinless
pink salmon
1 egg white (beaten)
100g/4oz seasoned breadcrumbs
100g/4oz onions (chopped)
½ teaspoon dried thyme

½ teaspoon cracked pepper
1 teaspoon salt
1 tablespoon corn oil
4 iceberg lettuce leaves
1 tomato (sliced)
2 small pitta breads (halved crossways)

- Drain the canned salmon, reserving 2 tablespoons of the liquid.
- In a mixing bowl combine the reserved liquid, egg white, breadcrumbs, onion, thyme, pepper and salt. Add the drained salmon and mix well. Then shape the mixture into 4 x 1cm/½in-thick patties.

$\rightarrow$

←

- In a frying pan, cook the patties in the oil over a medium heat for 2 to 3 minutes or until brown on the underside. Turn and cook for a further 2 minutes.
- Serve each patty with lettuce and tomato in half a pitta bread.

Barbecued pork

SERVES 6

260 calories per serving

INGREDIENTS:

3 tablespoons honey
2 tablespoons hoisin sauce
2 tablespoons low-calorie ketchup
1 tablespoon soy sauce

⅛ teaspoon Chinese five-spice powder
2 pork tenderloins, 350g/12oz each

- Combine all the ingredients except the pork in a mixing bowl, stir well and set aside.
- Trim any fat from the pork and place in a large shallow dish. Pour the honey mixture over the pork, cover and marinate in the refrigerator for 8 hours, turning the pork occasionally.
- Remove the pork from the marinade, reserving the marinade.
- Place the pork on a grill pan or barbecue and cook until cooked through, basting occasionally with marinade. Serve with boiled rice.

Irish bacon with cabbage

SERVES 4

350 calories per serving

INGREDIENTS:

1kg/2¼lb very lean unsmoked collar bacon
1 bay leaf
4 onions (peeled)
6 black peppercorns

1 green cabbage (quartered and thick stalk removed)
450g/1lb potatoes (chopped into large pieces)

- Place the bacon in a large saucepan and just cover with water. Bring to the boil, then discard the water. Add fresh water, the bay leaf, onions and peppercorns.

- Bring to the boil, cover, reduce the heat and simmer gently for 1½ hours.
- Add the cabbage and potatoes and continue cooking for 30 minutes. Lift out the cabbage, potatoes and onions with a slotted spoon and keep warm.
- Carve half the joint, trimming off any remaining fat. Place on warmed plates with the potatoes, cabbage and onions and spoon a little of the broth over.

Thai red chicken

SERVES 4
250 calories per serving

INGREDIENTS:

1 tablespoon sunflower oil
450g/1lb lean boneless, skinless chicken (thinly sliced)
2 garlic cloves (crushed)
2 tablespoon Thai red curry paste
2 tablespoons grated root ginger
1 tablespoon tamarind paste

4 lime leaves
600ml/1pt coconut milk
225g/8oz sweet potato (peeled and diced)
225g/8oz cherry tomatoes (halved)
3 tablespoons chopped fresh coriander

- Heat the oil in a large preheated wok. Add the chicken and stir-fry for 5 minutes.
- Add the garlic, curry paste, ginger, tamarind and lime leaves to the wok and stir-fry for about 1 minute.
- Add the coconut milk and sweet potato to the mixture in the wok and bring to the boil. Allow to bubble over a medium heat for 20 minutes, or until the juices start to thicken and reduce.
- Add the cherry tomatoes and coriander to the curry and cook for a further 5 minutes, stirring occasionally. Transfer to serving plates and serve hot with rice.

Spiced rainbow trout

SERVES 4
190 calories per serving

INGREDIENTS:

4 large rainbow trout fillets, about 150g/5oz each
1 tablespoon ground coriander
1 garlic clove (crushed)

2 tablespoons finely chopped fresh mint
1 teaspoon paprika
175g/6oz natural yogurt

→

←
- With a sharp knife, slash the flesh of the fish fillets through the skin fairly deeply at intervals.
- Mix together the coriander, garlic, mint, paprika and yogurt. Spread this mixture evenly over the fish and leave to marinate for about an hour.
- Cook the fish under a moderately hot grill or on a barbecue, turning occasionally, until crisp and golden. Serve hot.

Chicken curry

SERVES 6
155 calories per serving

INGREDIENTS:

75g/3oz red lentils
2 tablespoons mild curry powder
2 teaspoons ground coriander
1 teaspoon ground cumin
450ml/³/₄pt vegetable stock

8 chicken thighs (skinned)
225g/8oz fresh spinach (shredded)
1 tablespoon chopped fresh coriander
Salt and pepper

- Rinse the lentils under cold running water. Put in a large heavy-based saucepan with the curry powder, ground coriander, cumin and stock. Bring to the boil, then lower the heat. Cover and simmer gently for 10 minutes.
- Add the chicken and spinach. Replace the cover and simmer gently for a further 40 minutes, or until the chicken has cooked.
- Stir in the fresh coriander and season to taste. Serve with basmati rice.

Trout with almonds

SERVES 4
350 calories per serving

INGREDIENTS:

4 small rainbow trout (cleaned)
50g/2oz low-fat spread
25g/1oz flaked almonds
2 tablespoons chopped fresh parsley

Salt and pepper
1 tablespoon lemon juice
450g/1lb potatoes (boiled)

- Rinse the trout and pat dry with kitchen paper. Remove the heads if preferred.
- Melt 25g/1oz low-fat spread in a large frying pan and fry the fish for 5 minutes

on each side until golden brown and cooked through. Transfer to serving plates and keep warm.

- Melt the remaining low-fat spread in the juices in the pan. Add the almonds and fry until golden brown. Throw in the parsley, a little salt and pepper and the lemon juice. Spoon over the trout and serve with the potatoes.

Chicken in cashew nut sauce

SERVES 4

285 calories per serving

INGREDIENTS:

2 onions
2 tablespoons tomato purée
50g/2oz cashew nuts
1½ teaspoons garam masala
1 garlic clove (crushed)
1 teaspoon chilli powder
1 tablespoon lemon juice
¼ teaspoon ground turmeric
1 teaspoon salt

1 tablespoon low-fat natural yogurt
2 tablespoons corn oil
1 tablespoon chopped fresh coriander
1 tablespoon sultanas
450g/1lb skinned, boned chicken breast (cubed)
175g/6oz button mushrooms
300ml/½pt water

- Cut the onions into quarters, place in a blender or food processor and blend for about 1 minute. Add the tomato purée, cashew nuts, garam masala, garlic, chilli powder, lemon juice, turmeric, salt and yogurt. Blend for a further 1 to 1½ minutes.
- In a saucepan, heat the oil, lower the heat to medium and pour in the spice mixture from the food processor. Fry the mixture for about 2 minutes.
- Add the coriander, sultanas and chicken, and continue to stir-fry for a further 1 minute.
- Add the mushrooms, pour in the water and bring to a simmer. Cover the pan and cook over a low heat for 10 minutes. Check that the chicken is thoroughly cooked and the sauce is thick. Serve hot.

Garlic & lime chicken

SERVES 4

285 calories per serving

INGREDIENTS:

4 large skinless, boneless chicken breasts
50g/2oz garlic butter (softened)
3 tablespoon chopped fresh coriander

1 tablespoon sunflower oil
Finely grated zest and juice of 2 limes
25g/1oz demerara sugar

- Place each chicken breast between 2 sheets of clingfilm and pound with a rolling pin until flattened to about 1cm/½in thick.
- Mix together the garlic butter and coriander and spread over each chicken breast. Roll the chicken up like a Swiss roll and secure with a cocktail stick.
- Heat the oil in a preheated wok or heavy-based frying pan. Add the chicken to the wok and cook, turning, for 15 to 20 minutes or until cooked through.
- Remove the chicken from the wok and transfer to a board. Cut each chicken roll into slices.
- Add the lime zest, juice and sugar to the wok and heat gently, stirring, until the sugar has dissolved. Raise the heat and allow to bubble for 2 minutes.
- Arrange the chicken on warmed serving plates and spoon the pan juices over to serve. Serve warm with boiled rice.

Stuffed cabbage leaves

SERVES 6

260 calories per serving

INGREDIENTS:

12 large cabbage leaves
450g/1lb minced turkey
1 medium onion (minced)
Dash of pepper
100g/4oz long-grain rice (cooked)

1 egg white (lightly beaten)
225ml/8fl oz tomato juice
2 tablespoons malt vinegar
3 tablespoons vegetable oil
50g/2oz demerara sugar

- Preheat the oven to 180°C/350°F/Gas mark 4.
- Wash the cabbage leaves and steam in a colander over boiling water for 5 to 10 minutes until they are soft enough to roll. Remove from the heat.

- Mix the turkey, onion, pepper, rice and egg. Place a spoonful of the meat mixture in the centre of each cabbage leaf. Fold the sides up over the filling, tucking in the edges, and secure with a cocktail stick. Repeat until all the leaves are filled. Place in a greased 1.2 litre/2pt baking dish.
- Mix the tomato juice, vinegar and oil and pour over the stuffed cabbage.
- Sprinkle with sugar and bake, covered, for 45 minutes, removing the cover slightly before the end of baking to brown the top.

Chicken jalfrezi

SERVES 4
280 calories per serving

INGREDIENTS:

1 teaspoon mustard oil
3 tablespoons vegetable oil
1 large onion (finely chopped)
3 garlic cloves (crushed)
1 tablespoon tomato purée
2 tomatoes (skinned and chopped)
1 teaspoon ground turmeric
½ teaspoon ground cumin seeds
½ teaspoon ground coriander seeds

½ teaspoon chilli powder
½ teaspoon garam masala
1 teaspoon red wine vinegar
1 small red pepper (chopped)
100g/4oz frozen broad beans
500g/1lb 2oz cooked chicken (cut into bite-sized pieces)
Salt

- Heat the mustard oil in a large frying pan set over a high heat for about 1 minute until it begins to smoke. Add the vegetable oil, reduce the heat and then add the onion and garlic. Fry until they are golden.
- Add the tomato purée, chopped tomatoes, turmeric, cumin, coriander, chilli powder, garam masala and vinegar to the frying pan. Stir the mixture until fragrant.
- Add the pepper and beans and stir for 2 minutes, until the pepper is softened.
- Stir in the chicken and add salt to taste.
- Simmer gently for 6 to 8 minutes, until the chicken is heated through and the beans are tender. Serve hot.

Thai green fish curry

SERVES 4

220 calories per serving

INGREDIENTS:

2 tablespoons vegetable oil
1 garlic clove (chopped)
1 small aubergine (diced)
125ml/4fl oz coconut cream
2 tablespoons Thai fish sauce
1 teaspoon granulated sugar
225g/8oz cod fillet (cut into pieces)
125ml/4fl oz fish stock
2 kaffir lime leaves (finely shredded)
15 fresh Thai basil leaves

For the curry paste:
5 fresh green chillies (deseeded and chopped)
2 teaspoons chopped lemon grass
1 large shallot (chopped)
2 garlic cloves (chopped)
1 teaspoon freshly grated root ginger
2 fresh coriander roots (chopped)
1/2 teaspoon ground coriander
1/4 teaspoon ground cumin
1 kaffir lime leaf (finely chopped)
1/2 teaspoon salt

- To make the curry paste, put all the ingredients into a blender or food processor and blend to a smooth paste, adding a little water if necessary.
- Heat the vegetable oil in a large frying pan or preheated wok over a medium heat until almost smoking. Add the garlic and fry until golden. Add the curry paste and stir-fry for a few seconds before adding the aubergine. Stir-fry for about 4 to 5 minutes until softened.
- Add the coconut cream, bring to the boil and stir until the cream thickens and curdles slightly. Add the fish sauce and sugar to the frying pan and stir well.
- Add the cod and stock. Simmer for 3 to 4 minutes, stirring occasionally, until the fish is just tender. Add the lime leaves and basil, then cook for a further minute.
- Transfer to a large, warmed serving dish and serve immediately.

Sage & cheese pork fillets

SERVES 4

340 calories per serving

INGREDIENTS:

4 pieces pork fillet (about 100g/4oz each)
2 teaspoons low-fat spread (melted)

8 sage leaves (chopped)
Salt and pepper
50g/2oz Emmental cheese (grated)

- Put the pork pieces in a plastic bag one at a time and beat flat with a rolling pin or meat mallet. Place on a grill rack and brush with half the low-fat spread. Grill for about 4 minutes until golden. Turn over and brush with the remaining spread.
- Grill for a further 4 minutes, until cooked through.
- Sprinkle with the sage, salt and pepper and cheese and return to the grill until the cheese bubbles. Serve with new potatoes and vegetables.

Fish with coconut & basil

SERVES 4
210 calories per serving

INGREDIENTS:

2 tablespoons vegetable oil
450g/1lb skinless cod fillet
25g/1oz plain flour (seasoned with salt and pepper)
1 garlic clove (crushed)

2 tablespoons red curry paste
1 tablespoon fish sauce
300ml/¹/₂pt coconut milk
175g/6oz cherry tomatoes (halved)
20 fresh basil leaves

- Heat the oil in a large preheated wok. Using a sharp knife, cut the fish into large cubes, removing any bones.
- Place the flour in a bowl, add the fish and mix until well coated. Add to the wok and stir-fry over a high heat for 3 to 4 minutes, or until the fish begins to brown.
- Mix together the garlic, curry paste, fish sauce and coconut milk. Pour the mixture over the fish and bring to the boil.
- Add the tomatoes to the mixture in the wok and leave to simmer for 5 minutes.
- Roughly chop or tear the basil leaves. Add the basil to the wok and stir.
- Transfer to serving plates and serve hot with fragrant rice.

Cider baked rabbit

SERVES 4
170 calories per serving

INGREDIENTS:

450g/1lb rabbit joints
1 tablespoon plain flour
1 teaspoon dry mustard powder
3 medium leeks (thickly sliced)

250ml/9fl oz dry cider
2 sprigs rosemary
Salt and pepper
Fresh rosemary, to garnish

→

←

- Preheat the oven to 180°C/350°F/Gas mark 4.
- Place the rabbit joints in a bowl and sprinkle the flour and mustard powder over them. Toss to coat evenly.
- Arrange the rabbit in one layer in a wide casserole dish. Blanch the leeks in boiling water, then drain and add to the casserole dish.
- Add the cider, rosemary and seasoning to taste. Cover, then bake for 1 to 1¼ hours or until the rabbit is tender. Garnish with fresh rosemary and serve with jacket potatoes and vegetables.

Stir-fried lamb with orange

SERVES 4

215 calories per serving

INGREDIENTS:

450g/1lb minced lamb
2 garlic cloves (crushed)
1 teaspoon cumin seeds
1 teaspoon ground coriander
1 red onion (sliced)

Finely grated zest and juice of
1 orange
2 tablespoons soy sauce
1 orange (peeled and segmented)
Salt and pepper

- Heat a wok or large, heavy-based frying pan, without adding any oil. Add the lamb to the wok and dry fry for 5 minutes until evenly browned. Drain away any excess fat from the wok.
- Add the garlic, cumin, coriander and onion to the wok and stir-fry for a further 5 minutes.
- Stir in the orange zest and juice and the soy sauce, mixing thoroughly. Cover, reduce the heat and leave to simmer, stirring occasionally, for 15 minutes. Remove the lid, increase the heat and add the orange segments. Stir to mix. Season with salt and pepper to taste and heat through for a further 2 to 3 minutes.
- Transfer the stir-fry to warm serving plates and serve immediately.

Aromatic & crispy duck

SERVES 4
180 calories per serving

INGREDIENTS:

2 large duckling quarters
1 teaspoon salt
3 pieces star anise
1 teaspoon Szechuan red peppercorns
1 teaspoon cloves

2 cinnamon sticks (broken into pieces)
3 spring onions (cut into short pieces)
5 small slices ginger root
4 tablespoons rice wine
Vegetable oil for deep-frying

- Rub the duck with the salt and arrange the star anise, peppercorns, cloves and cinnamon on top. Sprinkle with the spring onions, ginger and wine and marinate for at least 3 to 4 hours.
- Arrange the duck pieces on a plate that will fit inside a bamboo steamer. Pour some hot water into a wok, and place the bamboo steamer above it, sitting on a trivet.
- Add the duck and cover with the bamboo lid. Steam the duck over a high heat for 2 to 3 hours, until tender and cooked through. Top up the hot water from time to time as required. Remove the duck and leave to cool for at least 4 to 5 hours so it becomes crispy.
- Pour off the water and wipe the wok dry. Pour in the oil and heat until smoking.
- Deep-fry the duck pieces, skin-side down, for 4 to 5 minutes or until crisp and brown. Remove and drain.

Neapolitan pork steaks

SERVES 4
360 calories per serving

INGREDIENTS:

2 tablespoons olive oil
1 large onion (sliced)
1 garlic clove (chopped)
400g/14oz canned chopped tomatoes
2 teaspoons yeast extract

4 pork loin steaks (about 100g/4oz each)
75g/3oz black olives (stoned)
2 tablespoons shredded fresh basil

- Heat the oil in a large frying pan. Add the onion and garlic and cook, stirring, for 3 to 4 minutes, or until they just begin to soften.

→

- Add the tomatoes and yeast extract to the frying pan and leave to simmer for about 5 minutes, or until the sauce starts to thicken.
- Cook the pork steaks under a preheated grill for 5 minutes on both sides, or until the meat is golden and cooked through. Set the pork steaks aside and keep warm.
- Add the olives and basil to the sauce in the frying pan and stir briefly.
- Transfer the pork steaks to warm serving plates. Top the steaks with the sauce and serve immediately with vegetables of your choice.

Pork steaks with gremolata

SERVES 4

275 calories per serving

INGREDIENTS:

2 tablespoons olive oil
4 lean pork shoulder steaks, about
175g/6oz each
1 onion (chopped)
2 garlic cloves (crushed)
2 tablespoons tomato purée
400g/14oz canned chopped tomatoes
150ml/¼pt dry white wine
Bouquet garni

3 anchovy fillets (drained and chopped)
Salt and pepper

For the gremolata:
3 tablespoons chopped fresh parsley
Grated zest of ½ lemon
Grated zest of 1 lime
1 garlic clove (chopped)

- Heat the oil in a large flameproof casserole dish, add the pork steaks and brown on both sides. Remove the steaks from the dish.
- Add the onion to the dish and cook until soft and beginning to brown. Add the garlic and cook for 1 to 2 minutes, then stir in the tomato purée, tomatoes and wine. Add the bouquet garni. Bring to the boil, then boil rapidly for a further 3 to 4 minutes to reduce the sauce and thicken slightly.
- Return the pork to the casserole dish, then cover and cook for about 30 minutes.
- Stir in the anchovies. Cover the casserole and cook for a further 15 minutes, or until the pork is tender.
- For the gremolata, mix together the parsley, lemon and lime zests and garlic.
- When ready, remove the pork steaks and discard the bouquet garni. Reduce the sauce over a high heat, if it is not already thick. Taste and adjust the seasoning if required.
- Return the pork to the casserole dish, then sprinkle with the gremolata. Cover and cook for a further 5 minutes, then serve hot.

Tuna almondine

SERVES 11

210 calories per serving

INGREDIENTS:

Vegetable oil for greasing
1½ teaspoons powdered gelatine
125ml/4fl oz cold water
225ml/8fl oz boiling water
450g/1lb low-fat cottage cheese
(whipped)
2 tablespoons lemon juice
½ teaspoon garlic powder

¼ teaspoon salt
75g/3oz onions (finely chopped)
2 tablespoons chopped red pepper
400g/14oz canned tuna (drained and flaked)
225g/8oz almonds (sliced and lightly toasted)

- Grease a 1.2 litre/2pt fish mould and set aside.
- In a large bowl, sprinkle the gelatine over the cold water and leave to stand for 1 minute. Add the boiling water and stir until the gelatine is completely dissolved.
- With a rotary beater, blend in the cottage cheese until smooth.
- Stir in the lemon juice, garlic powder and salt. Fold in the onions, red pepper, tuna and half the almonds.
- Pour the mixture into the mould and chill until firm. Before serving, unmould on to a platter and garnish with the remaining almonds.

Curried prawns in coconut milk

SERVES 4

190 calories per serving

INGREDIENTS:

600ml/1pt coconut milk
2 tablespoons Thai curry paste
1 tablespoon fish sauce
½ teaspoon salt
1 teaspoon granulated sugar

450g/1lb shelled king prawns
(deveined, with tails left intact)
225g/8oz cherry tomatoes
1 red chilli (seeded and chopped)
Juice of ½ lime

→

←

- Pour half the coconut milk into a pan or wok and bring to the boil. Add the curry paste, stir until it disperses, then simmer for about 10 minutes.
- Add the fish sauce, salt, sugar and remaining coconut milk. Simmer for another 5 minutes.
- Add the prawns, cherry tomatoes and chilli. Simmer gently for about 5 minutes, until the prawns are pink and tender. Serve sprinkled with lime juice.

Chicken, tomato & herbs

SERVES 4
315 calories per serving

INGREDIENTS:

1.3kg/3lb chicken (skinned and cut into bite-sized chunks)
75g/3oz plain flour
Salt and pepper
50ml/2fl oz olive oil
1 garlic clove (crushed)
3 tablespoons chopped onion
4 tomatoes (quartered)

225ml/8fl oz white wine
Bouquet garni
25g/1oz margarine
225g/8oz mushrooms (sliced)
100g/4oz black olives (sliced)
125ml/4fl oz chicken stock
25g/1oz cornflour

- Rinse the chicken and pat dry. Shake the chicken in a bag with the flour and seasoning to taste.
- Heat the oil in a large frying pan and brown the chicken in it. Add the garlic and onion and continue to cook over a medium heat. Add the tomatoes, wine and bouquet garni. Cover and simmer over a low heat for 30 minutes.
- In a small frying pan, melt the margarine and fry the mushrooms. Add to the chicken with the olives.
- To thicken, put the chicken stock and cornflour in a screw-top jar and shake.
- Remove the chicken and vegetables from the pan and discard the bouquet garni.
- Gradually add the stock mixture to the cooking liquid in the frying pan, stirring constantly. Boil for 3 to 5 minutes, until the mixture thickens. Arrange the chicken on serving plates and top with the sauce.

Salt cod fritters

SERVES 6
150 calories per serving

INGREDIENTS:

100g/4oz self-raising flour
1 egg (beaten)
150ml/¼pt milk
250g/9oz salt cod (soaked overnight)

1 small red onion (finely chopped)
1 small fennel bulb (finely chopped)
1 red chilli (finely chopped)
2 tablespoons vegetable oil

- Sift the flour into a large bowl. Make a well in the centre of the flour and add the egg. Using a wooden spoon, gradually draw in the flour, slowly adding the milk, and mix to form a smooth batter. Leave to stand for 10 minutes. Drain the salt cod and rinse it under cold running water. Drain again thoroughly. Remove and discard the skin and any bones from the fish, then mash the flesh with a fork.
- Place the fish in a large bowl and combine with the onion, fennel and chilli. Add the mixture to the batter and blend together.
- Heat the oil in a large frying pan and, taking about 1 tablespoon of the mixture at a time, spoon it into the hot oil. Cook the fritters, in batches, for 3 to 4 minutes on each side until golden and slightly puffed. Keep warm while cooking the remaining mixture. Serve with vegetables and rice.

Jambalaya

SERVES 4
290 calories per serving

INGREDIENTS:

2 tablespoons vegetable oil
2 onions (roughly chopped)
1 green pepper (roughly chopped)
2 celery sticks (roughly chopped)
3 garlic cloves (roughly chopped)
1 teaspoon paprika
300g/11oz skinless, boneless chicken breasts (chopped)
100g/4oz kabanos sausage (chopped)

3 tomatoes (peeled and chopped)
450g/1lb long-grain rice
850ml/1½pt hot chicken stock
1 teaspoon dried oregano
2 bay leaves
12 large raw prawns, including tails
4 spring onions (finely chopped)
2 tablespoons chopped fresh parsley
Salt and pepper

- Heat the vegetable oil in a large frying pan over a low heat. Add the onions,

→

←

pepper, celery and garlic and cook for 8 to 10 minutes until all the vegetables have softened. Add the paprika and cook for a further 30 seconds. Add the chicken and sausage and cook for 8 to 10 minutes until lightly browned. Add the tomatoes and cook for 2 to 3 minutes.

- Add the rice to the pan and stir well. Pour in the stock, oregano and bay leaves and stir well. Cover and simmer for 10 minutes.
- Add the prawns and stir. Cover again and cook for a further 6 to 8 minutes until the rice is tender and the prawns are cooked through.
- Stir in the spring onions and parsley and season to taste with salt and pepper.
- Transfer to a large serving dish and serve immediately.

Beef & mushroom burgers

SERVES 4
200 calories per serving

INGREDIENTS:

1 small onion (chopped)
150g/5oz small cup mushrooms
450g/1lb lean minced beef
50g/2oz fresh wholemeal breadcrumbs

1 teaspoon dried mixed herbs
1 tablespoon tomato purée
Salt and pepper
Flour for shaping

- Place the onion and mushrooms in a blender or food processor and blend until finely chopped. Add the beef, breadcrumbs, herbs, tomato purée and seasoning. Blend for a few seconds, until the mixture binds together but still has some texture.
- Divide the mixture into 8 to 10 pieces, then press into burger shapes using lightly floured hands.
- Cook the burgers in a non-stick frying pan or under a hot grill for 12 to 15 minutes, turning once, until evenly cooked.

Grilled chicken kievs

SERVES 4
340 calories per serving

INGREDIENTS:

4 boneless chicken breasts, about
175g/6oz each
50g/2oz low-fat spread

2 garlic cloves (crushed)
Salt and pepper
1 tablespoon lemon juice

- Make a slit in the side of each chicken breast to form a pocket.
- Reserving 1 teaspoon of the low-fat spread, mash the rest with the garlic, salt and pepper. Spoon into the chicken breasts and secure with cocktail sticks.
- Place on aluminium foil on a grill pan and smear the reserved low-fat spread over, adding a sprinkling of lemon juice. Place under a hot grill for about 15 minutes, or until cooked through. Serve with rice.

Tamarind beef balti

SERVES 4
280 calories per serving

INGREDIENTS:

100g/4oz tamarind block (broken into pieces)
150ml/¹/₄pt water
2 tablespoons tomato purée
1 tablespoon granulated sugar
2.5cm/1in piece root ginger (chopped)
1 garlic clove (chopped)
¹/₂ teaspoon salt
1 onion (chopped)
2 tablespoons vegetable oil
1 teaspoon cumin seeds

1 teaspoon coriander seeds
1 teaspoon brown mustard seeds
4 curry leaves
750g/1lb 10oz lean braising steak (cut into 2.5cm/1in cubes and par-cooked)
1 red pepper (sliced)
2 green chillies (deseeded and sliced)
1 teaspoon garam masala
1 tablespoon chopped fresh coriander, to garnish

- Soak the tamarind overnight in the water. Strain the soaked tamarind, keeping the liquid.
- Put the tamarind, tomato purée, sugar, ginger, garlic, salt and onion into a blender or food processor and mix to a smooth purée.
- Heat the oil in a wok, add the cumin, coriander, mustard seeds and curry leaves, and cook until the spices start popping.
- Stir the beef into the spices and stir-fry for 2 to 4 minutes until the meat is browned.
- Add the red pepper, chillies, garam masala, tamarind mixture and reserved tamarind liquid and cook for 20 to 25 minutes. Serve garnished with fresh coriander.

Grilled sole & white sauce

SERVES 6

300 calories per serving

INGREDIENTS:

6 pieces of sole, 175g/6oz each
Juice of 1 lemon
1 tablespoon corn oil
1 teaspoon grated lemon zest
3 tablespoons dry white wine
175g/6oz tomatoes (finely chopped)
2 tablespoons chopped fresh dill

25g/1oz low-fat spread

For the white sauce:
25g/1oz margarine
50g/2oz wholewheat flour
700ml/1¼pt skimmed milk

- To make the white sauce, melt the margarine in a saucepan and stir until golden brown. Stir in the flour until crumbly. Whisk in the milk and stir over a medium heat, beating with a whisk until thickened.
- Brush the fish with the lemon juice and corn oil. Grill for about 15 minutes, until the fish flakes easily.
- Heat the sauce in a saucepan and stir in the remaining ingredients. Serve hot.

Apple chicken

SERVES 6

225 calories per serving

INGREDIENTS:

1 chicken (weighing 2kg/4½lb)
Vegetable oil for brushing
2 dessert apples
15g/½oz butter
1 tablespoon redcurrant jelly

For the stuffing:
15g/½oz butter
1 small onion (finely chopped)

50g/2oz mushrooms (finely chopped)
50g/2oz lean smoked ham (finely chopped)
25g/1oz fresh breadcrumbs
1 tablespoon chopped fresh parsley
1 dessert apple (cored and coarsely grated)
1 tablespoon lemon juice
Salt and pepper

- Preheat the oven to 190°C/375°F/Gas mark 5.
- To make the stuffing, melt the butter and fry the onion gently, stirring until softened. Stir in the mushrooms and cook over a moderate heat for 2 to 3 minutes.

- Remove from the heat and stir in the ham, breadcrumbs and chopped parsley.
- Add the apple to the stuffing mixture with the lemon juice. Season to taste.
- Loosen the breast side of the chicken and carefully spoon the stuffing mixture under it, smoothing evenly with your hands.
- Place the chicken in a roasting tin and brush lightly with oil. Roast in the oven for 25 minutes per 500g/1lb 2oz plus 25 minutes, or until the juices run clear.
- Core and slice the apples and sauté in the butter until golden. Stir in the redcurrant jelly and warm through until melted. Serve the chicken garnished with the redcurrant apples.

Chinese spicy chicken

SERVES 6
235 calories per serving

INGREDIENTS:

200g/7oz wholemeal spaghetti
500ml/18fl oz boiling water
250g/9oz chicken fillets (all skin and
fat removed, cut into thin strips)
1 tablespoon cornflour
1 tablespoon soybean oil
300g/11oz courgette (sliced)
250g/9oz cauliflower (diced)
150g/5oz onion (sliced)
15g/¹/₂oz garlic clove (crushed)
200g/7oz celery sticks (sliced)

100g/4oz tomato purée
250ml/9fl oz boiling water
1 tablespoon soy sauce
1 tablespoon hoisin sauce
¹/₄ teaspoon ground cumin
¹/₄ teaspoon cayenne pepper
¹/₄ teaspoon mustard seeds
¹/₄ teaspoon curry powder
¹/₄ teaspoon ground ginger
¹/₄ teaspoon celery seeds

- Place the spaghetti in a large saucepan with the boiling water. Cook uncovered until the spaghetti is just tender. Strain any remaining liquid.
- Toss the chicken in the cornflour.
- Heat the oil in a wok or non-stick frying pan. Add the chicken to the wok or pan and stir-fry until chicken is tender. Add vegetables and stir fry until just tender.
- Mix the tomato purée with the boiling water, the soy sauce, hoisin sauce and spices together. Stir into the wok. Add the spaghetti and stir until heated through.

Lamb & lemon chops

SERVES 4

275 calories per serving

INGREDIENTS:

4 lamb chops
1 tablespoon vegetable oil
15g/½oz butter
150ml/¼pt white wine

150ml/¼pt lamb stock
2 bay leaves
Pared zest of 1 lemon
Salt and pepper

- Using a sharp knife, carefully remove the bone from each lamb chop, keeping the meat intact. Shape the meat into rounds and secure with a length of string.
- In a large frying pan, heat together the oil and butter until the mixture starts to froth. Add the lamb to the frying pan and cook for 2 to 3 minutes on each side.
- Remove the frying pan from the heat, remove the meat, drain off all the excess fat and discard. Place the lamb back in the pan.
- Return the frying pan to the heat. Add the wine, stock, bay leaves and lemon zest to the frying pan and cook for 20 to 25 minutes or until the lamb is tender.
- Season the lamb and sauce to taste with salt and pepper. Transfer to serving plates. Remove the string from the lamb and serve with the sauce.

Chicken liver nests

SERVES 4

350 calories per serving

INGREDIENTS:

450g/1lb potatoes (cut into
even-sized pieces)
50g/2oz low-fat spread
1 tablespoon skimmed milk
2 onions (finely chopped)

300ml/½pt dry vermouth
450g/1lb chicken livers (trimmed)
1 teaspoon chopped fresh sage
Salt and pepper

- Boil the potatoes in lightly salted water until tender. Drain and mash with 1 tablespoon low-fat spread and the milk. Spoon into 4 'nests' on flameproof serving plates. Place briefly under a hot grill to brown slightly. Keep warm.
- Melt the remaining spread in a frying pan. Add the onions and fry, stirring, for 4 minutes until golden and soft. Add the vermouth and boil until almost all the liquid has evaporated. Stir in the chicken livers, sage and seasoning and cook,

stirring, for about 5 minutes until the livers are browned but still tender.
- Spoon the livers into the 'nests' and serve immediately.

Cajun-style cod

SERVES 4
155 calories per serving

INGREDIENTS:

4 cod steaks (about 175g/6oz each)
2 tablespoons low-fat natural yogurt
1 tablespoon lime juice
1 garlic clove (crushed)
1 teaspoon ground cumin
1 teaspoon paprika

1 teaspoon mustard powder
½ teaspoon cayenne pepper
½ teaspoon dried thyme
½ teaspoon dried oregano
1 teaspoon vegetable oil

- Pat the cod dry on kitchen paper. Mix together the yogurt and lime juice and brush lightly over both sides of the cod.
- Mix together the garlic, spices and herbs. Coat both sides of the fish with the seasoning mix, rubbing in well.
- Heat the oil in a heavy-based frying pan until very hot. Add the fish and cook over a high heat for 4 minutes, or until the undersides are well browned.
- Turn the steaks over and cook for a further 4 minutes. Serve immediately with new potatoes and a green salad.

Noodles with cod & mango

SERVES 4
280 calories per serving

INGREDIENTS:

250g/9oz dried egg noodles
450g/1lb skinless cod fillet (cut into thin strips)
1 tablespoon paprika
2 tablespoons sunflower oil
1 red onion (diced)
1 yellow pepper (sliced)
1 red pepper (sliced)

1 green pepper (sliced)
100g/4oz baby corn cobs (halved)
1 mango (peeled, stoned and sliced)
100g/4oz beansprouts
2 tablespoons tomato ketchup
2 tablespoons soy sauce
2 tablespoons medium sherry
1 teaspoon cornflour

→

- Place the noodles in a large bowl and pour over enough boiling water to cover. Leave to stand for about 10 minutes.
- Place the cod in a large bowl, add the paprika and toss well to coat the fish.
- Heat the oil in a preheated wok or large, heavy-based frying pan over a medium heat.
- Add the onion, peppers and baby corn cobs to the wok and stir-fry for about 5 minutes.
- Add the cod to the wok together with the sliced mango and stir-fry for a further 2 to 3 minutes or until the fish is tender. Add the beansprouts to the wok and toss well to combine.
- Mix the tomato ketchup, soy sauce, sherry and cornflour together. Add the mixture to the wok and cook, stirring occasionally, until the juices thicken.
- Drain the noodles well and transfer to 4 warmed serving bowls. Transfer the cod and mango stir-fry to separate serving bowls and serve immediately.

Tofu & beef dinner

SERVES 4
240 calories per serving

INGREDIENTS:

550g/1lb 4oz tofu (cut into 2.5cm/1in cubes)
3 tablespoons vegetable oil
100g/4oz coarsely minced beef
½ teaspoon finely chopped garlic
1 leek (chopped into short sections)
½ teaspoon salt

1 tablespoon black bean sauce
1 tablespoon soy sauce
1 teaspoon chilli bean sauce
4 tablespoons water
1 teaspoon cornflour (mixed with 1½ teaspoons water to form a paste)
A few drops sesame oil

- Bring some water to the boil in a small pan or wok, add the tofu and blanch for 2 to 3 minutes to harden. Remove and drain well.
- Heat the oil in a preheated wok. Add the beef and garlic and stir-fry for about 1 minute, or until the colour of the beef changes. Add the leek, salt and sauces and blend well.
- Add the water followed by the tofu. Bring to the boil and braise for 2 to 3 minutes.
- Add the cornflour paste and stir until the sauce has thickened. Sprinkle with sesame oil and serve hot.

Cinnamon pork

SERVES 4

345 calories per serving

INGREDIENTS:

4 small lean pork steaks (about
150g/5oz each)
25g/1oz low-fat spread
1 tablespoon lemon juice

3 tablespoons chopped fresh mint
1 teaspoon ground cinnamon
Salt and pepper

- Put the pork in a shallow dish.
- Melt the low-fat spread with the lemon juice and stir in the mint and cinnamon.
- Season lightly, pour over the pork and turn the meat over in the mixture. Leave to stand for 1 hour.
- Grill, brushing with the remaining marinade, for 10 minutes on each side until golden and cooked through. Serve immediately.

Spicy lamb roast

SERVES 6

200 calories per serving

INGREDIENTS:

1.6kg/3½lb lean leg spring lamb
1 teaspoon chilli powder
1 garlic clove (crushed)
1 teaspoon ground coriander
1 teaspoon ground cumin
1 teaspoon salt

2 teaspoons desiccated coconut
2 teaspoons ground almonds
3 tablespoons low-fat natural yogurt
2 tablespoons lemon juice
2 tablespoons sultanas
2 tablespoons corn oil

- Preheat the oven to 180°C/350°F/Gas mark 4.
- Trim the fat from the lamb, rinse and pat dry, then set aside on a sheet of aluminium foil large enough to enclose the whole joint.
- In a medium-sized bowl, mix together the chilli powder, garlic, spices and salt.
- In a blender or food processor, blend the desiccated coconut, almonds, yogurt, lemon juice and sultanas until smooth. Add the contents of the food processor to the spice mixture together with the corn oil and mix together. Pour this on to the leg of lamb and rub over the meat.
- Enclose the meat in the foil and place in an ovenproof dish. Bake for 1½ hours.

→

← • Remove the lamb from the oven, open the foil and, using the back of a spoon, spread the mixture evenly over the meat again. Return the lamb, uncovered, to the oven for a further 45 minutes, or until it is cooked right through. Slice the meat and serve.

Chilli chicken meatballs

SERVES 4

200 calories per serving

INGREDIENTS:

450g/1lb lean chicken (minced)
4 spring onions (finely chopped)
1 small red chilli (deseeded and finely chopped)
2.5cm/1in piece root ginger (finely chopped)
100g/4oz canned sweetcorn (drained)
Salt and white pepper

For the sauce:
150ml/¹/₄pt chicken stock
100g/4oz canned cubed pineapple (drained, with 4 tablespoons reserved juice)
1 medium carrot (cut into thin strips)
1 small red pepper (diced)
1 small green pepper (diced)
1 tablespoon soy sauce
2 tablespoons rice vinegar
1 tablespoon caster sugar
1 tablespoon tomato purée
2 teaspoons cornflour (mixed with 4 teaspoons cold water to form a paste)

• To make the meatballs, place the chicken in a bowl and mix with the spring onions, chilli, ginger, sweetcorn and seasoning.
• Divide into 16 portions and form each into a ball. Bring a saucepan of water to the boil. Arrange the meatballs on baking parchment in a steamer or large sieve, place over the water, cover and steam for 10 to 12 minutes.
• To make the sauce, pour the stock and pineapple juice into a pan and bring to the boil. Add the carrot and peppers, cover and simmer for 5 minutes. Add the remaining ingredients, stirring until thickened. Season and set aside.
• Drain the meatballs and transfer to a serving plate. Serve with boiled rice and the sauce.

Veal chops & mushrooms

SERVES 4

301 calories per serving

INGREDIENTS:

25g/1oz margarine
4 lean loin veal chops
1 medium onion (chopped)
450g/1lb mushroom caps
225g/8oz white onions
1 tablespoon plain flour
1 tablespoon tomato purée

175ml/6fl oz chicken stock
150ml/¼pt dry white wine
50g/2oz chopped chives
1 teaspoon tarragon
1 teaspoon chopped fresh basil
1 small bay leaf
1 tablespoon chopped fresh parsley

- Preheat the oven to 170°C/325°F/Gas mark 3.
- Melt the margarine in a large, heavy-based frying pan. Brown the veal chops in the pan over a high heat, then transfer to a shallow casserole dish.
- In the same frying pan, fry the onions. Add the remaining ingredients except the parsley. Cover the pan and cook for 5 minutes.
- Pour the mixture over the chops. Cover the casserole dish and bake in the oven for 1 hour. Sprinkle with parsley before serving.

Fried venison steaks

SERVES 4

260 calories per serving

INGREDIENTS:

1 orange
1 lemon
75g/3oz fresh cranberries
1 teaspoon grated fresh root ginger
1 thyme sprig
1 teaspoon Dijon mustard

4 tablespoons redcurrant jelly
150ml/¼pt ruby port
2 teaspoons sunflower oil
4 venison steaks (about 100g/4oz each)
2 shallots (finely chopped)
Salt and pepper

- Pare the zest from half the orange and half the lemon using a vegetable peeler, then cut into very fine strips.
- Blanch the strips in a small pan of boiling water for about 5 minutes until tender. Drain the strips and refresh under cold water.
- Squeeze the juice from the orange and lemon, then pour into a small pan. Add

→

←

the cranberries, ginger, thyme sprig, mustard, redcurrant jelly and port. Cook over a low heat until the jelly melts.

- Bring the sauce to the boil, stirring occasionally, then cover the pan and reduce the heat. Cook gently for about 15 minutes, until the cranberries are just tender.
- Heat the oil in a heavy-based frying pan, add the steaks and cook over a high heat for 2 to 3 minutes.
- Turn the steak over and add the shallots to the pan. Cook the steaks on the other side for 2 to 3 minutes, depending on whether you want them rare or medium.
- Just before the end of cooking, pour in the sauce and add the strips of zest.
- Leave the sauce to bubble for a few seconds to thicken slightly, then remove the thyme sprig and adjust the seasoning to taste. Transfer the steaks to serving plates and spoon the sauce over. Serve with mashed potato and broccoli.

Marinara pizza

SERVES 4
360 calories per serving

INGREDIENTS:

For the base:
225g/8oz peeled boiled potatoes
50g/2oz butter
100g/4oz self-raising flour
½ teaspoon salt

For the tomato sauce:
1 small onion (chopped)
1 garlic clove (crushed)
2 tablespoons olive oil
225g/8oz tomatoes
1 tablespoon tomato purée
1 teaspoon demerara sugar
2 teaspoons chopped fresh basil
½ teaspoon dried oregano

1 bay leaf
Salt and pepper

For the topping:
200g/7oz frozen seafood cocktail (thawed)
1 tablespoon capers
12 black olives
1 small yellow pepper (chopped)
1 tablespoon fresh marjoram
½ teaspoon dried oregano
50g/2oz Mozzarella cheese (grated)
15g/½oz Parmesan cheese (grated)
Olive oil for drizzling

- Preheat the oven to 200°C/400°F/Gas mark 6.
- To make the base, mash the potatoes then stir in the butter until it has melted and is distributed evenly throughout the potatoes. Leave to cool.
- Sift the flour and salt together and stir into the mashed potato to form a soft dough.
- Either roll out or press the dough into a 25cm/10in circle on a lightly greased baking tray, pushing the edge up slightly to form a ridge.
- To make the sauce, fry the onion and garlic gently in the oil for 5 minutes, until

softened but not browned.

- Cut a cross in the base of each tomato and place them in a bowl. Pour on boiling water and leave for about 45 seconds. Drain, then plunge in cold water.
- Skin and chop the tomatoes, discarding any hard cores.
- Add the tomatoes to the onion mixture with the tomato purée, sugar, herbs and seasoning. Stir well. Bring to the boil, cover and leave to simmer gently for about 30 minutes, stirring occasionally, or until you have a thickish sauce.
- Remove the bay leaf and adjust the seasoning to taste.
- Spread the tomato sauce over the pizza base, almost to the edge. Arrange the seafood cocktail, capers, black olives and yellow pepper over the top of the tomato sauce. Sprinkle over the herbs and cheeses and a little olive oil.
- Bake in the oven for 18 to 20 minutes or until the edge of the pizza is crisp and golden brown. Serve immediately.

Cod curry

SERVES 4
320 calories per serving

INGREDIENTS:

1 tablespoon vegetable oil
1 small onion (chopped)
2 garlic cloves (chopped)
2.5cm/1in piece fresh root ginger (roughly chopped)
2 large tomatoes (peeled and roughly chopped)
150ml/¼pt fish stock
1 tablespoon medium curry paste

1 teaspoon ground coriander
400g/14oz canned chickpeas (drained and rinsed)
750g/1lb 10oz cod fillet (cut into large chunks)
4 tablespoons chopped fresh coriander
4 tablespoons thick yogurt
Salt and pepper

- Heat the vegetable oil in a large saucepan over a low heat. Add the onion, garlic and ginger and fry for 4 to 5 minutes until softened. Remove from the heat. Put the onion mixture into a blender and food processor with the tomatoes and fish stock and process until smooth.
- Return to the saucepan with the curry paste, ground coriander and chickpeas.
- Mix together well, then simmer gently for 15 minutes until thickened.
- Add the pieces of fish and return to a simmer. Cook for 5 minutes until the fish is just tender. Remove from the heat and leave to stand for 2 minutes.
- Stir in the coriander and yogurt. Season to taste with salt and pepper and serve with steamed basmati rice.

Stir-fried cod with mango

SERVES 4

200 calories per serving

INGREDIENTS:

2 tablespoons vegetable oil
1 red onion (sliced)
175g/6oz carrots (cut into matchsticks)
1 red pepper (sliced)
1 green pepper (sliced)
450g/1lb skinless cod fillet

1 ripe mango
1 teaspoon cornflour
1 tablespoon soy sauce
125ml/4fl oz tropical fruit juice
1 tablespoon chopped fresh coriander,
to garnish

- Heat the oil in a preheated wok and stir-fry the onion, carrots and peppers for 5 minutes.
- Using a sharp knife, cut the cod into small cubes. Peel the mango, then carefully remove the flesh from the centre stone. Cut the flesh into thin slices.
- Add the cod and mango to the wok and stir-fry for a further 4 to 5 minutes, or until the fish is cooked through.
- Mix together the cornflour, soy sauce and fruit juice. Pour the mixture into the wok and stir until the mixture bubbles and the juices thicken. Scatter with coriander and serve immediately.

Stuffed plaice rolls

SERVES 4

165 calories per serving

INGREDIENTS:

1 medium courgette (grated)
2 medium carrots (grated)
4 tablespoons fresh wholemeal breadcrumbs

1 tablespoon lime juice
Salt and pepper
4 plaice fillets

- Preheat the oven to 200°C/400°F/Gas mark 6.
- Mix together the carrots and courgettes. Stir in the breadcrumbs and lime juice and season to taste.
- Lay the fillets skin side up and divide the stuffing between them, spreading evenly.
- Roll up the fish to enclose the stuffing and place in an ovenproof dish. Cover and bake for about 30 minutes, or until the fish flakes easily. Serve with new potatoes.

Oyster sauce noodles

SERVES 4
280 calories per serving

INGREDIENTS:

250g/9oz egg noodles
450g/1lb chicken thighs
2 tablespoons groundnut oil
100g/4oz carrots (sliced)

3 tablespoons oyster sauce
2 eggs
3 tablespoons cold water

- Place the egg noodles in a large bowl or dish. Pour enough boiling water over the noodles to cover and leave to stand for 10 minutes.
- Meanwhile, remove the skin from the chicken thighs. Cut the chicken flesh into small pieces, using a sharp knife.
- Heat the groundnut oil in a large preheated wok or frying pan. Add the chicken and carrot to the wok and stir-fry for 5 minutes.
- Drain the noodles, add to the wok and stir-fry for a further 2 to 3 minutes.
- Beat together the oyster sauce, eggs and cold water. Drizzle the mixture over the noodles and stir-fry for a further 2 to 3 minutes or until the eggs set. Serve hot.

Chicken Veronique

SERVES 4
275 calories per serving

INGREDIENTS:

2 whole chicken breasts (skinned)
25g/1oz margarine
225g/8oz mushrooms (sliced)
3 tablespoons sliced onion
50g/2oz red pepper (minced)
125ml/4fl oz chicken stock

25g/1oz plain flour
225g/8oz seedless white grapes
(halved)
125ml/4fl oz dry white wine
475g/1lb 1oz long-grain rice (cooked)

- Remove the bones from the chicken breasts and cut the flesh into 2.5cm/1in pieces.
- In a frying pan, melt the margarine over a medium-high heat. Fry the mushrooms and onions for 3 minutes or until soft. Add the red pepper. Add the chicken pieces and sauté for about 5 minutes until the chicken is cooked.
- Blend the chicken stock and the flour and add to the pan. Cook until thickened, and allow to simmer for 1 minute. Stir in the grapes and wine. Serve with the rice.

Vegetarian

Sometimes cutting down on meat forms a vital part of a diet plan, whereas for some it is a lifestyle choice. Others may just fancy a change – and in this chapter there are choices for you, no matter what your reasons for going meat-free. Satay noodles, Broccoli with feta & tomato sauce and Tofu with mushrooms & peas are just a few of the delicious recipes.

Spring vegetable stir-fry

SERVES 4

110 calories per serving

INGREDIENTS:

1 tablespoon groundnut oil
1 garlic clove (sliced)
2.5cm/1in piece fresh root ginger
(finely chopped)
100g/4oz baby carrots
100g/4oz patty-pan squash (roughly chopped)
100g/4oz baby corn
100g/4oz green beans (topped and tailed)
100g/4oz sugar-snap peas (topped and tailed)

100g/4oz young asparagus (cut into 7.5cm/3in pieces)
8 spring onions (trimmed and cut into 5cm/2in pieces)
100g/4oz cherry tomatoes

For the dressing:
Juice of 2 limes
1 tablespoon clear honey
1 tablespoon soy sauce
1 teaspoon sesame oil

- Heat the groundnut oil in a wok or large frying pan. Add the garlic and ginger and stir-fry for about 1 minute.
- Add the carrots, patty-pan squash, baby corn and beans and stir-fry for a further 3 to 4 minutes.
- Add the peas, asparagus, spring onions and cherry tomatoes and stir-fry for a further 1 to 2 minutes.
- For the dressing, mix all the ingredients together and add to the pan.
- Stir well then cover the pan. Cook for 2 to 3 minutes more until the vegetables are tender but still crisp.

Pasta with Sicilian sauce

SERVES 4

290 calories per serving

INGREDIENTS:

50g/2oz sultanas
450g/1lb tomatoes (halved)
25g/1oz pine kernels
50g/2oz canned anchovies (drained and halved lengthways)

2 tablespoons tomato purée
675g/1lb 8oz fresh penne

- Soak the sultanas in a bowl of warm water for about 20 minutes. Then drain them thoroughly.
- Cook the tomatoes under a preheated grill for about 10 minutes. Leave to cool slightly, then peel off the skin and dice the flesh.
- Place the pine kernels on a baking tray and lightly toast under the grill for 2 to 3 minutes, or until golden brown.
- Place the tomatoes, pine kernels and sultanas in a small saucepan and gently heat through.
- Add the anchovies and tomato purée, heating the sauce for a further 2 to 3 minutes or until hot. Keep warm.
- Cook the pasta in a saucepan of salted boiling water for 8 to 10 minutes or until it is cooked through. Drain thoroughly.
- Transfer the pasta to a serving dish and serve with the hot sauce.

Blue cheese hotpot

SERVES 4
340 calories per serving

INGREDIENTS:

2 carrots (sliced)
1 turnip (diced)
2 celery sticks (sliced)
8 small leeks (quartered)
25g/1oz low-fat spread
25g/1oz plain flour
450ml/³/₄pt vegetable stock

1 teaspoon yeast extract
425g/15oz canned haricot beans
(drained)
Salt and pepper
3 tablespoons chopped fresh parsley
450g/1lb potatoes (thinly sliced)
50g/2oz blue cheese (crumbled)

- Preheat the oven to 180°C/350°F/Gas mark 4.
- Fry the carrots, turnip, celery and leeks in the low-fat spread in a flameproof casserole dish for 3 minutes, stirring. Stir in the flour.
- Remove from the heat and gradually blend in the stock and yeast extract. Return to the heat, bring to the boil and cook for 2 minutes, stirring. Stir in the beans, salt and pepper to taste and the parsley. Cover with the potatoes in a layer.
- Cover with a lid and bake in the oven for 1 hour. Remove the lid, sprinkle with the cheese and continue cooking for a further 30 minutes. Serve straight from the pot.

Thai fragrant rice

SERVES 4

270 calories per serving

INGREDIENTS:

Zest of 2 limes
225g/8oz brown basmati rice
1 tablespoon olive oil
1 onion (chopped)
1 lemon grass stalk (finely chopped)
2.5cm/1in piece fresh root ginger
(peeled and finely chopped)

1½ teaspoons coriander seeds
1½ teaspoons cumin seeds
750ml/1¼pt vegetable stock
4 tablespoons chopped fresh coriander
Lime wedges, to serve

- Rinse the rice in cold water and drain through a sieve.
- Heat the oil in a large saucepan, add the onion, lemon grass and spices and cook gently for about 2 to 3 minutes.
- Add the rice and cook for a further 1 minute, then add the stock and bring to the boil. Reduce the heat to very low and cover the pan. Cook gently for about 30 minutes, or until the rice is tender. Remove from the heat.
- Stir in the fresh coriander, fluff up the grains, cover and leave for 10 minutes.
- Serve with lime wedges.

Vegetable fried rice

SERVES 4

180 calories per serving

INGREDIENTS:

100g/4oz long-grain white rice
3 tablespoons groundnut oil
2 garlic cloves (crushed)
½ teaspoon Chinese five-spice powder
50g/2oz green beans
1 green pepper (chopped)

4 baby corn cobs (sliced)
25g/1oz bamboo shoots (chopped)
3 tomatoes (skinned and chopped)
50g/2oz cooked peas
1 teaspoon sesame oil

- Bring a large saucepan of water to the boil. Add the rice to the saucepan and cook for about 15 minutes. Drain the rice well, rinse under cold running water and drain thoroughly again.
- Heat the groundnut oil in a preheated wok. Add the garlic and five-spice powder

and stir-fry for approximately 30 seconds.
- Add the green beans, green pepper and corn cobs and stir-fry the ingredients in the wok for 2 minutes.
- Stir the bamboo shoots, tomatoes, peas and rice into the mixture in the wok and stir-fry for 1 minute.
- Sprinkle with sesame oil and transfer to serving dishes. Serve immediately.

Vegetable curry

SERVES 10
110 calories per serving

INGREDIENTS:

1 tablespoon olive oil	*¼ teaspoon ground turmeric*
1 teaspoon yellow mustard seeds	*¼ teaspoon ground coriander*
1 teaspoon cumin seeds	*1 teaspoon chilli powder*
100g/4oz finely diced onion	*25g/1oz finely chopped garlic*
500g/1lb 2oz diced potato	*15g/½oz fresh ginger*
500g/1lb 2oz diced aubergine	*125ml/4fl oz water*
250g/9oz tomatoes (finely diced)	*Fresh coriander*
1 teaspoon curry powder	

- Heat the oil in a large wok or non-stick frying pan. Add the mustard and cumin seeds. Add the onion and sauté. Add the remaining ingredients and cook until the vegetables are tender.
- Garnish with fresh coriander before serving.

Honey-fried spinach

SERVES 4
150 calories per serving

INGREDIENTS:

3 tablespoons groundnut oil	*2 tablespoons dry sherry*
350g/12oz shiitake mushrooms (sliced)	*2 tablespoons clear honey*
2 garlic cloves (crushed)	*4 spring onions (chopped)*
350g/12oz baby leaf spinach	

- Heat the oil in a large preheated wok or heavy-based frying pan. Add the

→

←

mushrooms to the wok and stir-fry for about 5 minutes, or until they have softened.

- Stir the garlic into the mushrooms. Add the spinach and stir-fry for a further 2 to 3 minutes, or until the spinach leaves have just wilted.
- Mix together the sherry and honey in a small bowl until well combined. Drizzle the sherry and honey mixture over the spinach and heat through, stirring to coat the spinach leaves thoroughly in the mixture.
- Transfer the stir-fry to warm serving dishes, scatter with the chopped onions and serve immediately.

Vegetable biryani

SERVES 6
180 calories per serving

INGREDIENTS:

175g/6oz long-grain rice
2 whole cloves
Seeds of 2 cardamom pods
450ml/³/₄pt vegetable stock
2 garlic cloves
1 small onion (roughly chopped)
1 teaspoon cumin seeds
1 teaspoon ground coriander
½ teaspoon ground turmeric

½ teaspoon chilli powder
Pinch of salt and pepper
75ml/3fl oz water (plus 2 tablespoons)
1 large potato (peeled and cut into
2.5cm/1in cubes)
2 carrots (sliced)
½ cauliflower (broken in florets)
2 tablespoons chopped fresh coriander
2 tablespoons lime juice

- Put the rice, cloves and cardamom seeds into a large, heavy-based saucepan.
- Pour the stock over and bring to the boil.
- Reduce the heat, cover and simmer for 20 minutes, or until all the stock has been absorbed.
- Meanwhile, put the garlic cloves, onion, cumin seeds, coriander, turmeric, chilli powder and seasoning into a blender or food processor together with the 2 tablespoons of water and blend to a smooth paste.
- Preheat the oven to 180°C/350°F/Gas mark 4.
- Spoon the spicy paste into a flameproof casserole dish and cook over a low heat for 2 minutes, stirring occasionally. Add the potato, carrots, cauliflower florets and 75ml/3fl oz water. Cover and cook over a low heat for a further 12 minutes, stirring occasionally. Add the chopped coriander.
- Remove the cloves and spoon the rice over the vegetables. Sprinkle the lime juice over. Cover and cook in the oven for 25 minutes, or until the vegetables are tender.

Pasta & chilli tomatoes

SERVES 4
360 calories per serving

INGREDIENTS:

275g/10oz pappardelle pasta
3 tablespoons groundnut oil
2 garlic cloves (crushed)
2 shallots (sliced)
225g/8oz green beans (sliced)

100g/4oz cherry tomatoes (halved)
1 teaspoon chilli flakes
4 tablespoons crunchy peanut butter
150ml/¼pt coconut milk
1 tablespoon tomato purée

- Cook the pappardelle in a large saucepan of lightly salted boiling water for 5 to 6 minutes. Drain thoroughly and set aside.
- Heat the groundnut oil in a large saucepan or preheated wok. Add the garlic and shallots and stir fry for 1 minute. Add the green beans and drained pasta to the wok and stir-fry for 5 minutes. Add the cherry tomatoes to the wok and mix.
- Mix together the chilli flakes, peanut butter, coconut milk and tomato purée.
- Pour the chilli mixture over the pasta, toss well to combine and heat through.
- Transfer to a warm serving dish. Serve immediately while still hot.

Spanish rice

SERVES 6
90 calories per serving

INGREDIENTS:

2 tablespoons olive oil
100g/4oz green pepper (chopped)
50g/2oz onion (chopped)
1 garlic clove (crushed)
½ teaspoon dried basil

½ teaspoon dried rosemary
500ml/18fl oz water
225g/8oz long-grain rice
225g/8oz tomato (peeled and chopped)
2 tomatoes (sliced), to garnish

- Heat the olive oil in a frying pan and cook the pepper, onion, garlic, basil and rosemary until the vegetables are tender.
- Stir in the water, rice, chopped tomato and pepper. Cover and cook over a low heat for about 20 minutes or until the rice is done. Garnish with the tomato slices and serve.

Carrot & poppy seed bake

SERVES 4

145 calories per serving

INGREDIENTS:

700g/1½lb carrots (cut into matchsticks)
1 leek (sliced)
300ml/½pt fresh orange juice
2 tablespoons clear honey

1 garlic clove (crushed)
1 teaspoon mixed spice
2 teaspoons dried thyme
Salt and pepper
1 tablespoon poppy seeds

- Preheat the oven to 180°C/350°F/Gas mark 4.
- Cook the carrots and leek in a saucepan of boiling salted water for 5 to 6 minutes. Drain well and transfer to a shallow baking dish until required.
- Mix together the orange juice, honey, garlic, mixed spice and thyme and pour the mixture over the vegetables. Add salt and pepper to taste.
- Cover the baking dish and cook in the oven for 30 minutes or until the vegetables are tender.
- Remove the lid and sprinkle with poppy seeds. Serve immediately.

Courgette & asparagus parcels

SERVES 4

115 calories per serving

INGREDIENTS:

2 medium courgettes
1 medium leek
225g/8oz young asparagus (trimmed)
4 tarragon sprigs

4 whole garlic cloves (unpeeled)
Salt and pepper
1 egg (beaten, to glaze)

- Preheat the oven to 200°C/400°F/Gas mark 6.
- Using a potato peeler, carefully slice the courgettes lengthways into thin strips.
- Cut the leek into very fine julienne strips and cut the asparagus evenly into 5cm/2in lengths.
- Cut out 4 sheets of baking parchment measuring 30 x 38cm/12 x 15in and fold

in half. Draw a large curve to make a heart shape when unfolded. Cut along the line and open out.

- Divide the courgettes, asparagus and leek evenly between each paper heart, positioning the filling on one side of the fold line and topping each with a tarragon sprig and a garlic clove. Season to taste.
- Brush the edges lightly with the egg and fold over. Twist the edges together so each parcel is completely sealed. Lay the parcels on a baking tray and cook for 10 minutes. Serve immediately.

Vegetable pie

SERVES 6
260 calories per serving.

INGREDIENTS:

100g/4oz carrot (grated)
200g/7oz potato (grated)
25g/1oz chopped shallots
200g/7oz red pepper (diced)
200g/7oz celery sticks (thinly sliced)
100g/4oz fresh wholemeal breadcrumbs
1 tablespoon finely chopped fresh parsley
Freshly ground black pepper
2 eggs (lightly beaten)
375ml/13fl oz evaporated skimmed milk
2 egg whites

For the sauce topping:
25g/1oz margarine
1 tablespoon plain flour
250ml/9fl oz skimmed milk
50g/2oz low-fat Cheddar cheese (grated)
1 teaspoon grated Parmesan cheese

- Preheat the oven to 180°C/350°F/Gas mark 4.
- Place the carrot, potato, shallots, pepper, celery, breadcrumbs, parsley and pepper into a casserole dish.
- Combine the beaten egg and evaporated milk and pour over the vegetables.
- Stiffly beat the egg whites and lightly fold into the vegetable mixture.
- For the sauce topping, place the margarine in a saucepan and melt over a low heat. Remove from the heat and stir in the flour. Return to the heat and cook for 30 seconds. Remove from the heat and gradually stir in the milk. Return to the heat and cook, stirring continuously until the sauce boils and thickens.
- Pour the sauce over the vegetables and sprinkle the cheeses over. Bake for 40 minutes, or until firm.

Baked potatoes with salsa

SERVES 4

280 calories per serving

INGREDIENTS:

4 baking potatoes (225g/8oz each)
1 large avocado
1 teaspoon lemon juice
175g/6oz smoked tofu (diced)
2 garlic cloves (crushed)
1 onion (finely chopped)
1 tomato (finely chopped)
100g/4oz mixed salad leaves

For the salsa:
2 tomatoes (diced)
1 tablespoon chopped fresh coriander
1 shallot (finely diced)
1 green chilli (diced)
1 tablespoon lemon juice
Salt and pepper

- Preheat the oven to 190°C/375°F/Gas mark 5.
- Scrub the potatoes and prick the skins with a fork. Rub a little salt into the skins and place them on a baking tray.
- Cook in the oven for 1 hour, or until cooked through and the skins are crisp.
- Cut the potatoes in half lengthways and scoop the flesh into a bowl, leaving a thin layer of potato inside the shells.
- Halve and stone the avocado. Using a spoon, scoop out the avocado flesh and add to the bowl containing the potato. Stir in the lemon juice and mash the mixture together with a fork. Mix in the tofu, garlic, onion and tomato. Spoon the mixture into one half of the potato shells.
- Arrange the mixed salad leaves on top of the guacamole mixture and place the other half of the potato shell on top.

Ratatouille

SERVES 12

180 calories per serving

INGREDIENTS:

175ml/6fl oz olive oil
450g/1lb onions (thinly sliced)
450g/1lb red peppers (cut into large chunks)
4 garlic cloves (finely chopped)
750g/1lb 11oz courgettes (sliced)

750g/1lb 11oz aubergines (cut into chunks)
250g/9oz mushrooms (sliced)
2 teaspoons thyme
2 teaspoons salt
350ml/12fl oz tomato purée

- Preheat the oven to 200°C/400°F/Gas mark 6.
- In a large frying pan, heat the olive oil and sauté the onions, pepper and garlic until softened. Transfer to a large casserole dish.
- In the pan, sauté the courgettes, aubergines and mushrooms. Add to the casserole dish.
- Season with thyme and salt. Stir in tomato purée, mixing well.
- Bake for 30 minutes and serve hot.

Roasted Mediterranean vegetables

SERVES 6
130 calories per serving

INGREDIENTS:

1 red pepper (cut into chunks)
1 yellow pepper (cut into chunks)
2 Spanish onions (cut into wedges)
2 large courgettes (cut into chunks)
1 large aubergine (cut into chunks)
1 fennel bulb (thickly sliced)

Vegetable oil for greasing
2 beef tomatoes
8 garlic cloves
2 tablespoons olive oil
Fresh rosemary sprigs
Black pepper

- Preheat the oven to 220°C/425°F/Gas mark 7.
- Spread the peppers, onions, courgettes, aubergine and fennel in a lightly oiled, shallow ovenproof dish or roasting pan.
- Cut each tomato in half and place, cut side up, with the vegetables.
- Tuck the garlic cloves among the vegetables, then brush them with the olive oil.
- Place some sprigs of rosemary among the vegetables and grind over some black pepper.
- Roast for 20 to 25 minutes, turning the vegetables halfway through. Serve hot.

Swedish pasta

SERVES 4
350 calories per serving

INGREDIENTS:

1 onion (thinly sliced)
100g/4oz mushrooms (quartered)
175g/6oz tofu
450ml/³/₄pt vegetable stock
½ teaspoon soy sauce
1 teaspoon yeast extract

1 tablespoon chopped basil
Salt and pepper
1 tablespoon plain flour
100g/4oz low-fat quark
100g/4oz pasta shapes

- Put the onion, mushrooms and tofu in a saucepan with 300ml/½pt vegetable stock. Bring to the boil. Add the soy sauce, yeast extract, basil and seasoning and simmer for 1 hour.
- Blend the remaining stock with the flour and quark. Stir into the pan, bring back to the boil and cook, stirring, for 2 minutes.
- Meanwhile, cook the pasta according to the package instructions and drain. Add to the pan and toss well. Spoon on to warm plates and serve.

Vegetable paella

SERVES 6
235 calories per serving

INGREDIENTS:

350g/12oz broccoli (sliced)
2 small courgettes (thinly sliced)
1 green pepper (chopped)
1 red pepper (chopped)
100g/4oz onions (chopped)
2 garlic cloves (minced)
50ml/2fl oz olive oil

450g/1lb canned chopped tomatoes
600ml/1pt vegetable stock
350g/12oz long-grain rice
1 tablespoon lemon juice
225g/8oz frozen peas (thawed)
150g/5oz Parmesan cheese (grated)

- Preheat the oven to 180°C/350°F/Gas mark 4.
- Cook the broccoli in a small amount of boiling water for 5 minutes or until al dente. Drain well and reserve.
- In a paella pan or a large, deep heavy-based frying pan, cook the courgette, peppers, onions and garlic in the olive oil, until the onion is tender. Stir in the

canned tomatoes and their juice, the stock, rice and lemon juice and mix well. Bring to the boil. Reduce the heat and simmer for about 20 minutes, or until the rice is tender.

- Bake, covered, in the oven for 10 minutes. Stir in the broccoli, peas and cheese and serve.

Broccoli & cauliflower gratin

SERVES 4
150 calories per serving

INGREDIENTS:

1 small cauliflower
1 small head broccoli
150g/5oz low-fat natural yogurt
75g/3oz low-fat Cheddar cheese (grated)

1 teaspoon wholegrain mustard
Freshly ground black pepper
2 tablespoons wholemeal breadcrumbs

- Break the cauliflower and broccoli into florets and cook in lightly salted, boiling water for 8 to 10 minutes, until just tender. Drain well and transfer to a flameproof dish.
- Mix together the yogurt, grated cheese and mustard, then season the mixture with pepper and spoon over the cauliflower and broccoli.
- Sprinkle the breadcrumbs over the top and place under a medium-hot grill until golden brown. Serve hot.

Basil & tomato pasta

SERVES 4
180 calories per serving

INGREDIENTS:

1 tablespoon olive oil (plus extra for drizzling)
2 sprigs rosemary
2 garlic cloves
450g/1lb tomatoes (halved)

1 tablespoon tomato purée
12 fresh basil leaves (plus extra to garnish)
Salt and pepper
675g fresh farfalle pasta

→

←

- Place the oil, rosemary, garlic and tomatoes – skin side up – in a shallow roasting tin.
- Drizzle with a little more of the oil and cook under a preheated grill for 20 minutes or until the tomato skins are slightly charred. Peel the skin from the tomatoes. Roughly chop the tomato flesh and place in a pan.
- Squeeze the pulp from the garlic cloves and mix with the tomato flesh and tomato purée.
- Roughly tear the basil leaves into small pieces and then stir them into the sauce.
- Season with a little salt and pepper to taste.
- Cook the farfalle in a saucepan of boiling water for 8 to 10 minutes or until it is cooked through. Drain well.
- Gently re-heat the tomato and basil sauce, stirring. Transfer the farfalle to serving plates and pour the basil and tomato sauce over the top. Serve immediately.

Spicy bean hotpot

SERVES 4
285 calories per serving

INGREDIENTS:

1 tablespoon sunflower oil
2 onions (sliced)
1 garlic clove (crushed)
1 tablespoon red wine vinegar
400g/14oz canned chopped tomatoes
1 tablespoon tomato purée
1 tablespoon Worcestershire sauce
1 tablespoon wholegrain mustard
1 tablespoon demerara sugar
250ml/9fl oz vegetable stock

400g/14oz canned red kidney beans (drained)
400g/14oz canned haricot beans (drained)
1 bay leaf
75g/3oz raisins
225g/8oz button mushrooms (cut into small pieces)
Salt and pepper

- Heat the oil in a large saucepan or flameproof casserole dish, add the onions and garlic and cook over a gentle heat for 10 minutes, until soft.
- Add all the remaining ingredients except the mushrooms and seasoning. Bring to the boil, lower the heat and simmer for 10 minutes.
- Add the mushrooms and simmer for 5 minutes more. Stir in salt and pepper to taste. Transfer to serving plates and serve immediately.

Leek & herb soufflé

SERVES 4
190 calories per serving

INGREDIENTS:

Vegetable oil for greasing
1 tablespoon olive oil
350g/12oz baby leeks (finely chopped)
125ml/4fl oz vegetable stock
50g/2oz walnuts

2 eggs (separated)
2 tablespoons chopped fresh mixed herbs
2 tablespoons natural yogurt
Salt and pepper

- Preheat the oven 180°C/350°F/Gas mark 4. Lightly grease a 900ml/1½pt soufflé dish.
- Heat the olive oil in a frying pan. Add the leeks and sauté over a medium heat, stirring occasionally, for 2 to 3 minutes.
- Add the stock to the pan, lower the heat and simmer gently for a further 5 minutes.
- Place the walnuts in a blender or food processor and process until finely chopped. Add the leek mixture to the nuts and process briefly to form a purée. Transfer to a mixing bowl.
- Mix together the egg yolks, herbs and yogurt until thoroughly combined. Pour the egg mixture into the leek purée. Season with salt and pepper to taste and mix well.
- In a separate mixing bowl, whisk the egg whites until firm peaks form.
- Fold the egg whites into the leek mixture. Spoon the mixture into the prepared dish and place on a warmed baking tray. Bake in the oven for 35 to 40 minutes, or until risen and set. Serve immediately.

Chilli tagliatelle

SERVES 4
310 calories per serving

INGREDIENTS:

50g/2oz butter
1 onion (finely chopped)
1 garlic clove (crushed)
2 red chillies (deseeded and diced)
450g/1lb tomatoes (skinned, deseeded and diced)

200ml/7fl oz vegetable stock
2 tablespoons tomato purée
1 teaspoon granulated sugar
Salt and pepper
675g/1½lb fresh green and white tagliatelle

→

←
- Melt the butter in a large saucepan. Add the onion and garlic and cook for 3 to 4 minutes, or until softened. Add the chillies to the pan and continue cooking for about 2 minutes.
- Add the tomatoes and stock, then reduce the heat and simmer for 10 minutes, stirring occasionally.
- Pour the sauce into a blender or food processor and blend for 1 minute, until smooth. Return the sauce to the saucepan and add the tomato purée, sugar and seasoning to taste. Gently reheat over a low heat, until piping hot.
- Cook the tagliatelle in a saucepan of lightly salted boiling water, according to the packet instructions. Drain the tagliatelle, transfer to serving plates and top with the sauce.

Roast pepper tart

SERVES 8
245 calories per serving

INGREDIENTS:

For the pastry:
175g/6oz plain flour
Pinch of salt
75g/3oz butter
2 tablespoons finely chopped green olives
3 tablespoons cold water

For the filling:
1 red pepper (halved lengthways and deseeded)

1 green pepper (halved lengthways and deseeded)
1 yellow pepper (halved lengthways and deseeded)
2 garlic cloves (crushed)
2 tablespoons olive oil
100g/4oz Mozzarella cheese (grated)
2 eggs
150ml/¼pt milk
1 tablespoon chopped basil
Salt and pepper

- Preheat the oven to 200°C/400°F/Gas mark 6.
- To make the pastry, sift the flour and salt into a bowl. Rub in the butter until the mixture resembles breadcrumbs. Add the olives and cold water, bringing the mixture together to form a dough.
- Roll the dough out on a floured surface and use to line a 20cm/8in loose-bottomed flan tin. Prick the base with a fork and leave to chill.
- Place the peppers, skin side uppermost, on a baking tray. Mix the garlic and oil and brush over the peppers. Cook in the oven for 20 minutes, or until beginning to char. Let the peppers cool slightly, then slice them thinly. Arrange in the base of the pastry case and sprinkle the Mozzarella over.
- Beat the egg and milk and add the basil. Season and pour over the peppers. Put the tart on a baking tray and return to the oven for 20 minutes, or until set.

Tomato rice

SERVES 4
360 calories per serving

INGREDIENTS:

2 tablespoons corn oil
½ teaspoon onion seeds
1 onion (sliced)
2 tomatoes (sliced)
1 yellow pepper (chopped)
1 teaspoon grated fresh root ginger
1 garlic clove (crushed)

1 teaspoon chilli powder
2 tablespoons chopped fresh coriander
1 potato (diced)
1½ teaspoons salt
50g/2oz frozen peas
400g/14oz basmati rice
750ml/1¼pt water

- Heat the oil and fry the onion seeds for about 30 seconds. Add the sliced onion and fry for about 5 minutes.
- Add the tomatoes, pepper, ginger, garlic, chilli powder, coriander, potato, salt and peas and stir-fry over a medium heat for a further 5 minutes. Add the rice and stir-fry for about 1 minute.
- Pour in the water and bring to the boil, then lower the heat to medium. Cover and cook for a further 12 to 15 minutes. Leave the rice to stand for 5 minutes and serve.

Satay noodles

SERVES 4
285 calories per serving

INGREDIENTS:

275g/10oz rice noodles
3 tablespoons groundnut oil
2 garlic cloves (crushed)
2 shallots (sliced)
225g/8oz green beans (sliced)

100g/4oz cherry tomatoes (halved)
1 teaspoon chilli flakes
4 tablespoons crunchy peanut butter
150ml/¼pt coconut milk
1 tablespoon tomato purée

- Place the rice noodles in a large bowl and pour over enough boiling water to cover. Leave to stand for 10 minutes.
- Heat the groundnut oil in a large preheated wok or frying pan. Add the garlic and shallots to the wok and stir-fry for 1 minute.
- Drain the rice noodles thoroughly. Add the green beans and drained noodles to

→

←

the wok and stir-fry for about 5 minutes. Add the cherry tomatoes to the wok and mix well.

- Mix together the chilli flakes, peanut butter, coconut milk and tomato purée.
- Pour the chilli mixture over the noodles, toss well until all the ingredients are thoroughly combined and heat through.
- Transfer the satay noodles to warm serving dishes and serve immediately.

Macaroni & four cheeses

SERVES 6
400 calories per serving

INGREDIENTS:

225g/8oz macaroni
25g/1oz margarine
100g/4oz Parmesan cheese (grated)
100g/4oz Romano cheese (grated)
350ml/12fl oz skimmed milk
100g/4oz low-fat cottage cheese

25g/1oz plain flour
¼ onion (sliced)
½ teaspoon dry mustard
100g/4oz low-fat Mozzarella cheese (grated)
75g/3oz fresh breadcrumbs

- Preheat the oven to 180°C/350°F/Gas mark 4.
- Cook the macaroni in boiling water and drain. Toss with half the margarine.
- In a 1.2 litre/2pt baking dish, layer half the macaroni and the Parmesan and Romano cheeses. Repeat with the remaining macaroni and Parmesan and Romano cheeses.
- In a blender or food processor, blend the milk, cottage cheese, flour, onion and mustard. Blend until smooth. Pour the mixture over the macaroni. Sprinkle Mozzarella over the top.
- Combine the breadcrumbs and remaining margarine and sprinkle over the top. Bake for 40 minutes.

Tofu with mushrooms & peas

SERVES 4

220 calories per serving

25g/1oz dried Chinese mushrooms
450g/1lb tofu
25g/1oz cornflour
Vegetable oil for deep-frying

2 garlic cloves (finely chopped)
2.5cm/1in piece root ginger (grated)
100g/4oz fresh peas

INGREDIENTS:

- Place the Chinese mushrooms in a large bowl. Pour in enough boiling water to cover and leave to stand for about 10 minutes.
- Meanwhile, cut the tofu into bite-sized cubes using a sharp knife. Place the cornflour in a large bowl. Add the tofu to the bowl and toss in the cornflour until evenly coated.
- Heat the oil for deep-frying in a large preheated wok. Add the cubes of tofu to the wok and deep-fry in batches, for 2 to 3 minutes or until golden and crispy.
- Remove the tofu with a slotted spoon and leave to drain on kitchen paper.
- Drain off all but 2 tablespoons of oil from the wok. Add the garlic, ginger and Chinese mushrooms to the wok and stir-fry for 2 to 3 minutes.
- Return the cooked tofu to the wok and add the peas. Heat through for 1 minute and serve hot.

Tagliatelle with mushrooms

SERVES 4

245 calories per serving

1 small onion (finely chopped)
2 garlic cloves (crushed)
150ml/1/4pt vegetable stock
225g/8oz mixed fresh mushrooms
4 tablespoons white wine
2 teaspoons tomato purée
1 tablespoon soy sauce

1 teaspoon fresh thyme leaves
2 tablespoons chopped fresh parsley, plus extra to garnish
225g/8oz fresh sun-dried tomato and herb tagliatelle
Salt and pepper

INGREDIENTS:

- Put the onion and garlic into a pan with the stock, then cover and cook for 5

→

←

- minutes or until tender.
- Add the mushrooms, wine, tomato purée and soy sauce. Cover and cook for 5 minutes.
- Remove the lid from the pan and boil until the liquid has reduced by half. Stir in the fresh herbs and season to taste.
- Cook the fresh pasta in a large pan of boiling, salted water for 2 to 5 minutes until al dente. Drain thoroughly and toss lightly with the mushroom sauce.
- Serve, garnished with parsley.

Chive omelette stir-fry

SERVES 4
200 calories per serving

2 eggs
2 tablespoons snipped fresh chives
Salt and pepper
2 tablespoons groundnut oil
1 garlic clove (chopped)
1cm/½in piece fresh root ginger (chopped)

2 celery sticks (cut into shreds)
2 carrots (cut into shreds)
2 small courgettes (cut into shreds)
1 bunch radishes (sliced)
100g/4oz Chinese leaves (shredded)
1 tablespoon sesame oil

INGREDIENTS:

- Whisk together the eggs, chives and seasoning in a bowl. Heat about 1 teaspoon of the groundnut oil in an omelette pan and pour in just enough of the egg mixture to cover the base of the pan. Cook for about 1 minute until set, then turn the omelette over and cook for a further minute.
- Tip out the omelette on to a plate and cook the rest of the egg mixture in the same way to make several omelettes, adding extra oil to the pan if necessary. Roll up each omelette and slice thinly. Keep the omelettes warm in the oven until required.
- Heat the remaining oil in a wok or large frying pan, add the chopped garlic and ginger and stir-fry for a few seconds to flavour the oil.
- Add the shredded celery, carrots and courgettes and stir-fry the vegetables for about 1 minute. Add the radishes and Chinese leaves and stir-fry for a further 2 to 3 minutes, until all the vegetables are tender but still crunchy. Sprinkle a little sesame oil over the vegetables and toss gently.
- Serve the stir-fried vegetables at once with the sliced chive omelettes scattered over the top.

Casseroled beans & penne

SERVES 4
330 calories per serving

225g/8oz dried haricot beans (soaked overnight and drained)
850ml/1¼pt vegetable stock
2 large onions (sliced)
2 garlic cloves (chopped)
2 bay leaves
1 teaspoon dried oregano
1 teaspoon dried thyme
5 tablespoons red wine
2 tablespoons tomato purée

225g/8oz dried penne
90ml/3¼fl oz olive oil
2 celery sticks (sliced)
1 fennel bulb (sliced)
100g/4oz mushrooms (sliced)
225g/8oz tomatoes (sliced)
1 teaspoon muscovado sugar
4 tablespoons dry white breadcrumbs
Salt and pepper

INGREDIENTS:

- Preheat the oven to 180°C/350°F/Gas mark 4.
- Put the haricot beans in a large saucepan and add sufficient cold water to cover.
- Bring to the boil and continue to boil vigorously for 20 minutes. Drain, set aside and keep warm.
- Put the beans in a large, flameproof casserole dish. Add the vegetable stock and stir in 75ml/3fl oz olive oil, the onions, garlic, bay leaves, oregano, thyme, wine and tomato purée. Bring to the boil, then cover and cook in the oven for 2 hours.
- Bring a large saucepan of lightly salted water to the boil. Add the penne and the remaining olive oil and cook for about 3 minutes. Then drain.
- Add the penne, celery, fennel, mushrooms and tomatoes to the casserole dish and season to taste with salt and pepper. Stir in the muscovado sugar and sprinkle the breadcrumbs over. Cover the dish and cook in the oven for a further 1 hour.
- Serve hot.

Baked tomatoes

SERVES 6
50 calories per serving

INGREDIENTS:

675g/1lb 8oz large tomatoes (thickly sliced)
2 teaspoons red wine vinegar
½ teaspoon wholegrain mustard
1 garlic clove (crushed)

Salt and pepper
2 teaspoons cold water
2 teaspoons chopped fresh parsley
2 teaspoons snipped fresh chives
25g/1oz fresh white breadcrumbs

- Preheat the oven to 200°C/400°F/Gas mark 6.
- Arrange half the tomato slices in a 900ml/1½pt ovenproof dish.
- Mix the vinegar, mustard, garlic and seasoning together in a small bowl. Stir in the water.
- Sprinkle the tomatoes with half the parsley and chives, then drizzle half the dressing over them.
- Lay the remaining tomato slices on top, overlapping them slightly. Drizzle with the remaining dressing.
- Sprinkle the breadcrumbs over the top. Bake for 25 minutes or until the topping is golden. Sprinkle with the remaining parsley and chives. Serve immediately.

Vegetables in black bean & soy sauce

SERVES 4
120 calories per serving
INGREDIENTS:

- Heat the groundnut oil in a preheated wok or large frying pan until it is almost

2 tablespoons groundnut oil
6 spring onions (sliced)
3 garlic cloves (crushed)
1 green pepper (diced)
1 red pepper (diced)
1 red chilli (diced)
2 tablespoons chopped water chestnuts
1 courgette (chopped)

100g/4oz oyster mushrooms
3 tablespoons black bean sauce
2 teaspoons Chinese rice wine
4 tablespoons soy sauce
1 teaspoon demerara sugar
2 tablespoons water
1 teaspoon sesame oil

smoking. Lower the heat slightly, add the spring onions and garlic and stir-fry for about 30 seconds.

- Add the peppers, chilli, water chestnuts and courgette to the wok and stir-fry for 2 to 3 minutes, or until the vegetables are just beginning to soften. Add the oyster mushrooms, black bean sauce, Chinese rice wine, soy sauce, sugar and water to the wok and stir-fry for a further 4 minutes.
- Sprinkle the stir-fry with sesame oil and serve immediately.

Broccoli with feta & tomato sauce

SERVES 4
350 calories per serving

INGREDIENTS:

450g/1lb broccoli (cut into florets)	*2.5cm/1in piece of cinnamon stick*
25g/1oz low-fat spread	*Salt and pepper*
1 large onion (finely chopped)	*1 tablespoon lemon juice*
3 garlic cloves (crushed)	*100g/4oz Feta cheese (crumbled)*
850g/1³/₄lb canned chopped tomatoes	*100g/4oz Emmental cheese (grated)*
1 teaspoon dried oregano	

- Preheat the oven to 190°C/375°F/Gas mark 5.
- Cook the broccoli in lightly salted boiling water for 5 minutes until just tender. Drain and place in an ovenproof serving dish.
- Melt the low-fat spread in the saucepan. Fry the onion and garlic for 3 minutes, stirring. Add the tomatoes, oregano and cinnamon. Season with a little salt and pepper. Bring to the boil and simmer for 5 minutes. Discard the cinnamon stick.
- Pour the sauce over the broccoli and sprinkle with the lemon juice, then cover with the cheeses. Bake in the oven for 25 minutes and serve immediately.

Irish colcannon

SERVES 4

225 calories per serving

INGREDIENTS:

225ml/8fl oz water
1 tablespoon low-fat margarine
¼ teaspoon salt
650g/1lb 7oz cabbage (chopped)

75ml/3fl oz skimmed milk
150g/5oz instant mashed potato flakes
1 onion (finely chopped)

- In a medium-sized saucepan, combine the water, margarine and salt. Bring to the boil. Stir in the cabbage and return to the boil.
- Reduce the heat, cover and simmer for 4 to 6 minutes, until the cabbage is tender.
- Remove from the heat and stir in the milk and potato flakes with a fork. Stir in the onion. Cover and leave to stand for 3 minutes before serving.

Asparagus pie

SERVES 2

235 calories per serving

INGREDIENTS:

100g/4oz fresh asparagus
225g/8oz low-fat cottage cheese
1 tablespoon lemon juice
25g/1oz onion (minced)
1 tablespoon fresh dill (minced)

1 egg (lightly beaten)
2 sheets filo pastry
Vegetable oil for greasing
75g/3oz fresh parsley (snipped)

- Preheat the oven to 180°C/350°F/Gas mark 4.
- Snap off the tough ends of the asparagus. Cook the asparagus, covered, in a small amount of boiling water for 8 minutes, or until al dente. Drain well.
- Combine the cottage cheese, lemon juice, onion, dill and egg and stir well.
- Lightly oil a sheet of filo pastry and fold in half crossways. Repeat with the other sheet of pastry.
- Place the sheets, one on top of the other, on a baking tray. Spoon the cottage cheese mixture over half of the pastry to within 1cm/½in of the edges. Top with the asparagus. Place the other half of the pastry over the asparagus, tucking the edges under to seal.
- Bake for 40 minutes, until golden. Remove from the oven and serve warm.

Mixed mushroom ragout

SERVES 4
50 calories per serving

INGREDIENTS:

1 small onion (finely chopped)
1 garlic clove (crushed)
1 teaspoon coriander seeds (crushed)
1 tablespoon red wine vinegar
1 tablespoon soy sauce
1 tablespoon dry sherry
2 teaspoons tomato purée

2 teaspoons brown sugar
150ml/¼pt vegetable stock
100g/4oz baby button mushrooms
100g/4oz chestnut mushrooms
(quartered)
100g/4oz oyster mushrooms (sliced)
Salt and pepper

- Place the onion, garlic, coriander seeds, vinegar, soy sauce, sherry, tomato purée, sugar and stock into a large saucepan. Bring to the boil and reduce the heat.
- Cover and simmer for 5 minutes. Uncover the saucepan and simmer for 5 more minutes, or until the liquid has reduced by half.
- Add the button and chestnut mushrooms and simmer for 3 minutes. Stir in the oyster mushrooms and cook for a further 2 minutes. Remove the mushrooms from the pan with a slotted spoon, transfer them to a serving dish and keep warm.
- Boil the juices for about 5 minutes, or until reduced to about 75ml/3fl oz. Season to taste.
- Allow to cool for 2 to 3 minutes, then pour over the mushrooms. Serve hot or well chilled.

Penne with broccoli & chilli

SERVES 4
400 calories per serving

INGREDIENTS:

350g/12oz penne pasta
Salt and pepper
450g/1lb small broccoli florets
2 tablespoons vegetable stock

1 garlic clove (crushed)
1 small red chilli (sliced)
4 tablespoons low-fat natural yogurt
2 tablespoons toasted pine nuts

- Add the pasta to a large pan of lightly salted boiling water and return to the boil. Place the broccoli in a steamer basket over the top. Cover and cook for 8 to

→

← 10 minutes until both are just tender. Drain.
- Heat the stock and add the crushed garlic and chilli. Stir over a low heat for 2 to 3 minutes.
- Stir in the broccoli, pasta and yogurt. Adjust the seasoning, sprinkle with pine nuts and serve hot.

Oriental vegetable noodles

SERVES 4
200 calories per serving

INGREDIENTS:

175g/6oz thread noodles
1 teaspoon sesame oil
2 tablespoons crunchy peanut butter
2 tablespoons soy sauce
1 tablespoon white wine vinegar
1 teaspoon clear honey
Pinch of salt and pepper

100g/4oz Japanese radish (grated)
100g/4oz carrot (grated)
100g/4oz cucumber (finely shredded)
1 bunch spring onions (finely shredded)
1 tablespoon dry-roasted peanuts (crushed)

- Bring a large saucepan of water to the boil, add the noodles and cook according to the package instructions. Drain well and rinse in cold water. Leave in a bowl of cold water until required.
- To make the peanut butter sauce, put the sesame oil, peanut butter, soy sauce, vinegar, honey and seasoning into a screw-top jar. Seal and shake well to mix thoroughly.
- Drain the noodles well, place in a large serving bowl and mix in half the peanut sauce.
- Using 2 forks, toss in the radish, carrot, cucumber and spring onions. Sprinkle with crushed peanuts and serve with the remaining peanut sauce.

Chargrilled kebabs

SERVES 4
80 calories per serving

INGREDIENTS:

2 tablespoons lemon juice
1 tablespoon olive oil
1 garlic clove (crushed)
1 tablespoon chopped fresh rosemary
Salt and pepper
1 red pepper (sliced into
2.5cm/1in pieces)
1 green pepper (sliced into
2.5cm/1in pieces)

1 yellow pepper (sliced into
2.5cm/1in pieces)
1 courgette (sliced into
2.5cm/1in pieces)
4 baby aubergines (quartered
lengthways)
2 red onions (each cut into 8 wedges)

- In a large bowl, whisk together the lemon juice, olive oil, garlic, rosemary and seasoning. Pour the mixture over the vegetables and stir to coat evenly.
- Preheat the grill to medium. Thread the peppers, courgettes, aubergines and onion on to 8 skewers. Arrange the kebabs on the grill rack and cook for 10 to 12 minutes, turning frequently until the vegetables are lightly charred.

Lentil Bolognese

SERVES 6
110 calories per serving

INGREDIENTS:

3 tablespoons olive oil
1 onion (chopped)
2 garlic cloves (crushed)
2 carrots (coarsely grated)
2 celery sticks (chopped)
100g/4oz red lentils

400g/14oz canned chopped tomatoes
2 tablespoons tomato purée
450ml/3/4pt vegetable stock
1 tablespoon chopped fresh marjoram
(chopped)
Salt and pepper

- Heat the oil in a large saucepan and gently fry the onion, garlic, carrots and celery for about 5 minutes, until they are soft.
- Add the lentils, tomatoes, tomato purée, stock, marjoram and seasoning to the pan.
- Bring the mixture to the boil, then partially cover with a lid and simmer for 20 minutes until thick and soft. Serve with noodles.

Vegetable-stuffed pasta shells

SERVES 8
400 calories per serving

INGREDIENTS:

24 jumbo pasta shells
275g/10oz chopped spinach
1 egg white
350g/12oz low-fat cottage cheese
350g/12oz Mozzarella cheese (grated)
100g/4oz onion (finely chopped)
2 garlic cloves (minced)
50g/2oz fresh parsley (chopped)
275g/10oz broccoli (chopped)

For the sauce:
1 tablespoon olive oil
3 garlic cloves
½ medium onion (chopped)
400g/14oz canned chopped tomatoes
75g/3oz mushrooms (sliced)
½ tablespoon shredded fresh basil
½ tablespoon chopped fresh oregano
1 tablespoon chopped fresh parsley
50g/2oz Parmesan cheese (grated)

- Preheat the oven to 180°C/350°F/Gas mark 4. Grease a 33 x 23cm/13 x 9in tin.
- To make the marinara sauce, place the olive oil and garlic in a large saucepan.
- Sauté the garlic in the oil until the garlic begins to brown. Remove the garlic from the oil with a slotted spoon. Add the onion to the oil and sauté lightly.
- Add the tomatoes and mushrooms and cook over a medium heat for about 30 minutes. Add the basil, oregano and parsley and bring to a boil. Remove from the heat and stir in the Parmesan. Put aside.
- Prepare the pasta shells according to packet directions. Combine the spinach, egg white, cottage cheese, Mozzarella, onion, garlic, parsley and broccoli. Blend well.
- Stuff the shells with the cheese mixture, using about 2 tablespoons for each shell. Arrange in the prepared tin. Pour the sauce over the shells. Bake for 30 to 40 minutes.

Chilled noodles & peppers

SERVES 6
265 calories per serving

INGREDIENTS:

250g/9oz ribbon noodles
Salt
1 tablespoon sesame oil
1 red pepper
1 yellow pepper
1 green pepper
6 spring onions (cut into
matchstick strips)

For the dressing:
5 tablespoons sesame oil
2 tablespoons soy sauce
1 tablespoon tahini
4 drops hot pepper sauce

- Preheat the grill to medium. Cook the noodles in a large pan of boiling, salted water until they are almost tender. Drain them in a colander, run cold water through them and drain thoroughly. Tip the noodles into a bowl, stir in the sesame oil, cover and chill.
- Cook the peppers under the grill, turning them frequently, until they are blackened on all sides. Plunge into cold water, then skin them. Cut in half, remove the core and seeds and cut the flesh into thick strips. Set aside in a covered container.
- To make the dressing, mix together the sesame oil, soy sauce, tahini and pepper sauce until well combined.
- Pour the dressing on the noodles, reserving 1 tablespoon, and toss well. Turn the noodles and spoon on the reserved dressing. Scatter on the spring onion and serve.

Tofu & green bean curry

SERVES 4
110 calories per serving

INGREDIENTS:

350ml/12fl oz coconut milk
1 tablespoon red curry paste
3 tablespoons fish sauce
2 teaspoons granulated sugar
225g/8oz button mushrooms

100g/4oz French beans (trimmed)
175g/6oz tofu (rinsed and cut into
2cm/³/4in cubes)
4 kaffir lime leaves (torn)
2 red chillies (seeded and sliced)

→

←
- Put about one-third of the coconut milk in a wok or saucepan. Cook until it starts to separate and an oily sheen appears.
- Add the red curry paste, fish sauce and sugar to the coconut milk. Mix together thoroughly.
- Add the mushrooms. Stir and cook for 1 minute. Stir in the rest of the coconut milk and bring back to the boil.
- Add the French beans and cubes of tofu and simmer gently for another 4 to 5 minutes.
- Stir in the kaffir lime leaves and chillies. Serve hot,

Ratatouille penne bake

SERVES 6
210 calories per serving

INGREDIENTS:

1 small aubergine
2 courgettes (thickly sliced)
Salt and pepper
200g/7oz firm tofu (cubed)
3 garlic cloves (crushed)
2 teaspoons sesame seeds
1 small red pepper (sliced)

1 onion (finely chopped)
150ml/¼pt vegetable stock
3 tomatoes (skinned, deseeded and quartered)
1 tablespoon chopped fresh mixed herbs
225g/8oz penne

- Cut the aubergine into 2.5cm/1in cubes. Put into a colander with the courgettes, sprinkle with salt and leave to drain for 30 minutes.
- Mix the tofu with the soy sauce, 1 garlic clove and the sesame seeds. Cover and marinate for 30 minutes.
- Put the pepper, onion and remaining garlic into a saucepan with the stock. Bring to the boil, cover and cook for 5 minutes until tender. Remove the lid and boil until all the stock has evaporated. Add the tomatoes and herbs to the pan and cook for a further 3 minutes, then add the rinsed aubergine and courgette and cook until tender. Season to taste.
- Meanwhile, cook the pasta in a large pan of boiling, salted water according to the packet instructions until al dente, then drain thoroughly. Preheat the grill.
- Toss the pasta with the vegetables and tofu. Transfer to a shallow ovenproof dish and grill until lightly toasted.

Vegetable & goat's cheese pizza

SERVES 4

395 calories per serving

INGREDIENTS:

For the base:
15g/½oz fresh yeast
75ml/3fl oz tepid water
½ teaspoon granulated sugar
1 tablespoon olive oil
175g/6oz plain flour
1 teaspoon salt

For the tomato sauce:
1 small onion (chopped)
1 red pepper (chopped)
1 garlic clove (crushed)
2 tablespoons olive oil
225g/8oz tomatoes
1 tablespoon tomato purée
1 teaspoon demerara sugar

2 teaspoons chopped fresh basil
½ teaspoon dried oregano
1 bay leaf
Salt and pepper

For the topping:
2 baby courgettes (halved lengthways)
2 baby aubergines (halved lengthways)
½ red pepper (cut into 4 strips)
½ yellow pepper (cut into 4 strips)
1 small onions (cut into wedges)
2 garlic cloves (unpeeled)
4 tablespoons olive oil
1 tablespoon red wine vinegar
1 tablespoon fresh thyme leaves
75g/3oz goat's cheese

- Preheat the oven to 200°C/400°F/Gas mark 6.
- To make the base, combine the yeast with the water and sugar in a bowl. Leave the mixture to rest in a warm place for 5 to 6 minutes until frothy on the surface. Stir in the olive oil. Sift the flour and salt into a large bowl. Make a well in the centre and pour in the yeast liquid. Using either floured hands or a wooden spoon, mix together to form a dough. Turn out on to a floured work surface and knead for about 5 minutes, until smooth and elastic. Place the dough in a large greased plastic bag and leave for about 1 hour, or until doubled in size.
- For the sauce, fry the onion, pepper and garlic gently in the oil for 5 minutes until softened. Cut a cross in the base of each tomato and place them in a bowl.
- Pour on boiling water and leave for about 45 seconds. Drain, and then plunge in cold water. The skins will peel off easily. Chop the tomatoes, discarding any hard cores. Add the tomatoes to the onion mixture with the tomato purée, sugar, herbs and seasoning. Stir well. Bring to the boil, cover and leave to simmer gently for about 30 minutes, stirring occasionally, until it forms a thick sauce.
- Place all of the vegetables for the topping in a large roasting tin. Mix together

→

←

- the olive oil, vinegar and thyme and pour over, coating the vegetables well.
- Roast the vegetables in the oven for 15 minutes, or until the skins have started to blacken in places, turning halfway through. Leaving the oven on, carefully peel the skins from the peppers and the garlic. Slice the garlic.
- When the sauce is ready, remove the bay leaf and adjust the seasoning to taste. Leave to cool completely.
- Turn the dough out on to a lightly floured work surface and knock back by punching the dough. This releases air bubbles, which would make the pizza uneven. Knead 4 or 5 times, then roll out into a circle. Place on a baking tray.
- Spread the tomato sauce evenly over the base.
- Arrange the roasted vegetables on top and dot with the cheese. Drizzle the oil and juices from the roasting tin over the pizza and season.
- Bake in the oven for 18 to 20 minutes, then serve immediately.

Quorn-stuffed marrow

SERVES 4
350 calories per serving

INGREDIENTS:

1 small marrow
Salt and pepper
2 tablespoons water
25g/1oz low-fat spread
1 onion (finely chopped)
1 carrot (finely chopped)
1 celery stick (finely chopped)
225g/8oz mushrooms (roughly chopped)

200g/7oz minced quorn
2 tablespoons tomato purée
150ml/¼pt vegetable stock
½ teaspoon dried mixed herbs
50g/2oz low-fat Cheddar cheese (grated)

- Preheat the oven to 180°C/350°F/Gas mark 4.
- Peel the marrow and cut into 8 slices. Discard the pith and seeds. Place in a single layer in a baking tin and sprinkle with salt and pepper. Add the water.
- Cover with aluminium foil and bake in the oven for 30 minutes.
- To make the filling, melt the low-fat spread in a saucepan. Add the onion, carrot and celery and cook, stirring, for 2 minutes. Add the mushrooms, quorn, tomato purée, stock, herbs and a little seasoning, and stir well. Bring to the boil, reduce the heat and simmer gently for 20 minutes until the mixture is tender and the liquid is well reduced, stirring occasionally.
- Spoon the mixture into the marrow rings, top each with a little cheese and bake uncovered in the oven for a further 25 minutes or until tender and golden. Serve hot.

Red curry with cashews

SERVES 4
280 calories per serving

INGREDIENTS:

1 tablespoon vegetable oil
250ml/9fl oz coconut milk
1 kaffir lime leaf
¼ teaspoon soy sauce
50g/2oz baby corn cobs (halved lengthways)
100g/4oz broccoli florets
100g/4oz French beans (cut into 5cm/2in pieces)
25g/1oz cashew nuts
15 fresh Thai basil leaves
1 tablespoon chopped fresh coriander
1 tablespoon chopped roast peanuts, to garnish

For the red curry paste:
7 red chillies (halved, seeded and blanched)
2 teaspoons cumin seeds
2 teaspoons coriander seeds
2.5cm/1in piece galangal (chopped)
½ stalk lemon grass (chopped)
1 teaspoon salt
Grated zest of 1 lime
4 garlic cloves (chopped)
3 shallots (chopped)
2 kaffir lime leaves (shredded)

- To make the curry paste, grind all the ingredients together in a large mortar with a pestle or a grinder. Alternatively, process briefly in a blender or food processor.
- Put the oil a wok or large, heavy-based frying pan over a high heat, add 3 tablespoons of the red curry paste and stir until it gives off its aroma. Reduce the heat to medium.
- Add the coconut milk, kaffir lime leaf, soy sauce, baby corn cobs, broccoli florets, French beans and cashew nuts. Bring to the boil and simmer for about 10 minutes, until the vegetables are cooked, but still firm and crunchy.
- Remove and discard the lime leaf and stir in the basil leaves and coriander.
- Transfer to a warmed serving dish, garnish with peanuts and serve immediately.

Leek & carrot gratin

SERVES 6
325 calories per serving

INGREDIENTS:

700g/1½lb leeks (cut into 5cm/2in pieces)
150ml/¼pt vegetable stock
3 tablespoons white wine
1 teaspoon caraway seeds
Pinch of salt
300ml/½pt skimmed milk
25g/1oz margarine

25g/1oz plain flour

For the topping:
100g/4oz fresh wholemeal breadcrumbs
100g/4oz carrot (grated)
2 tablespoons chopped fresh parsley
75g/3oz Edam cheese (coarsely grated)
2 tablespoons flaked almonds

- Place the leeks in a large saucepan and add the stock, wine, caraway seeds and salt. Bring to a simmer, cover and cook for about 5 to 7 minutes until the leeks are just tender.
- With a slotted spoon, transfer the leeks to an ovenproof dish. Boil the remaining liquid to half the original volume, then make up to 350ml/12fl oz with the skimmed milk.
- Preheat the oven to 180°C/350°F/Gas mark 4.
- Melt the margarine in a flameproof casserole dish, stir in the flour and cook without allowing it to colour for about 1 to 2 minutes. Gradually add the stock and milk, stirring well after each addition, until you have a smooth sauce.
- Simmer the sauce for about 5 to 6 minutes, stirring constantly until thickened and smooth, then pour the sauce over the leeks in the dish.
- For the topping, mix all the ingredients together in a bowl and sprinkle over the leeks. Bake for about 20 to 25 minutes until golden.

Pasta pesto

SERVES 4
330 calories per serving

INGREDIENTS:

40 fresh basil leaves
3 garlic cloves (crushed)
25g/1oz pine nuts
50g/2oz Parmesan cheese (grated)

3 tablespoons extra-virgin olive oil
Salt and pepper
700g/1½lb fresh pasta

- Rinse the basil leaves and pat them dry with kitchen paper. Put the basil leaves, garlic, pine nuts and Parmesan cheese into a blender or food processor and blend for about 30 seconds or until smooth. Keep the motor running and slowly add the olive oil. Season with salt and pepper.
- Cook the pasta in a saucepan of lightly salted boiling water according to the packet instructions. Drain thoroughly.
- Transfer the pasta to a serving plate and serve with the pesto. Toss to mix well and serve hot.

Layered vegetable gratin

SERVES 6
240 calories per serving

INGREDIENTS:

225g/8oz large carrots (cut into thin strips lengthways)
225g/8oz baby parsnips (cut into thin strips lengthways)
1 fennel bulb (thinly sliced)
Salt and pepper
500g/1lb 2oz potatoes (diced into 2cm/³/₄in cubes)

100g/4oz low-fat spread
25g/1oz plain flour
300ml/¹/₂pt skimmed milk
¹/₂ teaspoon ground nutmeg
1 egg (beaten)
25g/1oz Parmesan cheese (grated)

- Preheat the oven to 180°C/350°F/Gas mark 4.
- Cook the carrots and parsnips in boiling water for 5 minutes. Drain well and transfer to an ovenproof baking dish.
- Cook the fennel in boiling water for 2 to 3 minutes. Drain well, add to the carrots and parsnips and season.
- Cook the potatoes in boiling water for 6 minutes. Drain well.
- Gently melt half the low-fat spread and stir in the flour. Remove from the heat and gradually mix in the milk. Return to the heat and stir until thickened.
- Season and stir in the nutmeg. Cool for 10 minutes.
- Beat the egg into the sauce and spoon over the vegetables. Arrange the potatoes on top and sprinkle the cheese over.
- Dot the potatoes with the remaining low-fat spread. Bake in the oven for 1 hour, until the vegetables are tender. Serve hot.

Vegetarian chilli

SERVES 5
200 calories per serving

INGREDIENTS:

225g/8oz kidney beans
225g/8oz canned chickpeas
750ml/1¼pt water
1 onion (diced)
1 large carrot (diced)
1 celery stick (diced)
175g/6oz mushrooms

½ green pepper (diced)
2 garlic cloves (minced)
175ml/6fl oz tomato purée
2 tomatoes (skinned and deseeded)
1 teaspoon ground cumin
1½ teaspoons chilli powder
½ teaspoon black pepper

- Place the kidney beans in a saucepan and cover with water. Bring to the boil.
- Boil for 15 minutes and remove from the heat. Cover and leave to stand for 1 hour.
- Drain and place in a large heavy-based saucepan. Repeat the process with the chickpeas in a separate saucepan. Divide half of the water between the 2 saucepans. Cook the kidney beans for 20 minutes. Cook the chickpeas for 30 minutes, then add to the kidney beans together with any liquid.
- Sauté the onion, carrot, celery, mushrooms and pepper in a frying pan. Add the garlic and sauté for a few seconds. Add the tomato purée, tomatoes, cumin, chilli powder, pepper and sautéed vegetable mixture to the kidney beans and chickpeas.
- Simmer for 40 minutes, adding water as needed to keep moist.

Aubergine cake

SERVES 4

210 calories per serving

INGREDIENTS:

1 large aubergine
300g/11oz tricolour pasta shapes
100g/4oz low-fat soft cheese with
garlic and herbs
350ml/12fl oz passata

4 tablespoons grated Parmesan cheese
1½ teaspoons dried oregano
Salt and pepper
2 tablespoons dry white breadcrumbs

- Preheat the oven to 190°C/375°F/Gas mark 5. Grease and line a 20cm/8in round spring-form cake tin.
- Trim the aubergine and slice lengthways into slices about 5mm/¼in thick. Place in a bowl, sprinkle with salt, and set aside for 30 minutes to remove any bitter juices. Rinse well under cold running water and drain.
- Bring a saucepan of water to the boil and blanch the aubergine for 1 minute.
- Drain and pat dry with kitchen paper.
- Cook the pasta shapes according to the instructions on the packet. Drain well and return to the saucepan. Add the soft cheese and allow it to melt over the pasta.
- Stir in the passata, Parmesan, oregano and salt and pepper.
- Arrange the aubergine over the base and sides of the tin, overlapping the slices and making sure there are no gaps.
- Pile the pasta mixture into the tin, packing down well, and sprinkle with the breadcrumbs. Bake for 20 minutes and leave to stand for 15 minutes.
- Loosen the cake around the edge with a palette knife and release from the tin.
- Turn out the pasta cake, aubergine side uppermost, and serve hot.

Desserts

This chapter proves that a diet does not mean denying yourself
dessert. A calorie count is provided for each treat – and you may
find yourself pleasantly surprised. Whether you would prefer Baked
satsumas in brandy, Boozy banana soufflé, Pears with strawberry
sauce or Custard tart – they are all here so you can relax and
enjoy without feeling guilty.

Nectarines with spiced ricotta

SERVES 4
100 calories per serving

INGREDIENTS:

4 ripe nectarines (halved and stoned)
100g/4oz ricotta cheese

1 tablespoon demerara sugar
½ teaspoon star anise, to decorate

- Arrange the nectarine halves cut-side upwards in a shallow flameproof dish.
- Place the ricotta cheese in a small mixing bowl. Stir the sugar into the cheese.
- Using a teaspoon, spoon equal amounts of the mixture into the hollow of each nectarine half.
- Sprinkle with the star anise. Cook under a moderately hot grill for 6 to 8 minutes, or until the nectarines are hot. Serve warm.

Mango & lime sorbet in lime shells

SERVES 4
55 calories per serving

INGREDIENTS:

4 large limes
1 medium-ripe mango
½ teaspoon powdered gelatine

2 egg whites
1 tablespoon granulated sugar

- Cut a thick slice from the top of each of the limes and a thin slice from the bottom end so that the limes will stand upright. Squeeze out the juice, then use a small knife to remove all the white membrane from the centre.
- Halve, stone, peel and chop the mango, then purée the flesh in a blender or food processor with 2 tablespoons of the lime juice. Dissolve the gelatine in 3 tablespoons of the lime juice and stir it into the mango mixture.
- Whisk the egg whites until they hold soft peaks. Whisk in the sugar, then fold the egg white mixture into the mango mixture. Spoon the sorbet into the lime shells.
- Wrap the shells in clingfilm and put in the freezer until the sorbet is firm.
- Before serving, let the shells stand at room temperature for about 10 minutes.

Coconut dumplings with apricot sauce

SERVES 4
120 calories per serving

INGREDIENTS:

75g/3oz low-fat cottage cheese
1 egg white
15g/½ oz low-fat spread
1 tablespoon muscovado sugar
2 tablespoons self-raising wholemeal
flour

Finely grated zest of ½ lemon
1 tablespoon desiccated coconut

For the sauce:
225g/8oz canned apricots in juice
1 tablespoon lemon juice

- Half-fill a steamer with boiling water and put it on to boil. If you do not have a steamer, place a heatproof plate over a pan of boiling water.
- Beat together the cottage cheese, egg white and low-fat spread until they are evenly mixed. Stir in the sugar, flour, lemon zest and coconut, mixing everything evenly to form a fairly firm dough.
- Place 8 to 12 spoonfuls of the mixture in the steamer or on the plate, leaving a space between them.
- Cover the steamer or pan tightly with a lid or plate and steam for about 10 minutes, until the dumplings have risen and are firm to the touch.
- Meanwhile, make the sauce. Purée the apricots and juice in a blender or food processor and stir in the lemon juice. Pour into a small pan and heat until boiling, then serve with the dumplings.

Raspberry parfait

SERVES 4
50 calories per serving

INGREDIENTS:

150ml/¼ pt skimmed milk
175g/6oz fresh raspberries

1 tablespoon honey
1 egg white

- Place the milk in the freezer for 2 hours, or until it just begins to freeze.
- Reserve 4 raspberries for garnish. In a blender or food processor, purée the

→

←

remaining raspberries with the honey.

- Whip the milk for about 8 minutes, or until thick. Beat the egg white until it holds stiff peaks. Fold the egg white into the milk. Stir in the raspberry purée and serve immediately, topping each serving with a raspberry.

Apple couscous pudding

SERVES 4
200 calories per serving

INGREDIENTS:

600ml/1pt unsweetened apple juice
100g/4oz couscous
50g/2oz sultanas
½ teaspoon mixed spice

2 cooking apples (peeled, cored and sliced)
2 tablespoons demerara sugar

- Preheat the oven to 200°C/400°F/Gas mark 6.
- Put the apple juice, couscous, sultanas and spice in a pan and bring to the boil, stirring. Lower the heat, cover and simmer for 5 minutes.
- Spoon half the couscous mixture into a 1.2 litre/2pt ovenproof dish. Arrange half the apple slices over the couscous. Top with the remaining couscous.
- Arrange the remaining apple slices over the top and sprinkle with the sugar.
- Bake for 25 to 30 minutes or until golden brown. Serve hot.

Baked satsumas in brandy

SERVES 4
100 calories per serving

INGREDIENTS:

50ml/2fl oz orange juice
1 teaspoon granulated sugar
25g/1oz low-fat spread

2 tablespoons brandy
8 small satsumas (peeled, with all pith removed)

- Preheat the oven to 180°C/350°F/Gas mark 4.
- Put the orange juice, sugar, low-fat spread and brandy in a flameproof casserole dish. Bring to the boil and simmer for 2 minutes.
- Add the satsumas and turn in the liquid. Cover and bake in the oven for about 30 minutes until just cooked, spooning the juices over twice during cooking.

Greek honey & lemon cake

SERVES 8
190 calories per serving

INGREDIENTS:

*50g/2oz margarine (plus extra
for greasing)
4 tablespoons clear honey
Finely grated zest and juice of 1 lemon
150ml/¼ pt skimmed milk
150g/5oz plain flour*

*1½ teaspoons baking powder
½ teaspoon grated nutmeg
50g/2oz semolina
2 egg whites
2 teaspoons sesame seeds*

- Preheat the oven to 200°C/400°F/Gas mark 6. Lightly grease a 19cm/7½in square cake tin and line the base with baking parchment.
- Place the margarine and 3 tablespoons of the honey in a saucepan and heat gently until melted. Reserve 1 tablespoon lemon juice, then stir in the rest with the lemon zest and milk.
- Sift together the flour, baking powder and nutmeg, then beat in the semolina.
- Whisk the egg whites until they form soft peaks, then fold evenly into the mixture. Spoon into the prepared tin and sprinkle with sesame seeds.
- Bake for 25 to 30 minutes, until golden brown. Mix the reserved honey and lemon juice and drizzle over the cake while warm. Cool in the tin and then cut into fingers to serve.

Eggless sponge

SERVES 6
200 calories per serving

INGREDIENTS:

*Butter for greasing
225g/8oz self-raising wholemeal flour
2 teaspoon baking powder
175g/6oz caster sugar (plus extra
for dusting)*

*90ml/3¼fl oz sunflower oil
250ml/9fl oz water
1 teaspoon vanilla essence
4 tablespoons strawberry jam*

- Preheat the oven to 180°C/350°F/Gas mark 4. Grease 2 x 20cm/8in sandwich cake tins and line them with baking parchment.
- Sieve the flour and baking powder into a large mixing bowl, stirring in any bran

→

←

remaining in the sieve. Stir in the caster sugar.

- Pour in the sunflower oil, water and vanilla essence. Mix well with a wooden spoon for about 1 minute until the mixture is smooth, then divide between the prepared tins.
- Bake in the oven for about 25 to 30 minutes until the centre springs back when lightly touched. Leave the sponges to cool in the tins before turning out and transferring to a wire rack.
- To serve, remove the baking parchment and place one of the sponges on to a serving plate. Spread with the jam and place the other sponge on top. Dust with caster sugar before serving.

Strawberries in raspberry & passion fruit sauce

SERVES 4
120 calories per serving

INGREDIENTS:

350g/12oz fresh raspberries
3 tablespoons caster sugar

1 passion fruit
700g/1½lb small strawberries

- Mix the raspberries and sugar in a saucepan and heat gently until the raspberries release their juices. Simmer for 5 minutes. Leave to cool.
- Cut the passion fruit in half and scoop out the seeds and juice into a bowl.
- Tip the raspberry mixture into a blender or food processor, add the passion fruit and blend to a smooth purée.
- Press the purée through a fine nylon sieve placed over a bowl to remove the seeds.
- Fold the strawberries into the sauce, then spoon into 4 stemmed glasses.

Melon, ginger & grapefruit

SERVES 4
80 calories per serving

INGREDIENTS:

500g/1lb 2oz diced watermelon flesh
2 pink grapefruit

2 pieces stem ginger in syrup
(reserving 2 tablespoons of the syrup)

- Remove any seeds from the watermelon and discard. Cut the fruit into bite-sized chunks.
- Using a small sharp knife, cut away all the peel and white pith from the grapefruit and carefully lift out the segments, catching any juice in a bowl.
- Finely chop the stem ginger and put in a serving bowl with the melon cubes and grapefruit segments, also adding the juice.
- Spoon the ginger syrup over and toss the fruits lightly to mix evenly. Chill before serving.

Exotic green fruit salad

SERVES 4
100 calories per serving

INGREDIENTS:

2 tablespoons lime juice
2 tablespoons clear honey
2 green dessert apples (cored and sliced)

1 small ogen melon (diced)
2 kiwi fruit (sliced)
1 star fruit (sliced)
Mint sprigs, to decorate

- Mix together the lime juice and honey in a large bowl, then toss the apple slices in the mixture.
- Stir in the melon, kiwi fruit and star fruit. Place in a glass serving dish and chill before serving. Decorate with mint sprigs.

Hot chocolate custard

SERVES 4
100 calories per serving

INGREDIENTS:

25g/1oz cornflour
25g/1oz cocoa powder

600ml/1pt skimmed milk
Artificial sweetener granules

- Blend the cornflour and cocoa with a little of the milk in a saucepan. Stir in the remaining milk. Bring to the boil and cook for 3 minutes, stirring until smooth and thick. Sweeten with granules to taste and serve immediately.

Souffléed rice pudding

SERVES 4
170 calories per serving

INGREDIENTS:

50g/2oz short-grain rice
3 tablespoons clear honey
750ml/1¼pt skimmed milk

½ teaspoon vanilla essence
2 egg whites
1 teaspoon freshly grated nutmeg

- Place the rice, honey and milk in a heavy or non-stick saucepan and bring to the boil.
- Reduce the heat and put the lid on the pan. Leave to simmer gently for about 1 to 1¼ hours, stirring occasionally to prevent sticking, until most of the liquid has been absorbed. Add the vanilla essence.
- Preheat the oven to 220°C/425°F/Gas mark 7.
- Place the egg whites in a bowl and whisk them until they hold soft peaks. Using a large metal spoon, carefully fold the egg whites evenly into the rice and milk mixture and tip into 1 litre/1³/₄pt ovenproof dish.
- Sprinkle with grated nutmeg and bake for about 15 to 20 minutes, until the pudding is well risen and golden brown. Serve hot.

Banana cake

SERVES 12
225 calories per serving

INGREDIENTS:

Low-fat spread for greasing
450g/1lb plain flour
25g/1oz granulated sugar
1 tablespoon baking powder
½ teaspoon salt
50ml/2fl oz vegetable oil

2 eggs
125ml/4fl oz skimmed milk
1 teaspoon vanilla essence
6 bananas (mashed)
225ml/8fl oz low-fat natural yogurt
1 banana (sliced), for decoration

- Preheat the oven to 180°C/350°F/Gas mark 4. Grease 2 x 20cm/8in round cake tins.
- Sift together the dry ingredients.
- Blend the oil, eggs, milk and vanilla essence until smooth. Stir in the bananas.
- Add to the dry ingredients and stir until the flour is thoroughly moistened.

- Pour equal amounts into the prepared cake tins. Bake in the oven for 20 minutes, or until a skewer inserted in the centre comes out clean.
- Spread one cake with the yogurt and place the other cake on top. Decorate with banana slices.

Green fruit salad

SERVES 6
75 calories per serving

INGREDIENTS:

3 galia melons
100g/4oz green seedless grapes
2 kiwi fruit
1 star fruit

1 green dessert apple
1 lime
175ml/6fl oz sparkling grape juice

- Cut the melons in half and scoop out the seeds. Keeping the shells intact, scoop out the fruit with a melon baller. Set aside the melon shells.
- Remove any stems from the grapes and peel and chop the kiwi fruit. Thinly slice the star fruit. Core and thinly slice the apple and place the slices in a bowl, with the melon, grapes, kiwi fruit and star fruit.
- Thinly pare the zest from the lime and cut it into fine strips. Blanch the strips in boiling water for 10 seconds, then drain them and rinse in cold water. Squeeze the juice from the lime and toss it into the fruit. Mix gently.
- Spoon the prepared fruit into the melon shells and chill in the refrigerator until required. Just before serving, spoon the sparkling grape juice over the fruit and scatter it with the lime zest.

Grapes in grape-yogurt jelly

SERVES 4
120 calories per serving

INGREDIENTS:

200g/7oz white seedless grapes
450ml/³/₄pt unsweetened white grape juice

1 tablespoon powdered gelatine
125ml/4fl oz low-fat natural yogurt

→

←

- Set aside 4 small sprigs of grapes for decoration. Pull the rest off their stalks and cut them in half.
- Divide the grapes among 4 stemmed glasses.
- Place the grape juice in a pan and heat it until almost boiling. Remove it from the heat and sprinkle the gelatine over the surface, stirring to dissolve the gelatine.
- Pour half the grape juice over the grapes and refrigerate until set.
- Cool the remaining grape juice until on the verge of setting, then stir in the yogurt. Pour the yogurt mixture over the set grape jelly. Chill for at least 1 hour.
- Decorate with a sprig of grapes per glass and serve.

Spiced red fruit compote

SERVES 4
95 calories per serving

INGREDIENTS:

4 red plums (halved)
225g/8oz strawberries (halved)
225g/8oz raspberries
25g/oz muscovado sugar
2 tablespoons cold water

1 cinnamon stick
3 pieces star anise
6 cloves
Natural yogurt or fromage frais, to serve

- Place the plums, strawberries and raspberries in a heavy-based pan with the sugar and water.
- Add the cinnamon stick, star anise and cloves to the pan and heat gently, without boiling, until the sugar dissolves and fruit juices run.
- Cover the pan and leave the fruit to infuse over a very low heat for about 5 minutes. Remove the spices from the compote before serving warm with natural yogurt or fromage frais.

Strawberry baked apples

SERVES 4
100 calories per serving

INGREDIENTS:

4 cooking apples
50ml/2fl oz reduced-sugar strawberry jam

1 teaspoon sugar

- Preheat the oven to 180°C/350°F/Gas mark 4.
- Remove the cores from the apples and cut a line around the centre of the fruit to prevent the skin from bursting. Place in an ovenproof dish.
- Fill the centres of the apples with jam and sprinkle with the sugar.
- Add about 2.5cm/1in of water to the dish. Bake in the oven for 1 hour, until tender but still holding their shape.

Chocolate brownies

SERVES 8
200 calories per serving

INGREDIENTS:

Low-fat spread for greasing
150g/5oz plain flour
100g/4oz low-calorie granulated
sweetener
1 teaspoon baking powder
¼ teaspoon salt

50g/2oz butter (softened)
2 eggs
1 teaspoon vanilla essence
100g/4oz unsweetened apple sauce
50g/2oz unsweetened cocoa powder

- Preheat the oven to 180°C/350°F/Gas mark 4. Grease a 20cm/8in square cake tin with low-fat spread.
- In a bowl, stir together the flour, sweetener, baking powder and salt.
- In a mixing bowl, beat the butter, eggs and vanilla essence for 1 minute. Add the apple sauce and beat just until blended. Fold in the flour mixture until just moistened.
- Using half the batter, drop by spoonfuls into the prepared tin. Fold the cocoa powder into the remaining batter until just combined. Gently spoon the remaining batter into the tin, covering the white batter and smoothing the surface.
- Bake in the oven for 15 minutes. Transfer to a wire rack to cool.

Strawberries romanoff

SERVES 4
100 calories per serving

INGREDIENTS:

350g/12oz strawberries (sliced)
½ teaspoon granulated sugar
2 tablespoons orange liqueur

Finely grated zest and juice of 1
orange

- Put the strawberries in a glass serving dish. Sprinkle with the sugar and add the liqueur, orange zest and juice. Toss gently, then leave to marinade for 2 hours before serving.

Iced apple
& blackberry terrine

SERVES 6
85 calories per serving

INGREDIENTS:

450g/1lb dessert apples
300ml/½pt sweet cider
1 tablespoon clear honey
1 teaspoon vanilla essence

200g/7oz fresh blackberries
1 tablespoon powdered gelatine
2 egg whites

- Peel, core and chop the apples and place them in a saucepan with half the cider. Bring to the boil, then cover the pan and simmer gently until tender.
- Tip the apples into a blender or food processor and blend to a smooth purée. Stir in the honey and vanilla essence. Add the blackberries to the apple purée and blend again until smooth. Sieve to remove the pips.
- Heat the remaining cider until almost boiling, then sprinkle the gelatine over and stir until the gelatine has completely dissolved. Add the gelatine to the apple and blackberry purée.
- Leave the purée to cool until almost set. Whisk the egg whites until they are stiff, then quickly fold them into the apple purée. Tip the purée into a 1.75 litre/3pt loaf tin, pressing down firmly and spread it evenly.
- Freeze until firm. Allow to stand at room temperature for 20 minutes and serve.

Rice pudding fruit sundae

SERVES 4

175 calories per serving

INGREDIENTS:

50g/2oz short-grain rice
600ml/1pt skimmed milk
1 teaspoon vanilla essence
½ teaspoon ground cinnamon

25g/1oz granulated sugar
200g/7oz mixed strawberries,
raspberries and blackberries

- Put the rice, milk, vanilla essence, cinnamon and sugar into a medium-sized saucepan. Bring to the boil, stirring constantly, and then turn down the heat so that the mixture barely simmers.
- Cook the rice for 30 to 40 minutes, stirring occasionally, until the grains are soft.
- Tip into a bowl and allow the rice to cool, stirring occasionally. When cold, chill the rice in the fridge.
- Just before serving, stir the rice and spoon into 4 sundae dishes. Top with the berries.

Cherry mousse

SERVES 8

95 calories per serving

INGREDIENTS:

1 egg
2 tablespoons powdered gelatine
1 tablespoon cornflour
150ml/¼pt cranberry juice
1 tablespoon cold water

225ml/8fl oz boiling water
450g/1lb fresh cherries (stoned)
225ml/8fl oz low-fat natural yogurt
150g/5oz granulated sugar

- Combine the egg, gelatine, cornflour, cranberry juice and cold water. Stir well to blend. Add the boiling water and mix together thoroughly.
- Purée the cherries in a blender or food processor, add the gelatine mixture, yogurt and sugar, and blend until smooth. Chill for 4 to 6 hours to set. Blend again just before serving.

Angel cake

SERVES 10
145 calories per serving

INGREDIENTS:

50g/2oz cornflour
50g/2oz plain flour
8 egg whites
225g/8oz caster sugar, plus extra for sprinkling

1 teaspoon vanilla essence
100ml/3½fl oz orange-flavoured glacé icing

- Preheat the oven to 180°C/350°F/Gas mark 4. Sift both flours on to a sheet of baking parchment.
- Whisk the egg whites in a large bowl until very stiff, then gradually add the sugar and vanilla essence, whisking until the mixture is thick and glossy.
- Gently fold in the flour mixture with a large metal spoon. Spoon into an ungreased 25cm/10in angel cake tin, smooth the surface and bake for about 45 to 50 minutes, until the cake springs back when lightly pressed.
- Allow the cake to cool in the tin. Sprinkle a piece of greaseproof paper with caster sugar and turn the cake out on to it. Turn the cake over so the sugar is on the top. Spoon the icing over the top and serve.

Sparkling pear cocktail

SERVES 4
100 calories per serving

INGREDIENTS:

4 pears
50ml/2fl oz brandy

Low-calorie ginger ale (chilled)

- Peel and slice the pears and place in 4 champagne glasses or wine goblets. Add the brandy and toss gently. Bring to the table and top up with ginger ale.

Apple rice pudding

SERVES 4
220 calories per serving

INGREDIENTS:

Low-fat spread for greasing
300g/11oz cooked short-grain rice
450ml/³/₄pt skimmed milk
225g/8oz dessert apples (chopped)
1 teaspoon vanilla essence

4 egg whites
Pinch of salt
25g/1oz granulated sugar, mixed with
¹/₂ teaspoon cinnamon

- Preheat the oven to 180°C/350°F/Gas mark 4. Grease a 20cm/8in ovenproof casserole dish.
- Combine the rice, milk, apples and vanilla essence in a medium-sized bowl.
- Slowly beat the egg whites and salt with an electric beater until soft peaks form.
- Then fold into the rice mixture and pour the mixture into the casserole dish.
- Place the casserole dish into a large pan of water and bake for 30 minutes.
- Remove from the oven and stir in the sugar and cinnamon mixture. Serve warm or cooled to room temperature.

Passion fruit & apple foam

SERVES 4
90 calories per serving

INGREDIENTS:

450g/1lb cooking apples
100ml/3¹/₂fl oz unsweetened apple juice

3 passion fruit
3 egg whites

- Peel, core and roughly chop the cooking apples. Put them in a pan with the apple juice. Bring the liquid to the boil, then lower the heat and cover the pan.
- Cook gently, stirring occasionally, until the apple is very tender.
- Remove from the heat and beat the apple mixture with a wooden spoon until it forms a fairly smooth purée.
- Cut the passion fruit in half and scoop out the flesh. Stir the flesh into the apple purée to mix thoroughly.
- Place the egg whites in a bowl and whisk them until they form soft peaks. Fold the egg whites into the apple mixture. Spoon the apple foam into 4 serving dishes. Leave to cool and serve cold.

Spiced pears in cider

SERVES 4
110 calories per serving

INGREDIENTS:

4 medium pears
250ml/9fl oz dry cider
Thinly pared strip of lemon zest
1 cinnamon stick

25g/1oz muscovado sugar
1 teaspoon arrowroot
1 tablespoon cold water
Ground cinnamon, to sprinkle

- Peel the pears thinly, leaving them whole with the stalks on. Place in a pan with the cider, lemon zest and cinnamon. Cover and simmer gently, turning the pears occasionally, for 15 to 20 minutes or until tender.
- Lift out the pears. Boil the syrup, uncovered, to reduce by half. Remove the lemon zest and cinnamon stick, then stir in the sugar.
- Mix the arrowroot with the water in a small bowl until smooth, then stir into the syrup. Bring to the boil and stir over the heat until thickened and clear.
- Pour the sauce over the pears and sprinkle with ground cinnamon. Leave to cool slightly, then serve.

Filo chiffon pie

SERVES 6
80 calories per serving

INGREDIENTS:

500g/1lb 2oz rhubarb
1 teaspoon mixed spice
Finely grated zest and juice of 1 orange

15g/$\frac{1}{2}$oz granulated sugar
15g/$\frac{1}{2}$oz butter
3 filo pastry sheets

- Preheat the oven to 200°C/400°F/Gas mark 6.
- Chop the rhubarb into 2.5cm/1in pieces and put them into a bowl. Add the mixed spice, orange zest and juice and sugar. Tip the rhubarb into a 1 litre/1³/₄pt pie dish.
- Melt the butter and brush it over the pastry. Lift the pastry on to the pie dish, butter-side up, and crumple it up decoratively to cover the pie.
- Put the dish on a baking tray and bake for 20 minutes, until golden brown.

- Reduce the heat to 180°C/350°F/Gas mark 4 and bake for a further 10 to 15 minutes, until the rhubarb is tender.

Apple foam & blackberries

SERVES 4
55 calories per serving

INGREDIENTS:

225g/8oz blackberries
150ml/¼pt apple juice
1 teaspoon powdered gelatine

1 tablespoon clear honey
2 egg whites

- Place the blackberries in a pan with 4 tablespoons of the apple juice and heat gently until the fruit is soft. Remove from the heat, cool and chill.
- Sprinkle the gelatine over the remaining apple juice in a small pan and stir over a low heat until dissolved. Stir in the honey.
- Whisk the egg whites until they hold stiff peaks. Continue whisking hard and pour in the hot gelatine mixture gradually, until well mixed.
- Quickly spoon the foam into rough mounds on individual plates. Chill. Serve with the blackberries and juice spooned around.

Rhubarb & orange layer

SERVES 4
100 calories per serving

INGREDIENTS:

1 orange
450g/1lb rhubarb (trimmed and cut into short lengths)
150ml/¼pt water

2 teaspoons granulated sugar
25g/1oz cornflour
300ml/½pt skimmed milk

- Thinly pare the zest off half the orange. Cut into thin strips and boil in water for 2 minutes. Drain, rinse with cold water, drain again and dry on kitchen paper.
- Finely grate the remaining orange zest and squeeze the juice.
- Put the rhubarb in the pan with the water and the sugar. Bring gently to the boil, reduce the heat, cover and cook until the rhubarb is tender. Remove the lid, bring

→

←

to the boil and boil rapidly until pulpy and most of the liquid has evaporated.
- Put the cornflour in a separate pan. Make the orange juice up to 300ml/½pt with the milk and stir into the cornflour until smooth. Add the grated orange zest. Bring to the boil and cook for 1 minute, stirring, until thickened and smooth.
- Layer the rhubarb and orange sauce in four heatproof glasses, sprinkle with the reserved orange zest and serve.

Spiced pear & blueberry parcels

SERVES 4
150 calories per serving

INGREDIENTS:

4 pears	*150g/5oz blueberries*
2 tablespoons lemon juice	*50g/2oz muscovado sugar*
15g/½oz low-fat spread (melted)	*Black pepper*

- Preheat the oven to 200°C/400°F/Gas mark 6.
- Peel the pears, cut in half lengthways and scoop out the core. Brush with lemon juice to prevent browning.
- Cut 4 squares of double-thickness aluminium foil, each large enough to wrap a pear, and brush with melted spread. Place 2 pear halves on each, cut-side upwards.
- Gather the foil around them to hold them level.
- Mix the blueberries and sugar together and spoon them on top of the pears.
- Sprinkle with black pepper. Wrap the foil over and cook for 20 to 25 minutes in the oven. Serve hot.

Oat crisps

SERVES 9
200 calories per serving

INGREDIENTS:

Butter for greasing	*1 egg*
175g/6oz rolled oats	*4 tablespoons sunflower oil*
75g/3oz muscovado sugar	*2 tablespoons malt extract*

- Preheat the oven to 190°C/375°F/Gas mark 5. Lightly grease 2 baking trays.
- Mix the rolled oats and sugar in a bowl, breaking up any lumps in the sugar.
- Add the egg, sunflower oil and malt extract, mix well, then leave to soak for 15 minutes.
- Using a teaspoon, place small heaps of the mixture well apart on the baking trays. Press the heaps into 7.5cm/3in rounds with the back of a dampened fork.
- Bake the biscuits for 10 to 15 minutes, until golden brown. Leave them to cool for 1 minute then remove to a wire to cool completely.

Raspberry vacherin

SERVES 6
200 calories per serving

INGREDIENTS:

3 egg whites
175g/6oz caster sugar
1 teaspoon chopped almonds
Icing sugar for dusting

For the filling:
175g/6oz low-fat soft cheese
2 tablespoons clear honey
2 tablespoons Cointreau
125ml/4fl oz low-fat fromage frais
225g/8oz raspberries

- Preheat the oven to 140°C/275°F/Gas mark 1. Draw a 20cm/8in circle on 2 pieces of baking parchment. Turn the paper over so the marking is on the underside and use it to line 2 baking trays.
- Whisk the egg whites in a bowl until very stiff, then gradually whisk in the caster sugar to make a stiff meringue mixture.
- Spoon the mixture on to the circles on the prepared baking trays, spreading the meringue evenly to the edges. Sprinkle 1 meringue round with the almonds.
- Bake for 1½ hours until crisp and dry, and then carefully lift the meringue rounds off the baking trays. Peel away the paper and cool the meringues on a wire rack.
- To make the filling, cream the soft cheese with the honey and Cointreau in a bowl. Gradually fold in the fromage frais and the raspberries, reserving 3 berries for decoration.
- Place the meringue round on a board, spread with the filling and top with the nut-covered round. Dust with the icing sugar, transfer to a serving plate and decorate with the reserved raspberries.

Baked apples in honey & lemon

SERVES 4
80 calories per serving

INGREDIENTS:

4 cooking apples
1 tablespoon clear honey

Grated zest and juice of 1 lemon
25g/1oz low-fat spread

- Preheat the oven to 180°C/350°F/Gas mark 4.
- Remove the cores from the apples, leaving them whole. With a sharp knife, cut lines through the skin of the apples at intervals and place them in an ovenproof dish.
- Mix together the honey, lemon zest and juice and low-fat spread.
- Spoon the mixture into the apples and cover the dish with aluminium foil or a lid. Bake for about 40 to 45 minutes, or until the apples are tender.

Banana & gingerbread slices

SERVES 10
300 calories per serving

INGREDIENTS:

Butter for greasing
275g/10oz plain flour
4 teaspoons ground ginger
2 teaspoons mixed spice
1 teaspoon bicarbonate of soda
100g/4oz demerara sugar
4 tablespoons sunflower oil

2 tablespoons molasses
2 tablespoons malt extract
2 eggs
4 tablespoons orange juice
3 bananas
100g/4oz raisins

- Preheat the oven to 180°C/350°F/Gas mark 4. Lightly grease and line an 18 x 28cm/7 x 11in baking tin.
- Sift the flour into a bowl with the spices, bicarbonate of soda and sugar. Make a well in the centre, add the oil, molasses, malt extract, eggs and orange juice and mix together thoroughly.
- Mash the bananas, add them to the bowl with the raisins and mix well together.

- Pour the mixture into the prepared tin and bake for about 35 to 40 minutes, until the centre springs back when lightly pressed.
- Leave the cake in the tin to cool for 5 minutes, then turn out on to a wire rack and leave to cool completely. Cut into 20 slices.

Strawberry almond shortcake

SERVES 8
180 calories per serving

INGREDIENTS:

*25g/1oz low-fat spread, plus extra
for greasing
450g/1lb strawberries (sliced)
40g/1½oz granulated sugar
400g/14oz plain flour*

*3 teaspoons baking powder
1 egg (beaten)
1 teaspoon almond essence
125ml/4fl oz skimmed milk*

- Preheat the oven to 230°C/450°F/Gas mark 8. Grease a 20cm/8in cake tin.
- Combine the strawberries and 25g/1oz sugar and refrigerate for at least 1 hour.
- In a medium-sized bowl, stir together the remaining sugar, the flour and the baking powder and cut in the low-fat spread until the mixture resembles breadcrumbs.
- Combine the egg, almond essence and milk and add to the flour mixture, stirring until mixed. With lightly floured hands, spread the dough in the prepared tin.
- Bake in the oven for about 10 minutes or until golden.
- Leave to cool, then split in half. Spread the bottom portion with some of the strawberries, top with the rest of the cake and spread the rest of the strawberries on the top.

Banana & pineapple soufflé

SERVES 6
115 calories per serving

INGREDIENTS:

*2 bananas
225g/8oz low-fat cottage cheese
425g/15oz canned pineapple chunks
in juice*

*4 tablespoons water
1 tablespoon powdered gelatine
2 egg whites*

→

←

- Tie a double band of baking parchment around a 600ml/1pt soufflé dish, to come approximately 5cm/2in above the rim.
- Peel and chop one banana and place it in a blender or food processor with the cottage cheese. Blend the mixture until smooth.
- Drain the pineapple and reserve a few pieces for decoration. Add the rest of the pineapple to the mixture in the blender and process until finely chopped.
- Pour the water into a small heatproof bowl and sprinkle the gelatine on top.
- Leave until spongy, then place the bowl over hot water, stirring occasionally, until all the gelatine has dissolved.
- Whisk the egg whites in a bowl until they hold soft peaks, then fold them lightly and evenly into the mixture. Tip the mixture into the prepared dish, smooth the surface and chill it in the fridge until set.
- When the soufflé has set, carefully remove the paper collar. Decorate the soufflé with the reserved banana and pineapple.

Apple & orange biscuits

SERVES 6
100 calories per serving

INGREDIENTS:

Low-fat spread for greasing
100g/4oz wholemeal self-raising flour
25g/1oz oat bran
25g/1oz skimmed milk powder
150g/5oz apple (grated)

2 teaspoons finely chopped fresh ginger root
125ml/4fl oz fresh orange juice
1½ tablespoons margarine (melted)
¼ teaspoon vanilla essence

- Preheat the oven to 180°C/350°F/Gas mark 4. Prepare two flat baking trays by greasing with low-fat spread.
- Place the flour, oat bran and milk powder into a large mixing bowl. Add the grated apple and ginger.
- Stir in the orange juice, margarine and vanilla essence and mix well.
- Using lightly floured hands, roll portions about the size of a walnut and place on to the prepared trays. Press down with a fork dipped in flour. Bake for approximately 15 minutes or until golden brown. When cooked, remove from oven and leave on trays for 2 minutes. Loosen the biscuits and leave to cool.
- When completely cold, store in an airtight container.

Custard tart

SERVES 4

200 calories per serving

INGREDIENTS:

100g/4oz plain flour
Pinch of salt
50g/2oz low-fat spread
2 eggs

½ teaspoon granulated sugar
300ml/½pt skimmed milk (warmed)
Grated nutmeg, for sprinkling

- Preheat the oven to 200°C/400°F/Gas mark 6.
- Put the flour and salt in a bowl. Add the low-fat spread and blend with your fingertips. Mix with enough cold water to form a firm dough. Knead gently on a lightly floured surface. Roll out and use to line an 18cm/7in flan tin. Prick the base with a fork. Fill with crumpled aluminium foil and place on a baking tray.
- Bake in the oven for 15 minutes, removing the foil after 10 minutes to allow the pastry to dry out. Lower the oven temperature to 190°C/375°F/Gas mark 5.
- Whisk together the eggs and sugar, then whisk into the milk. Strain into the pastry case and sprinkle with nutmeg. Bake for about 35 minutes until the custard is set. Serve warm.

Strawberries in grape jelly

SERVES 4

90 calories per serving

INGREDIENTS:

450ml/¾pt red grape juice
1 cinnamon stick
1 small orange

1 tablespoon gelatine
225g/8oz strawberries (chopped)

- Place the grape juice in a pan with the cinnamon. Thinly pare the zest from the orange and add to the pan. Infuse over a very low heat for 10 minutes, then remove the flavourings.
- Squeeze the juice from the orange and sprinkle the gelatine over it. Stir into the grape juice to dissolve. Allow to cool until just beginning to set.
- Stir in the strawberries and quickly tip into a 1 litre/1¾pt mould or serving dish. Chill until set.
- To turn out, dip the mould quickly into cold water and invert on to a serving plate.

Filo fruit scrunchies

SERVES 6
140 calories per serving

INGREDIENTS:

6 apricots
4 sheets filo pastry
15g/¹/₂oz low-fat spread (melted)

50g/2oz demerara sugar
2 tablespoons flaked almonds
Icing sugar for dusting

- Preheat the oven to 190°C/375°F/Gas mark 5.
- Halve the apricots, remove the stones and slice the fruit.
- Cut the filo pastry into 12 x 18cm/7in squares. Pile the squares on top of each other and cover with a clean tea towel to prevent the pastry from drying out.
- Remove one square of filo and brush it with melted spread. Lay a second square on top, then, using your fingers, mould the pastry into folds. Quickly make 5 more scrunchies in the same way so that the pastry does not dry out.
- Arrange a few slices of fruit in the folds of each scrunchie, then sprinkle generously with the sugar and almonds.
- Place the scrunchies on a baking tray. Bake for 8 to 10 minutes until golden brown, then loosen the scrunchies from the baking tray with a palette knife and transfer to a wire rack. Dust with icing sugar and serve at once.

Raspberry muesli layer

SERVES 4
120 calories per serving

INGREDIENTS:

225g/8oz fresh raspberries
225g/8oz low-fat natural yogurt

75g/3oz Swiss-style muesli

- Reserve 4 raspberries for decoration, then spoon a few raspberries into each of 4 stemmed glasses or glass dishes.
- Top the raspberries with a spoonful of yogurt in each glass. Sprinkle a layer of muesli over the yogurt.
- Repeat with the remaining raspberries and other ingredients, finishing with muesli.
- Top each dish with a raspberry.

Baked blackberry cheesecake

SERVES 5
100 calories per serving

INGREDIENTS:

175g/6oz cottage cheese
150g/5oz low-fat natural yogurt
1 tablespoon wholemeal flour
2 tablespoons caster sugar
1 egg

1 egg white
200g/7oz blackberries
Finely grated zest and juice of
½ lemon

- Preheat the oven to 180°C/350°F/Gas mark 4. Lightly grease a 18cm/7in cake tin and line the base.
- Purée the cottage cheese in a blender or food processor until smooth. Add the yogurt, flour, sugar, egg and egg white to the cottage cheese and mix. Add the blackberries, lemon zest and juice, reserving a few blackberries for decoration.
- Tip the mixture into the prepared tin and bake for about 30 to 35 minutes, or until just set. Turn off the oven and leave for 30 minutes.
- Run a knife around the edge of the cheesecake and turn it out.
- Remove the lining paper and place the cheesecake on a warm serving plate.
- Decorate with the reserved blackberries and serve warm.

Dried fruit fool

SERVES 4
185 calories per serving

INGREDIENTS:

300g/11oz ready-to-eat dried fruit,
such as apricots, peaches or apples
300ml/½pt fresh orange juice

250ml/9fl oz low-fat fromage frais
2 egg whites

- Put the dried fruit in a saucepan, add the orange juice and heat gently until boiling. Lower the heat, cover and simmer gently for 3 minutes.
- Cool slightly. Tip into a blender or food processor and blend until smooth. Stir in the fromage frais.
- Whisk the egg whites in a bowl until stiff enough to hold soft peaks, then slowly fold into the fruit mixture until it is all combined.
- Spoon into 4 stemmed glasses. Chill for at least 1 hour.

Almond cheesecakes

SERVES 4
365 calories per serving

INGREDIENTS:

12 Amaretti biscuits
1 egg white (lightly beaten)
225g/8oz skimmed-milk soft cheese
½ teaspoon almond essence
½ finely grated lime zest
25g/1oz ground almonds

25g/1oz caster sugar
50g/2oz sultanas
2 teaspoons powdered gelatine
2 tablespoons boiling water
2 tablespoons lime juice

- Preheat the oven to 180°C/350°F/Gas mark 4. Arrange 4 non-stick pastry rings or poached egg rings, 9cm/3½in across, on a baking tray.
- Place the biscuits in a clean plastic bag, seal the bag and, using a rolling pin, crush them into small pieces. Place the crumbs in a bowl and bind together with the egg white. Divide the mixture between the pastry rings, pressing down well.
- Bake for 10 minutes until crisp and leave to cool.
- Beat together the soft cheese, almond essence, lime zest, almonds, sugar and sultanas until well mixed.
- Dissolve the gelatine in the boiling water and stir in the lime juice. Fold into the cheese mixture and spoon over the biscuit bases. Smooth over the tops and chill for 1 hour, until set.
- Loosen the cheesecakes from the tins using a small palette knife or spatula and transfer to serving plates.

Apple fluff

SERVES 4
100 calories per serving

INGREDIENTS:

450g/1lb cooking apples (sliced)
2 tablespoons water

2 eggs (separated)
1½ teaspoons granulated sugar

- Preheat the oven to 180°C/350°F/Gas mark 4.
- Put the apples in a saucepan with the water and simmer until pulpy, then beat.
- Beat in the egg yolks, turn the mixture into an ovenproof dish and bake for about 30 minutes, until just set.

- Meanwhile, whisk the egg whites until stiff. Whisk in the sugar a little at a time.
- Pile on top of the apple and return to the oven for about 20 minutes until golden. Serve warm.

Pear & sultana tea bread

SERVES 8
200 calories per serving

INGREDIENTS:

Butter for greasing
25g/1oz rolled oats
50g/2oz muscovado sugar
2 tablespoons apple juice
2 tablespoons sunflower oil
1 large pear

100g/4oz self-raising flour
100g/4oz sultanas
½ teaspoon baking powder
2 teaspoons mixed spice
1 egg

- Preheat the oven to 180vC/350°F/Gas mark 4. Grease and line a 450g/1lb loaf tin with baking parchment.
- Put the oats in a bowl with the sugar, pour in the apple juice and oil, mix well and leave to stand for 15 minutes.
- Quarter, core and coarsely grate the pear. Add to the oat mixture with the flour, sultanas, baking powder, mixed spice and egg, then mix together thoroughly.
- Spoon the mixture into the prepared loaf tin and level the top. Bake for 50 to 60 minutes or until a skewer inserted in the centre comes out clean.
- Transfer the teabread on to a wire rack and peel off the lining paper. Leave to cool completely.

Perfumed pineapple salad

SERVES 4
135 calories per serving

INGREDIENTS:

1 small pineapple
1 tablespoon icing sugar
1 tablespoon orange-flower water
100g/4oz fresh dates (stoned and quartered)

225g/8oz strawberries (sliced)
Mint sprigs, to decorate

→

←

- Cut the skin from the pineapple and, using the tip of a vegetable peeler, remove as many brown 'eyes' as possible. Quarter the pineapple lengthways, remove the core from each wedge, then slice.
- Lay the pineapple slices in a shallow serving bowl. Sprinkle with icing sugar and drizzle the orange-flower water over.
- Add the dates and strawberries to the pineapple, cover and chill for at least 2 hours, stirring once or twice. Serve, decorated with a few mint sprigs.

Boozy banana soufflé

SERVES 6
200 calories per serving

INGREDIENTS:

50g/2oz low-fat spread (plus extra for greasing)
1 teaspoon artificial sweetener granules

2 eggs (separated)
150ml/¼pt white rum
4 bananas
4 tablespoons low-fat crème fraîche

- Preheat the oven to 190°C/375°F/Gas mark 5. Lightly grease a 20cm/8in soufflé dish.
- Purée the low-fat spread, sweetener, egg yolks, rum and bananas in a blender or food processor. Whisk the egg whites until stiff and fold into the mixture with a metal spoon.
- Turn into the prepared dish and bake in the oven for about 35 minutes until risen, golden and just set. Serve hot with the crème fraîche.

Orange raisin muffins

SERVES 12
160 calories per serving

INGREDIENTS:

Low-fat spread for greasing
450g/1lb wholewheat plain flour
1½ teaspoons baking powder
1 egg (beaten)
175ml/6fl oz orange juice

50ml/2fl oz canola oil
75ml/3fl oz clear honey
½ teaspoon vanilla essence
50g/2oz raisins
1 tablespoon grated orange zest

- Preheat the oven to 180°C/350°F/Gas mark 4. Grease a 12-hole muffin tray.
- In a large bowl, combine the flour and baking powder. In a small bowl, combine the egg, orange juice, oil, honey and vanilla essence. Add to the dry ingredients, with the raisins and orange zest and stir until combined.
- Pour the batter into the prepared tray and bake for 20 minutes until golden.

Pineapple wedges with lime

SERVES 4
100 calories per serving

INGREDIENTS:

1 pineapple, about 800g/1³/₄lb
1 lime

1 tablespoon muscovado sugar
1 teaspoon ground allspice

- Cut the pineapple lengthways into quarters and remove the hard core.
- Loosen the flesh on each wedge by sliding a knife between the flesh and the skin. Cut the flesh into slices, leaving it on the skin.
- Using a sharp-pointed knife, remove a few shreds of zest from the lime. Squeeze out the juice.
- Sprinkle the pineapple with the lime juice and zest, sugar and allspice. Chill for 1 hour and serve.

Grilled nectarines with Amaretto

SERVES 4
160 calories per serving

INGREDIENTS:

6 nectarines (halved and stoned)
2 tablespoons clear honey

4 tablespoons Amaretto

- Place the nectarines cut-side up in an ovenproof dish and drizzle with the honey and Amaretto. Preheat the grill to high and then grill the fruit until lightly charred.
- Serve hot.

Apple & blackcurrant pancakes

SERVES 10
120 calories per serving

INGREDIENTS:

100g/4oz plain wholemeal flour
300ml/¹/₂pt skimmed milk
1 egg (beaten)
1 tablespoon sunflower oil (plus extra
for greasing)

For the filling:
450g/1lb cooking apples
225g/8oz blackcurrants
2 tablespoons water
25g/1oz demerara sugar

- To make the pancake batter, put the flour in a mixing bowl and make a well in the centre.
- Add a little of the milk with the egg and the oil. Beat the flour into the liquid, then gradually beat in the rest of the milk, keeping the batter smooth and free from lumps. Cover the batter and chill while you prepare the filling.
- Quarter, peel and core the apples. Slice them into a pan and add the blackcurrants and water. Cook over a gentle heat for 10 to 15 minutes until the fruit is soft. Stir in the sugar.
- Lightly grease a pan. Heat it and pour in about 2 tablespoons of the batter, swirl it around and cook for about 1 minute. Flip the pancake over with a palette knife and cook the other side. Put on a sheet of kitchen paper and keep hot while cooking the remaining pancakes.
- Fill the pancakes with the apple and blackcurrant mixture and roll them up.

Fromage frais with hot plum sauce

SERVES 4
100 calories per serving

INGREDIENTS:

450g/1lb plums (halved and stoned)
2 tablespoons water

1 teaspoon granulated sugar
225g/8oz low-fat fromage frais

- Put the plums in a pan with the water and cook very gently until the juice runs.
- Cover and stew over a gentle heat until tender and pulpy. Purée in a blender or food processor and return to the pan. Add the sugar and reheat.
- Spoon the fromage frais into 4 individual dishes, spoon the hot sauce over.

Redcurrant filo baskets

SERVES 6
90 calories per serving

INGREDIENTS:

3 sheets filo pastry
1 tablespoon sunflower oil
175g/6oz redcurrants

250ml/9fl oz low-fat Greek yogurt
1 teaspoon icing sugar

- Preheat the oven to 200°C/400°F/Gas mark 6. Grease 6 small patty tins. Cut the sheets of pastry into 18 x 10cm/4in squares.
- Brush each filo square very thinly with oil, then arrange 3 squares in each of the patty tins, placing each one at a different angle so that they form star shaped baskets. Bake for 6 to 8 minutes, until crisp and golden. Lift the baskets out carefully and leave them to cool on a wire rack.
- Set aside a few sprigs of redcurrants on their stems for decoration and string the rest. Stir the redcurrants into the yogurt.
- Spoon the yogurt into the filo baskets. Decorate them with the reserved sprigs of redcurrants and sprinkle with the icing sugar.

Floating islands in hot plum sauce

SERVES 4
100 calories per serving

INGREDIENTS:

450g/1lb red plums
300ml/1/2pt apple juice
2 egg whites

2 tablespoons concentrated apple juice
Freshly grated nutmeg, to sprinkle

→

←
- Halve the plums and remove the stones. Place them in a wide saucepan, with the apple juice. Bring to the boil, then cover and simmer gently until the plums have become tender.
- Place the egg whites in a bowl and whisk them until they hold soft peaks.
- Gradually whisk in the concentrated apple juice, whisking until the meringue holds fairly firm peaks.
- Using a tablespoon, scoop the meringue mixture into the gently simmering plum sauce.
- Cover and simmer gently for about 2 to 3 minutes, until the meringues are set.
- Serve immediately, sprinkled with a little freshly grated nutmeg.

Figs with ricotta cheese

SERVES 4
100 calories per serving

INGREDIENTS:

4 ripe, fresh figs
100g/4oz ricotta cheese
3 tablespoons crème fraîche

1 tablespoon clear honey
½ teaspoon vanilla essence

- Using a small sharp knife, trim the stalks from the figs. Make four cuts through each fig from the stalk-end, cutting them almost through but being careful to leave them joined at the base.
- Place the figs on serving plates and open them out.
- In a bowl, mix the ricotta cheese, crème fraîche, honey and vanilla essence.
- Spoon a little ricotta cream mixture onto each plate with the fig and serve.

Minted melon & kiwi fruit salad

SERVES 4
100 calories per serving

INGREDIENTS:

1 small honeydew melon
4 kiwi fruit (peeled)

200ml/7fl oz apple juice
2 mint sprigs

- Halve the melon and scoop out the fruit using a melon baler. Place in a bowl.
- Slice 2 of the kiwi fruit and place in a bowl with the melon.
- Purée the remaining kiwi fruit in a blender or food processor with the apple juice and mint. Pour through a sieve to remove any seeds and mint stalks. Chill for at least 1 hour. Spoon over the melon mixture and serve.

Chocolate & orange angel cake

SERVES 10
70 calories per serving

INGREDIENTS:

25g/1oz plain flour
15g/½oz low-fat cocoa powder
15g/½oz cornflour
Pinch of salt
5 egg whites
½ teaspoon cream of tartar

100g/4oz caster sugar

For the icing:
200g/7oz caster sugar
75ml/3fl oz water
1 egg white

- Preheat the oven to 180°C/350°F/Gas mark 4.
- Sift the flour, cocoa powder, cornflour and salt together three times. Beat the egg whites in a large bowl until foamy. Add the cream of tartar, then whisk until soft peaks form.
- Add the caster sugar to the egg whites a spoonful at a time, whisking after each addition. Sift a third of the flour and cocoa mixture over the meringue and gently fold in. Repeat, sifting and folding in the flour and cocoa mixture 2 more times.
- Spoon the mixture into a non-stick 20cm/8in ring mould and level the top. Bake for 35 minutes or until springy to the touch. Turn upside-down on to a wire rack and leave to cool in the tin. Carefully ease out of the tin.
- For the icing, put the sugar in the pan with the water. Stir over a low heat until dissolved. Boil until the syrup reaches a temperature of 120°C/240°F on a sugar thermometer, or when a drop of the syrup makes a soft ball when dropped into a cup of cold water. Remove from the heat.
- Whisk the egg white until stiff. Add the syrup in a thin stream, whisking all the time. Continue to whisk until the mixture is very thick and fluffy.
- Spread the icing over the top and sides of the cooled cake.

Muffins

SERVES 12
180 calories per serving

INGREDIENTS:

1 teaspoon dry yeast
125ml/4fl oz warm water
50ml/2fl oz skimmed milk (warmed)
200g/7oz low-fat natural yogurt
2 tablespoons vegetable oil
50g/2oz sunflower seeds

50g/2oz raisins (finely chopped)
250g/9oz wholemeal flour
100g/4oz bran
50g/2oz wheat germ
½ teaspoon cinnamon
½ teaspoon nutmeg

- Place the yeast into a small bowl. Stir in the water and allow to stand for 10 minutes. Stir in the milk, yogurt and vegetable oil. Stir in the remaining ingredients and mix well.
- Place tablespoons of mixture into a 12-hole muffin tray. Set aside in a warm place for approximately 40 minutes or until the muffins have doubled in size.
- Preheat the oven to 230°C/450°F/Gas mark 8. Bake for approximately 12 minutes or until golden brown and cooked. Serve warm.

Chocolate vanilla moulds

SERVES 6
120 calories per serving

INGREDIENTS:

350ml/12fl oz skimmed milk
2 tablespoons cocoa powder (plus extra for sprinkling)
2 eggs (separated)
1 teaspoon vanilla essence
25g/1oz caster sugar

1 tablespoon powdered gelatine
3 tablespoons hot water

For the sauce:
125ml/4fl oz low-fat Greek yogurt
½ teaspoon vanilla essence

- Mix the milk and cocoa in a pan and stir over a moderate heat until the milk boils.
- Beat the egg yolks with the vanilla and sugar in a bowl, until smooth. Pour in the chocolate milk, beating well.
- Return the mixture to the pan and stir constantly over a gentle heat, without

boiling, until it thickens slightly and is smooth. Dissolve the gelatine in the hot water and then quickly stir it into the milk mixture. Let it cool until it is at the point of setting.

- Whisk the egg whites in a grease-free bowl until they hold soft peaks. Fold them quickly into the chocolate milk mixture, then divide among 6 individual moulds. Chill until set.
- For the sauce, stir the yogurt and vanilla essence together then spoon on to the plates with the inverted moulds.

Date & apple muffins

SERVES 12
170 calories per serving

INGREDIENTS:

150g/5oz self-raising wholemeal flour
150g/5oz self-raising white flour
1 teaspoon ground cinnamon
1 teaspoon baking powder
25g/1oz margarine
75g/3oz muscovado sugar

1 dessert apple
250ml/9fl oz apple juice
2 tablespoons pear and apple spread
1 egg (lightly beaten)
75g/3oz chopped dates
1 tablespoon chopped pecan nuts

- Preheat the oven to 200°C/400°F/Gas mark 6. Arrange 12 paper cake cases in a deep muffin tin.
- Put the wholemeal flour in a mixing bowl. Sift in the white flour with the cinnamon and baking powder.
- Rub in the margarine until the mixture resembles breadcrumbs, then stir in the sugar.
- Quarter and core the apple, chop the flesh finely and set aside. Stir a little of the apple juice with the pear and apple spread until smooth. Mix in the remaining juice, then add to the rubbed-in mixture with the egg.
- Add the chopped apple to the bowl with the dates. Mix quickly until just combined.
- Divide the mixture among the muffin cases. Sprinkle with the chopped pecan nuts.
- Bake the muffins for 20 to 25 minutes, until golden brown and firm in the middle.
- Remove to a wire rack and serve while still warm.

Apricot fool

SERVES 4
100 calories per serving

INGREDIENTS:

2 tablespoons cornflour
300ml/¹/₂pt skimmed milk
15g/¹/₂oz low-fat spread

¹/₄ teaspoon vanilla essence
¹/₂ teaspoon granulated sugar
400g/14oz canned apricots in juice

- To make the sauce, blend the cornflour with 2 tablespoons milk in a saucepan with a wooden spoon. Add the remaining milk, bring to the boil and cook for 2 minutes until thickened.
- Stir in the low-fat spread, vanilla essence and sugar. Leave to cool.
- Keeping half an apricot aside for decoration, purée the rest with the juice in a blender or food processor and fold into the sauce. Spoon into individual glasses and chill for 1 hour before serving.

Yogurt ring with tropical fruit

SERVES 6
105 calories per serving

INGREDIENTS:

175ml/6fl oz tropical fruit juice
1 tablespoon powdered gelatine
3 egg whites
150g/5oz low-fat natural yogurt
Finely grated zest of 1 lime

For the filling:
1 mango
2 kiwi fruit
12 cape gooseberries
Juice of 1 lime

- Place the fruit juice in a saucepan and sprinkle the gelatine over. Heat gently until the gelatine has dissolved.
- Whisk the egg whites in a bowl until they hold stiff peaks. Continue whisking hard, while gradually adding the yogurt and lime rind. Continue whisking hard and pour in the hot gelatine mixture. Mix in the gelatine mixture and quickly pour the mixture into a 1.5 litre/2¹/₂pt ring mould. Chill the mould in the refrigerator until set. The mixture will separate into 2 layers.

- For the filling, halve, stone, peel and dice the mango. Peel and slice the kiwi fruit. Remove the outer leaves from the gooseberries and cut in half. Toss all the fruits together and stir in the lime juice.
- Run a knife around the edge of the ring to loosen the mixture. Dip the mould quickly into cold water and then turn it out on to a serving plate. Spoon all the prepared fruit into the centre of the ring and serve immediately.

Strawberry rose-petal pashka

SERVES 4
155 calories per serving

INGREDIENTS:

350g/12oz cottage cheese
175g/6oz low-fat natural yogurt
2 tablespoons clear honey
½ teaspoon rose-water

275g/10oz strawberries
Handful of scented pink rose petals, to decorate

- Drain any free liquid from the cottage cheese and tip the cheese into a sieve. Use a wooden spoon to rub it through the sieve into a bowl.
- Stir the yogurt, honey and rose-water into the cheese.
- Roughly chop about half the strawberries and stir them into the cheese mixture.
- Line a new, clean flowerpot or a sieve with muslin and tip the cheese mixture in.
- Leave it to drain over a bowl for several hours, or overnight.
- Invert the flowerpot or sieve on to a serving plate, turn out the pashka and remove the muslin. Decorate with rose petals and serve chilled.

Peach cheese melba

SERVES 2
100 calories per serving

INGREDIENTS:

2 large ripe peaches
50g/2oz low-fat soft cheese
1 teaspoon granulated sugar

Grated zest and juice of 1 orange
100g/4oz raspberries

→

←
- Skin the peaches, cut them in half and remove the stones.
- Mash the cheese with the sugar and orange zest. Spoon the cheese mixture on to each peach half and place in a shallow serving dish.
- Purée the raspberries and orange juice in a blender or food processor and pass through a sieve to remove any seeds. Spoon over the peaches and serve.

Pears with strawberry sauce

SERVES 4
140 calories per serving

INGREDIENTS:

4 pears (pared, with stems attached)
50ml/2fl oz water
1 tablespoon orange juice
2 teaspoons low-fat spread (melted)
5cm/2in cinnamon stick (broken in half)

225g/8oz strawberries
1 tablespoon water
1 teaspoon granulated sugar
1 teaspoon cornflour
1 teaspoon lemon juice

- Preheat the oven 180°C/350°F/Gas mark 4.
- In a shallow 1.2 litre/2pt casserole dish, arrange the pears on their sides.
- In a bowl, combine the water, orange juice and low-fat spread and pour over the pears. Add the cinnamon stick and bake for 20 to 30 minutes until tender, basting occasionally. Using a slotted spoon, transfer each pear to a dessert dish, reserving the pan juices.
- In a small saucepan, combine the pan juices with the strawberries and bring to the boil.
- In a small bowl, combine the water, sugar, cornflour and lemon juice, stirring to dissolve. Add to the saucepan, stirring constantly, and bring to the boil. Reduce the heat and cook, stirring constantly, until thickened. Remove from the heat and pour over the pears.

Plum filo pockets

SERVES 4
190 calories per serving

INGREDIENTS:

100g/4oz skimmed milk soft cheese
1 tablespoon muscovado sugar
½ teaspoon ground cloves
8 large plums (halved and stoned)

8 sheets filo pastry
Sunflower oil for brushing
Icing sugar for sprinkling

- Preheat the oven to 220°C/425°F/Gas mark 7.
- Mix together the cheese, sugar and cloves.
- Sandwich the plum halves back together in twos with a spoonful of the cheese mixture.
- Spread out the pastry and cut into 16 pieces, about 23cm/9in square. Brush one lightly with oil and place a second diagonally on top. Repeat with the remaining squares.
- Place a plum on each pastry square and pinch the corners together. Place on a baking tray. Bake for 15 to 18 minutes until golden, then dust with icing sugar.

Apricot delice

SERVES 8
160 calories per serving

INGREDIENTS:

850g/1¾lb canned apricots in natural juice
50g/2oz granulated sugar
25ml/1fl oz lemon juice
5 teaspoons powdered gelatine

425g/15oz low-fat ready-to-serve custard
150ml/¼pt Greek-style yogurt
1 apricot (sliced, to decorate)

- Line the base of a 1.2 litre/2pt cake tin with baking parchment.
- Drain the apricots, reserving the juice. Put the apricots in a blender or food processor together with the sugar and 4 tablespoons of the apricot juice. Blend to a smooth purée.
- Measure 2 tablespoons of the apricot juice into a small bowl. Add the lemon juice, then sprinkle over 2 teaspoons of the gelatine. Leave for about 5 minutes, until spongy.

→

←

- Stir the gelatine into half of the purée and pour into the prepared tin. Chill in the refrigerator for 1½ hours or until firm.
- Sprinkle the remaining gelatine over 4 tablespoons of the apricot juice. Leave for about 5 minutes until spongy. Mix the remaining apricot purée with the custard, yogurt and gelatine. Pour on to the layer of set fruit purée and chill for 3 hours.
- Dip the cake tin into hot water for a few seconds and unmould the delice on to a serving plate and peel off the lining paper. Decorate with the sliced apricot.

Bananas with hot lemon sauce

SERVES 4
100 calories per serving

INGREDIENTS:

15g/½oz low-fat spread
2 teaspoons granulated sugar
15g/½oz cornflour

Grated zest and juice of ½ lemon
300ml/½pt low-fat plain yogurt
4 small bananas (sliced)

- Place the low-fat spread, sugar and cornflour in a saucepan. Make the lemon juice up to 150ml/¼pt with water and stir into the pan. Bring to the boil and cook, stirring, for 2 minutes.
- Divide the yogurt between 4 serving dishes and add the banana. Spoon the hot sauce over and serve immediately.

Blueberry sundae

SERVES 4
110 calories per serving

INGREDIENTS:

700g/1½lb fresh blueberries
2 tablespoons lemon juice
1 teaspoon vanilla essence

2 teaspoons cornflour
2 tablespoons water
150g/5oz granulated sugar

- Purée the blueberries in a blender or food processor. In a large saucepan, combine the blueberry purée, lemon juice and vanilla essence. Cook over a medium heat for 5 minutes, or until bubbly.
- Combine the cornflour and water. Add to the berry mixture, stirring constantly, for about 3 minutes until thickened. Remove from the heat and stir in the sugar.
- Divide between 4 glass dishes.

Poppy seed custard with red fruit

SERVES 6
115 calories per serving

INGREDIENTS:

Low-fat spread for greasing
600ml/1pt skimmed milk
2 eggs
1 tablespoon caster sugar
1 tablespoon poppy seeds

100g/4oz strawberries
100g/4oz raspberries
100g/4oz blackberries
1 tablespoon demerara sugar
60ml/2½fl oz red grape juice

- Preheat the oven to 150°C/300°F/Gas mark 2. Grease a soufflé dish very lightly with low-fat spread.
- Heat the milk until just below boiling point, but do not boil.
- Beat the eggs in a bowl with the caster sugar and poppy seeds until creamy.
- Whisk the milk into the egg mixture until very well mixed. Stand the prepared soufflé dish in a shallow roasting tin, then pour in hot water from the kettle to come halfway up the sides of the dish.
- Pour the custard into the soufflé dish and bake in the oven for 50 to 60 minutes, until the custard is just set and golden on top.
- While the custard is baking, mix the fruit with the sugar and fruit juice. Chill until ready to serve with the warm baked custard.

Apricot yogurt cookies

SERVES 8
200 calories per serving

INGREDIENTS:

3 tablespoons sunflower oil (plus extra for greasing)
175g/6oz plain flour
1 teaspoon baking powder
1 teaspoon ground cinnamon
75g/3oz rolled oats

75g/3oz muscovado sugar
100g/4oz ready-to-eat dried apricots (chopped)
1 tablespoon flaked hazelnuts
150g/5oz natural yogurt
Demerara sugar for sprinkling

- Preheat the oven to 190°C/375°F/Gas mark 5. Lightly oil a large baking tray.
- Sift together the flour, baking powder and cinnamon. Stir in the oats, sugar, apricots and nuts.
- Beat together the yogurt and oil, then stir evenly into the mixture to make a firm dough. If necessary, add a little more yogurt.
- Use your hands to roll the mixture into about 16 small balls, place on the baking sheet and flatten with a fork. Sprinkle with demerara sugar. Bake for 15 to 20 minutes, or until firm and golden brown. Leave to cool on a wire rack.

Cornflake-topped peach bake

SERVES 4
160 calories per serving

INGREDIENTS:

400g/14oz canned peach slices in juice
25g/1oz sultanas
1 cinnamon stick
Strip of pared orange zest

25g/1oz low-fat spread
50g/2oz cornflakes
2 teaspoons sesame seeds

- Preheat the oven to 200°C/400°F/Gas mark 6.
- Drain the peaches, reserving the juice in a small saucepan. Arrange the peach slices in a shallow ovenproof dish.
- Add the sultanas, cinnamon stick and orange zest to the juice and bring to the

boil. Lower the heat and simmer, for 3 to 4 minutes, to reduce the liquid by half.
- Remove the cinnamon stick and zest and spoon the syrup over the peaches.
- Melt the low-fat spread in a small pan, then stir in the cornflakes and sesame seeds.
- Spread the cornflake mixture over the fruit. Bake for 15 to 20 minutes, or until the topping is crisp and golden. Serve hot.

Lemon sponge fingers

SERVES 10
70 calories per serving

INGREDIENTS:

2 eggs
75g/3oz caster sugar (plus extra
for sprinkling)

Grated zest of 1 lemon
50g/2oz plain flour (sifted)

- Preheat the oven to 190°C/375°F/Gas mark 5. Line 2 baking trays with baking parchment.
- Whisk the eggs, sugar and lemon zest together with an electric whisk until the mixture is thick and mousse-like and leaves a thick trail on the surface for at least 15 seconds.
- Carefully fold in the flour with a large metal spoon. Place the mixture in a large piping bag fitted with a 1cm/½in nozzle and pipe into finger lengths on the baking trays.
- Dust the fingers with caster sugar and bake for 6 to 8 minutes until golden brown.

Apple tart

SERVES 10
110 calories per serving

INGREDIENTS:

Low-fat spread, for greasing
4 dessert apples (peeled and cut into
slices)
2 eggs
125ml/4fl oz low-fat yogurt

50ml/2fl oz clear honey
50g/2oz plain flour
¼ teaspoon vanilla essence
1 tablespoon apple sauce
2 tablespoons apple juice

→

←
- Preheat the oven to 190°C/375°F/Gas mark 5. Grease a 23cm/9in springform tart tin. Arrange the apple slices, overlapping each other slightly, in the pan.
- In a medium-sized bowl, combine the eggs, yogurt, honey, flour and vanilla essence. Spoon over the apple slices until they are covered. Bake for 30 minutes.
- In a small saucepan, combine the apple sauce and juice over a low heat. Brush evenly over the tart and bake for a further 10 minutes, or until golden brown.

Plum Charlotte

SERVES 4
200 calories per serving

INGREDIENTS:

450g/1lb plums (halved and stoned)
1 tablespoon water
1 teaspoon granulated sugar

4 slices white bread
25g/1oz low-fat spread

- Preheat the oven to 190°C/375°F/Gas mark 5.
- Put the plums in a saucepan with the water and stew until tender. Sweeten with the sugar.
- Spread the bread with the low-fat spread and use 2 of the slices to line a shallow ovenproof serving dish. Top with the plums.
- Cut the remaining bread into thin strips and arrange in a lattice on top of the plums. Bake in the oven for 30 to 40 minutes, until golden brown.

Apples & raspberries in rose syrup

SERVES 4
130 calories per serving

INGREDIENTS:

1 teaspoon rose pouchong tea
900ml/1½pt boiling water
1 teaspoon rose-water
50g/2oz granulated sugar

1 teaspoon lemon juice
5 dessert apples (peeled, cored and quartered)
175g/6oz fresh raspberries

- Warm a large tea pot. Add the rose pouchong tea, then pour on the boiling water, together with the rose-water, if using. Allow to infuse for 4 minutes.
- Measure the sugar and lemon juice into a stainless steel saucepan. Strain in the tea and stir to dissolve the sugar.
- Poach the apples in the syrup for about 5 minutes.
- Transfer the apples and syrup to a large metal tray and leave to cool to room temperature.
- Pour the cooled apples and syrup into a bowl, add the raspberries and mix to combine. Spoon into individual dishes or bowls and serve warm.

Cherry marmalade muffins

SERVES 12
160 calories per serving

INGREDIENTS:

225g/8oz self-raising flour
1 teaspoon ground mixed spice
75g/3oz caster sugar
100g/4oz glacé cherries (quartered)

2 tablespoons orange marmalade, plus
extra for brushing
150ml/¼pt skimmed milk
50g/2oz margarine

- Preheat the oven to 200∞C/400∞F/Gas mark 6. Lightly grease 12 deep muffin tins with oil. Sift together the flour and spice and then stir in the sugar and cherries.
- Mix the marmalade with the milk and beat into the dry ingredients with the margarine. Spoon into the greased tins. Bake for 20 to 25 minutes, until golden brown and firm.
- Turn out on to a wire rack and brush the tops with warmed marmalade. Serve warm or cold.

Ginger & honey syrup

SERVES 4
155 calories per serving

INGREDIENTS:

1 lemon
4 green cardamom pods
1 cinnamon stick
150ml/¼pt clear honey

3 pieces stem ginger, plus 2
tablespoons syrup from the jar
4 tablespoons water

- Thinly pare 2 strips of zest from the lemon with a potato peeler.
- Lightly crush the cardamom pods with the back of a heavy-bladed knife. Cut the lemon in half. Squeeze the juice from one half and set aside.
- Place the lemon zest, cardamoms, cinnamon stick, honey, ginger syrup and water in a heavy-based saucepan. Bring to the boil, then lower the heat and simmer for 2 minutes.
- Chop the ginger and stir it into the sauce with the lemon juice. Chill to serve. This syrup goes well with a winter fruit salad or a baked fruit compote.

Papaya & grapes with mint syrup

SERVES 4
125 calories per serving

INGREDIENTS:

2 large papayas
225g/8oz seedless green grapes
Juice of 3 limes
2.5cm/1in fresh root ginger (peeled
and finely grated)

1 tablespoon clear honey
5 fresh mint leaves (cut into
thin strips)

- Peel the papaya and cut into small cubes, discarding the seeds.
- Cut the grapes in half.
- In a bowl, mix together the lime juice, ginger, honey and mint leaves. Add the papaya and grapes and toss well. Cover and leave in a cool place to marinate.
- After an hour, serve in individual stemmed glasses.

Chocolate truffles

SERVES 12
175 calories per serving

INGREDIENTS:

175g/6oz dark chocolate
2 tablespoons Amaretto
50g/2oz butter

50g/2oz icing sugar
50g/2oz ground almonds
50g/2oz milk chocolate (grated)

- Melt the dark chocolate with the Amaretto in a bowl set over a saucepan of hot water, stirring until well combined.
- Add the butter and stir until it has melted. Stir in the sugar and the almonds.
- Leave the mixture in a cool place until firm enough to roll into 24 balls.
- Place the grated chocolate on a plate and roll each truffle to coat them. Chill for at least 30 minutes before serving.

Conversion
tables

Weights

Imperial	Approx. metric equivalent	Imperial	Approx. metric equivalent
$^1/_2$oz	15g	$1^1/_4$lb	600g
1oz	25g	$1^1/_2$lb	700g
$1^1/_2$oz	40g	$1^3/_4$lb	850g
2oz	50g	2lb	900g
$2^1/_2$oz	60g	$2^1/_2$lb	1.1kg
3oz	75g	3lb	1.4kg
4oz	100g	$3^1/_2$lb	1.6kg
5oz	150g	4lb	1.8kg
6oz	175g	$4^1/_2$lb	2kg
7oz	200g	5lb	2.3kg
8oz	225g	$5^1/_2$lb	2.5kg
9oz	250g	6lb	2.7kg
10oz	275g	$6^1/_2$lb	3kg
11oz	300g	7lb	3.2kg
12oz	350g	$7^1/_2$lb	3.4kg
13oz	375g	8lb	3.6kg
14oz	400g	$8^1/_2$lb	3.9kg
15oz	425g	9lb	4.1kg
16oz (1lb)	450g	$9^1/_2$lb	4.3kg
1lb 2oz	500g	10lb	4.5kg

The Imperial pound (lb), which is 16 ounces (oz), equals approximately 450 grams (g).

Oven temperatures

°C	°F	Gas mark	Temperature
130	250	$^1/_2$	Very cool
140	275	1	Very cool
150	300	2	Cool
160–170	325	3	Warm
180	350	4	Moderate
190	375	5	Fairly hot
200	400	6	Fairly hot
210–220	425	7	Hot
230	450	8	Very hot
240	475	9	Very hot

Fluid measures

Imperial	Approx. metric equivalent	Imperial	Approx. metric equivalent
1fl oz	25ml	9fl oz	250ml
2fl oz	50ml	10fl oz ($^1/_2$pt)	300ml
3fl oz	75ml	12fl oz	350ml
3$^1/_2$fl oz	100ml	15fl oz ($^3/_4$pt)	450ml
4fl oz	125ml	18 fl oz	500ml
5fl oz ($^1/_4$pt)	150ml	20fl oz (1pt)	600ml
6fl oz	175ml	30fl oz (1$^1/_2$pt)	900ml
7fl oz	200ml	35 fl oz (2pt)	1.2 litres
8fl oz	225ml	40 fl oz (2$^1/_2$pt)	1.5 litres

The Imperial pint (pt), which is 20 fluid ounces (fl oz), measures approximately 600 millilitres (ml).

Spoon measures

All the measurements given in the recipes are for levelled spoonfuls (British Imperial Standard)
1 teaspoon = 5ml
1 tablespoon = 15ml

The tablespoon measurements below are equivalent to approximately 1oz (25g) of the following ingredients:

Breadcrumbs (dried)	3	Flour, unsifted	3
Breadcrumbs (fresh)	7	Rice (uncooked)	2
Butter/margarine/lard	2	Sugar (granulated, caster)	2
Cheese, grated (Cheddar)	3	Sugar (icing)	3
Cheese, grated (Parmesan)	4	Honey/syrup	1
Cocoa powder	4	Yeast (dried)	2
Cornflour/custard powder	2$^1/_2$		

Calorie counter

Food

Calories
(Amounts are average raw per 100g/100ml)

FRUIT

Food	Calories
Apple	49Cals.
Banana	100Cals.
Blackcurrant	27.4Cals.
Grapefruit	45.9 Cals.
Grapes (green)	61.5Cals.
Lemon	7Cals.
Melons	10.6Cals.
Nectarines	35.9Cals.
Orange	37Cals.
Pineapple	44Cals.
Plums	35.3Cals.
Raspberry	26.3Cals.
Strawberry	27.6Cals.

VEGETABLES

Food	Calories
Broccoli	29.6Cals.
Cabbage	15.3Cals.
Carrot	20Cals.
Cauliflower	28Cals.
Celery	7.6Cals.
Corn	24Cals.
Lettuce	18Cals.
Potato	136Cals.
Spinach	22.6Cals.
Tomato	56.2Cals.

FISH

Food	Calories
Cod	96Cals.
Haddock	228Cals.
Mussels	104Cals.
Plaice	78.6Cals.
Prawns	219Cals.
Salmon	168Cals.
Sole	89Cals.
Squid	81.3Cals.
Trout	135Cals.
Tuna	107Cals.

Food

Calories
(Amounts are average raw per 100g/100ml)

MEAT & POULTRY

Beef	96Cals.
Beef curry	101Cals.
Chicken (breast fillets)	123Cals.
Chicken breast (fried)	136.5Cals.
Duck (breast fillets)	120Cals.
Ham	112Cals.
Lamb	246Cals.
Liver	113Cals.
Pork	133Cals.
Sausage (pork)	304.6Cals.
Turkey (breast fillets)	130.7Cals.

DAIRY

Cheese .	408.9Cals.
Cottage cheese	90Cals.
Custard	120Cals.
Double cream	438.3Cals.
Eggs (free range, medium)	147.3Cals.
Milk (semi-skimmed)	48.6Cals.

GRAINS & PULSES

Beans (baked)	75Cals.
Beans (green, frozen)	26Cals.
Beansprouts	32Cals.
Nuts (brazil, average)	687.4Cals.
Pasta	353.6Cals.
Rice (white, dry, average)	361.8Cals.
Tofu	118.7Cals.

MISCELLANEOUS

Butter Biscuits	486Cals.
Chocolate (Dairy Milk)	525Cals.
Chocolate sponge cake	355Cals.
Coffee (black)	2Cals.
Cola (average)	41Cals.
Tea (black)	0Cals.

Index